ADIRONDACK LOGGING

Stories, Memories, Cookhouse Chronicles,
Linn Tractors and Gould Paper Company History
from Adirondack and Tug Hill Lumber Camps

William J. O'Hern

Life and Times in the Early Years of Logging's Mechanization

ADIRONDACK LOGGING

Stories, Memories, Cookhouse Chronicles, Linn Tractors and
Gould Paper Company History from Adirondack and Tug Hill Lumber Camps

William J. O'Hern

Life and Times in the Early Years
of Logging's Mechanization

The book and cover design and typesetting
were created by Nancy Did It! (www.NancyDidIt.com)

Cover photograph courtesy of Ernest L. Portner
Back cover photograph courtesy of Dante O. Tranquille

For permission to reprint "A Bit of History About the NYS Woodsmen's
Field Days…" from the *67th Anniversary Celebration New York State
Woodsmen's Field Days*, grateful acknowledgment is made to Phyllis W. White,
Executive Coordinator, NYS Woodsmen's Field Days, Inc.

In the
Adirondacks

PO Box 526 • Camden, New York 13316-9998 • www.adkwilds.com

Printed in the United States of America by Bookmasters
ISBN 978-0-9890328-7-2

For permission to reprint Helen Escha Tyler's "Life in a Lumber Camp—1899" from *This-n-That* (The Currier Press, 1983), greatful acknowledgement is made to Dr. Martha Tyler John.

For permission to reprint the following material from the *Lumber Camp News*, grateful acknowledgment is made to Eric Johnson, executive editor at *The Northeastern Logger*, published by The Northeastern Loggers Association in Old Forge, N.Y.

Editorial, *Lumber Camp News*, August 1947.
"Planning One's Life," *Lumber Camp News*, August 1947.
"Logging in the Good Old Days," *Lumber Camp News*, August 1948.
Editorial, *Lumber Camp News*, February 1949.
"God's Work," *Lumber Camp News*, February 1949.
Editorial, *Lumber Camp News*, September 1949.

"The Camp Cook Says—," *Lumber Camp News*, January 1947; February 1947; August 1947; December 1947; June 1948; July 1948; August 1948; November 1948; December 1948; August 1948; March 1949; February 1949; September 1949; December 1949.

Editorial, *Lumber Camp News*, April 1953.

For permission to make lengthy quotations from "History and Heritage," December 18, 2001; January 8, 15, 29, 2002; June 18, August 13, 27, 2013; grateful acknowledgment is made to M. Lisa Monroe, Editor of the *Adirondack Express*, and Ken Sprague.

For permission to make lengthy quotations from "The History of the Linn Tractor," Issue 20, *TimberTimes* magazine, grateful acknowledgment is made to Eric Bracher and *TimberTimes* magazine.

For permission to make lengthy quotations from "Logging with Linn Tractors in Upstate New York," Issue 20, from *TimberTimes* magazine by Ernest L. Portner, grateful acknowledgment is made to *TimberTimes* magazine and Ernest L. Portner.

For permission to make lengthy quotations from "Good as Gould," March 1998, *Adirondack Life*, by Emily Williams, grateful acknowledgement is made to *Adirondack Life* magazine and Emily Williams.

For permission to reprint the following material from Ranger School Alumni Association's *Alumni News*, grateful acknowledgment is made to Gail M. Simmons, Office Manager of Alumni Affairs, Ranger School Alumni Association.

"Adirondack Lumbering," by Rev. Frank A. Reed, *Alumni News*, 1948.

For permission to reprint the following material from the *Watertown Daily Times*, grateful acknowledgment is made to the *Watertown Daily Times* and Lisa M. Carr, librarian, *Watertown Daily Times* Library.

Wells, Robert A. "Big Tracts in 3 Counties." *Watertown Daily Times*, Feb. 13, 1928
— "Snow Taxi Follows Forest Trail to Lumbering Camp." *Watertown Daily Times*, Feb. 14, 1928.
— "Many Difficulties Face Men Driving Tractor Log Trains." *Watertown Daily Times*, Feb. 15, 1928.
— "Thousands of Logs Piled on Ice Awaiting Spring Drive." *Watertown Daily Times*, Feb. 16, 1928.
— "Veteran Woodsmen Describe Entire Lumbering Operation." Watertown Daily Times, Feb. 17, 1928.
— "Colorful French-Canadian Lumbermen Disappearing." Watertown Daily Times, Feb. 18, 1928.

Episodes from *Calked Shoes* first appeared in *North Country Life* magazine between Spring 1951 and Summer 1952 as a long article titled "I Married a Forester." The installments dealt with Barbara K. Bird's experiences in the woods with her forester husband, Royal G. Bird.

The Lumber Camp News, August, 1949

CONTENTS

Dedication
Epigram

Adirondack Logging

The first Linn Tractor (1916) from an advertisement in *The American Agriculturist Farm Directory and Reference Book*, 1917. The Linn Mfg. Corporation (1916–1952) was in Morris, Otsego County, N.Y. *Public Domain. From Wikimedia Commons, the free media repository*

DEDICATION

*To the men and
women who earn their living
in the lumber woods.*

Unidentified Gould Paper Company workers in the Moose River Plains.
Courtesy of Lyons Falls History Association

The Northeastern Logger, November, 1952

EPIGRAM

Lumberjacks are Men
You'd like to Know

Ft. left: John "Jack" Donahue Sr. A sturdy, hard-talking lot but with hearts of gold, men who would give you the shirt off their back if you needed it but show you no mercy if you tangled with them. Men you'd like to know."—Conse R. Delutis.
Courtesy of John Donahue

STAND TO ONE SIDE WHEN TREE IS FALLING
WATCH FOR KICKBACKS

AMERICAN PULPWOOD ASSOCIATION SAFETY POSTER No. 1

The Northeastern Logger, December, 1952

PART ONE

The Mechanization of Logging

In the early days of old-style logging, horses not only figured in hauling out big timber; they formed the lifeline that kept lumber camps in operation until the introduction of the internal combustion engine, crawlers and motor trucks came into their own.
Author's collection

The old methods of using horses ended with the creation of "The Mary Anne," Lombard's first power-driven steam hauler. This iron hulk was the great-granddaddy of the modern Caterpillar.

"Alvin Orlando Lombard was a blacksmith building logging equipment in Waterville, Maine. He built 83 steam log haulers between 1901 and 1917. These log haulers resembled a saddle-tank steam locomotive with a small platform in front of the boiler where the cow-catcher might be expected. A steering wheel on the platform moved a large pair of skis beneath the platform. A set of tracked vehicle treads occupied the space beneath the boiler where driving wheels might be expected. The locomotive cylinders powered the treads through a gear train. The log haulers mechanically resembled 10- to 30-ton snowmobiles with a top speed of about 4.5 miles per hour."
—From Wikipedia, The Free Encyclopedia. *Courtesy of Ernest L. Portner*

Collection 1
Pioneer Movements in the Mechanization of Logging

From the early 1920s to the 1940s, tractors and trucks came into use in the lumber woods across America. The old-style horse-drawn methods of logging in the Adirondack Mountains were used until highway development, the growth of railroads, and tractor transportation made mechanical equipment the logical move to make.

Rev. Frank A. Reed was a supporter of the logging industry.[1] You might say he held many irons in the fire regarding the business of logging. One of his favorite studies was its history: loggers of the past, the care given to lumberjacks, lumber shanties in the woods, and life in the camps. The Bull Cook, who prepared food for the "Iron Men," the Barn Boss, swampers, whitewatermen, wood butchers, road monkeys, camp clerks, sawyers, log loaders, "walkers," cruisers and camp clerks: As minister to their spiritual needs, all of them were important to Rev. Reed. Skidding by oxen and horse and later the days of mechanical horsepower, logging railroads, road building, and other topics were of special interest to him as well.

By 1954 Reed had lived a lifetime with the ever-changing logging industry. "One of the pioneer movements in the mechanization of logging," he wrote in the September 1954 issue of *The Northern Logger* magazine, "was the invention of the steam log hauler, which was used extensively on log jobs in the early years" of the twentieth century."

The steam log haulers of days gone by were powerful machines. Their great power and weight made good roads essential. Reed concluded, "The cost of road construction and the investment in the machine itself meant that these machines could be used only on large jobs. Later, invention of the gasoline tractor reduced the weight and also operation cost."

Reed loved the history and he respected most companies and independent loggers who took good care of their workers. He also took a special interest in providing for the older men. The idea of a former logger dying in the poorhouse when he was too old to work the woods concerned him.

If the Adirondacks had bragging rights, the region could boast that one of the earliest steam haulers was used in the central Adirondacks near Inlet, N.Y. John O'Connell of Old Forge preserved how they were used in photographs he took.

Reed said, "The next step in the development of tractors on long hauls came in the use of Linn tractors on the Gould Paper Company operations and in the use of the Lombard gasoline tractors.

"At the invitation of John B. Todd, who was woodlands manager for the Gould Paper Company, Mr. Linn visited these operations in the winters of 1918–1919 and experimented in hauling logs from North Lake to the South Branch of the Moose River. That experiment was the beginning of a long period of tractor hauling."

On one trip to Gould Paper Company Camp 7 at the base of Ice Cave Mountain, Rev. Reed recalled he could hardly forget the day he stopped at Rev. A.L. Byron-Curtiss's Nat Foster Lodge on North Lake. Following a tour

The Lombard factory, Waterville, Maine. Circa 1927. Steam haulers were ugly, cumbersome monsters, but they could outdistance the horses on the long sleigh hauls. They towed trains of eight to twelve sleighs, and could travel over rough terrain and upgrades where horses could not work. *Courtesy of Ernest L. Portner*

STEAM LOMBARDS #1, 3, 7 & 8   GAS LOMBARD #13

Tractor repair shop of the Great Northern Paper Co., Cooper Brook Camp, 1927.
Lt. to Rt. steam Lombards #1, 3, 7 & 8 and gas Lombard #13.

The first steam-powered Lombard log hauler had an upright boiler, but it proved
to be too cumbersome. The redesigned steam-powered Lombard log haulers were
early machines with a horizontal boiler and were steered by a team of horses in a pair
of shafts attached in front of the engine. It must have been funny to see the puffing,
chattering, track-machine oddity followed by a train of huge loaded sleighs, the
whole thing led by horses.

The majority of these Lombard haulers were used in Maine and New Hampshire.
A few were used in Michigan, Wisconsin and Russia. *Courtesy of Ernest L. Portner*

around the reverend's newly developed lakeshore shrine, which he had named
St. Catherine's Calvary in honor of his youngest, recently-deceased daughter,
the two holy men visited.

"We talked about the North Lake [lumbering] operations," Reed recalled.
"Rev. Byron-Curtiss was quite a story-teller. I heard all about the day he witnessed a camp cook wearing caulked shoes with a side of bacon 'fastened to
each foot with hay wire, skating up and down the twenty-foot cook top greasing the cooking surface.'"

Reed left the folklore to "B-C," the name most often used for and by Reverend Byron-Curtiss. In conjunction with Leo Brandon, Edwin M. Kling and Dr. S.W. Nelson, the men penned a two-part educational lumber history that appeared in the April 1964 issue of *The Northern Logger*.

In 1965, Rev. Reed followed the comprehensive rise of the industry with his book, *Lumberjack Sky Pilot*.

Adirondack river-driving is now a thing of the past. Boiling masses of 13-foot peeled logs don't come tumbling down the white water to a mill any longer. Gone too are the hardy woodchoppers and sawyers and heroic men who built reputations on the size of the load they could carry and the speed at which they could make it through the woods to deliver ten- or twelve-foot high sleds of logs to the winter rolling banks where the landing crew would pile the logs with strategic precision on the frozen stillwater. Only a few faint traces remain of the old lumber roads that snaked throughout the backcountry and the lumber camps that stood there.

With all that in the past, the former old-time spirit of logging has not completely disappeared into history. Rev. Reed's and many others' memories have contributed to this informal history that brings to light a unique and interesting picture of old-time logging.

Lombard began building 6-cylinder gasoline-powered log haulers in 1914. A more powerful "Big 6" machine was produced later, and he built one Fairbanks-Morse diesel-engine hauler in 1934. The internal combustion log haulers were less powerful than the steam log haulers. *Courtesy of Ernest L. Portner*

Camp 7. Fred Worden was a highly respected mechanic for the Gould Paper Company. Fred had a reputation of being able to repair just about anything. During his retirement years he assembled an extensive photograph album filled with all things pertaining to Gould's machinery, camps, as well as more personal photos.

Fred was initially the only mechanic in charge of ten Linn tractors and four Lombard tractors at Gould Paper Company's Camp 9. In May 2006, Philomena Lawrence related in *The Northern Logger & Timber Processor's* "Old Tractors Live on in Unique Collection: New York Collector Specialized in Lombard & Linn Logging Tractors" that Worden of Forestport, N.Y. said "driving the tractors was the most prestigious job in the woods and it often took two men to turn the steering wheels of the older models. In a 1920's slide, Worden recognized the wires of the first radio he installed in the camp, the year of the Great Depression, when workers were clearing trees prior to the laying of railroad tracks in Glenfield (near the Black River). According to Worden's account, one of the owners walked into the woods and said, 'It's all over boys! Leave your axes where they are.'" The loggers quit then and there, leaving their axes and two-man saws right there in the woods. *Courtesy of Fred Worden*

A Lombard steam log hauler of days-gone-by with a load heading to the landing. Note the steersman in the front. Circa 1906. *Courtesy of Ernest L. Portner*

This 1907–08 Lombard is outfitted with a wooden cab on the front to better protect the steersman. *Courtesy of Ernest L. Portner*

Adirondack Logging

Lt. 4 cylinder Linn returning to Camp 7 with empty sleighs. Rt. 6 cylinder Linn hooking onto a train of sleighs. Tractor and truck drivers of the exciting early days of the mechanization of logging were commonly the practical but peppery "old-school" men of this modern movement of automotive machinery. *Courtesy of Ernest L. Portner*

Woodsmen's Field Days at Old Forge. Each and every driver had wild, adventurous and sometimes funny stories to tell about freak accidents. *Courtesy of John Donahue*

Linn hauling 12 sleighs—120 tons of logs. Descending the big hill to the Moose River Landing on the Canachagala Stillwater, circa early 1920s. There were ridiculous upsets, fruitlessly cranking cat engines, driving in such extreme cold that men's whiskers froze to metal parts in the cab. *Courtesy of Fred Worden*

Loading log sleighs to make up a train for the Linn. Long before daylight the sound of the cat engine could be heard. The cat driver's full attention was on navigation. A watchdog was needed to keep a sharp eye on the loads. His job was to jump from sleigh to sleigh, adjust the crotch chains when there was slack on the turns, and see that the binding chains held the loads tight so that they didn't shift. *Courtesy of John Donahue*

"Almost Over" Missing death by a split hair was all in a day's work and before anyone had heard of OSHA. *Courtesy Howard Wieman*

18-foot high load of logs piled on a Ford V-8. One day it was plain to Art as he shifted into lower gears that he was dragging hard in the mud-laden rock-strewn tote road and burning petro faster than usual. Fearing he would run out of gasoline before reaching the refueling stop, he sent Bedbug off with two empty five-gallon cans to Gould's landing to fill up with gas and run back to Ice Cave Creek bridge.

Tough, sinewy, hard-working and non-complaining, Rev. Frank Reed had great admiration for the "Men of Iron." *Courtesy of Eric Johnson, Executive Editor at The Northeastern Logger*

T.C. Williams' gas Lombard at Camp 7. The new mechanized internal-combustion machines changed the landscape of logging. *Courtesy of Fred Worden*

Caterpillar's Traxcavator 1950s answer to the logging industry. The new "cat" machines changed the landscape of logging all over the world. *Courtesy of the Town of Webb Historical Association, P5261*

This 1910 Phoenix at Benson Mines, N.Y. is a spinoff from the Lombard. The Phoenix Manufacturing Company brand was made under Lombard's patent. Lombard derived a thousand dollars for every Phoenix manufactured. Note the steersman's wheel is on an angle. Other, early machines similar to the Lombard and Phoenix were Linn, International TracTractor, Cletrac, and Allis Chalmers, which all came out in the 1920s and 30s. *Courtesy of Ernest L. Portner*

"Lumber Jill" waves to a crowd along a logging festival parade route from a flatbed trailer transporting a restored 6 cyl. duel brass carburator Lombard log hauler. This tractor is on display in the Augusta, Maine state museum. *Courtesy of Eric Johnson, Executive Editor at The Northeastern Logger*

Modern machinery brought greater efficiency. *Courtesy of Lyons Falls History Association*

A Barnhart steam log loader with an upright boiler and fixed log boom, circa 1917. The "cat," the automotive industry, and powerful steam and gasoline machinery brought about an end to an era that lionized the work horse as a beast of burden with nearly the same status in the logging camp as the lumberjacks. *Postcard image in Author's collection*

With the sky-high cost of machinery and energy, some people look back to the methods of old-style logging with nostalgia and practicability as they apply principles of good forest management on small wood lots. Properly handled, horses can do a lot of work. Their cost and upkeep is less than modern equipment and there is also a special connection between man and beast that one can never have with the best of the powerful logging machinery. *Courtesy of Special Collections, Feinberg Library, SUNY College at Plattsburgh*

  *Adirondack Logging*

CHAPTER 1

Adirondack Lumbering

Rev. Frank A. Reed

In 1948, Rev. Frank A. Reed, owner and editor of the *Lumber Camp News* and Presbyterian minister of the Adirondack and Northeast lumber camps, was asked to speak at the 13th annual New York State Ranger School Alumni Reunion held at the Wanakena school grounds on August 6 and 7. He spoke about the history of logging, as he knew of it, from his accumulated 32-year association with the lumbering industry in Northern New York. Reed's remarks addressed many interesting changes in methods and equipment, and were featured in the Ranger School's *Alumni News*. Reed's address, well over a half-century old, told of state-of-the-art methods for 1948. Today it helps us see how much the logging industry has continued to progress since he spoke.

Adirondack lumbering reached its peak during World War I. At that time 7,000 woodsmen were at work in 150 lumber camps, getting out strategic materials to meet the needs of the country in a time of stress. It declined to its lowest point about 1933, when the country was at the bottom of the Great Depression. In this period a few hundred men were employed in about 13 lumber camps which were then in operation.

In the earlier Adirondack days, the expert axeman had already been supplanted by the woodsman who was equally skilled in the use of the crosscut saw. The crosscut has continued to be the principal method of felling trees and the spud as the method of peeling. However, the development of newer methods of bark removal at the mill has, in some instances, eliminated the necessity of peeling the pulpwood in the woods. The wasteful rosser[2] of earlier times has given way to the drum barker and it, in turn, has been supplanted by more modern methods.

The work of the skidding seasons has involved more changes. In earlier years, most Adirondack pulpwood was cut in log length. Men cut the trees into logs at the point where they had been peeled, and skidded the logs into large skidways for the winter haul. They did this with the crosscut saw.

Rt. to Lt. Clarence J. Strife, Rev. Frank Reed and an unknown logger believed to be Joe Lindsey, C.J. Strife's camp clerk.

Rev. Reed was as passionate an advocate for logging and lumber industry history and the role trees played to benefit the lumberjacks and mankind as he was in being a preacher dedicated to the Ministry of the Gospel.

Sherman Adams, a reviewer of Reed's *Lumberjack Sky Pilot* book, said of the preacher that he devoted "himself to the spiritual welfare of those whose environment is too often far removed from spiritual experiences." *Courtesy of the Town of Webb Historical Association, P6546*

  *Adirondack Logging*

It was the cry from the outside world for lumber, lumber and more lumber which hastened the opening of the Adirondacks to increasing settlement," wrote Floy S. Hyde in *Adirondack Forests, Fields, and Mines.*

Shown is a Linn tractor hauling a train of sleds loaded with hardwood logs.

Courtesy of the Goff-Nelson Memorial (Tupper Lake) Library

> *As the custom of cutting pulpwood into four-foot lengths spread through part of the area, the bucksaw was introduced and became the principal tool on the four-foot jobs. The bucksaw era has produced a number of woodsmen who could saw and pile 8–10 cords per day. These men ordinarily cut by the cord and made excellent wages. Only young and rugged men could engage in this strenuous work, and their term of service would ordinarily be only 15–20 years.*

By 1948, Rev. Reed reported the bucksaw continued to be used extensively on the four-foot jobs but was "gradually giving way to the chain saw."

> *One chain saw of German make was used at Jerseyfield sometime before World War II. Daily production with this saw was low and the operator was subject to many jokes among his fellow woodsmen. In contrast to this early experiment, the crews in two camps on the Cedar River used 40*

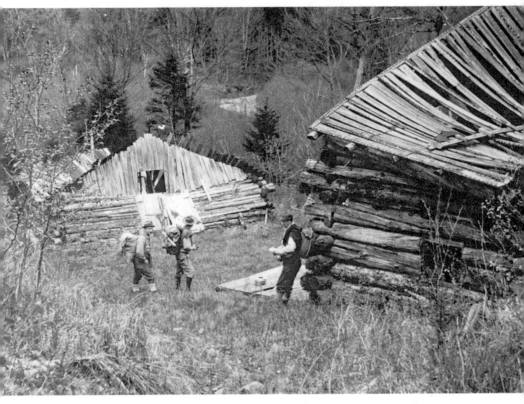

Records of the Santa Clara Lumber Company, tell the company was a major operator in New York's Tupper Lake area during the early 1900s, and was among the first to utilize the automobile in its woods operations. Back in 1912, the firm was running a half-dozen big lumbering camps in the wild Cold River country, logging the steep slopes of Mount Seward. Dr. CV Latimer Sr., Jay Gregory and an unidentified member of their deer hunting party relied on the Cold River derelict lumber camps for shelter. Circa late 1920s. *Courtesy of Dr. CV Latimer, Jr.*

chain saws in the fall of 1948. A skilled mechanic with a well-equipped shop and a good stock of spare parts kept these saws in operation. In the near future, other operators will no doubt approximate the high degree of efficiency in chain saw use which has been attained on the Cedar River.

The most marked changes have taken place in the field of transportation. In earlier years the horse was used entirely for both the skidding season and the winter haul. More than 100 teams were used the first winter on the long haul from North Lake to the landing on the [South

Branch of the] Moose River. On a one-trip haul, the earlier teamsters had breakfast at 2:30 and were soon out on the long trek to the landing. Late teamsters came in for supper at 7 or 8 in the evening. The log loaders had a long day of service and the cooking staff had little time for rest except the period from 9 to 1 o'clock at night.

This era produced some excellent teamsters—men who took great pride in their fine horses and treated them almost as friends. It also produced some skillful log rollers and a number of good cooks.

The invention of the caterpillar tractor by Samuel Holt laid the foundation for a new method of transportation. It became effective in the later days of World War I when surplus tractors became available. They proved to be very useful in plowing roads and hauling loads from the

Circa early 1900s. 'Jacks take time to pose before resuming work in the Seward Range. Getting the lumberjacks in to that territory used to require buckboard rigs consisting of a heavy running gear with long, springy hickory boards mounted on them, supporting four seats. With a load of eight lumberjacks aboard, those long buckboards bent in a graceful curve, touching the ground in the rough spots or where the wheels sunk in deep ruts. Old timers recalled the picture of a buckboard load of woodsmen, outfitted in colorful shirts and stag pants, and usually in uproariously good spirits, as something not readily forgotten. *Courtesy of the Goff-Nelson Memorial (Tupper Lake) Library*

woods to the yards. *Other tractors with steering sleighs became useful on the long hauls. Mr. Linn made his early experiments on the Moose River with tractors which John B. Todd had purchased for the Gould Paper Company. The great-grandsons of these early tractors are powerful machines which can haul trains of 15 or 20 loads to the landing. One of these could do the work of at least 20 teams.*

With the coming of the tractor, the breakfast hour was moved from 2:30 to 4:30. The Linn tractor drivers were out first in the morning for the long trek from the landing camp to the woods with a string of empty sleighs and then the return trip with a train of loaded ones for the landing on the Moose. With a daily schedule of two trips per day with each tractor, the crew was able to move logs rapidly from the woods to the landing.

With the advent of the automobile, the buckboard vanished quickly in the north woods. Tote roads were improved sufficiently to permit motorized travel, at least during dry weather, and the lumberjacks rode to the Cold River country in fine style.

Changing patterns in Adirondack logging, like the advent of mechanical methods of moving timber from steep terrain, also made it necessary to build log chutes. Frank Sykes of Emporium Lumber Co. had the patent on this log slide. Circa 1900.

Courtesy of Paul Sykes

The trademark, "O.W.D.," Oval Wood Dish Company's logo is displayed on an early Linn skid steer. The company was a generous and consistent supporter of projects throughout the Tupper Lake community. Once Franklin County's largest industry, it sold its mill site and buildings in 1964. *Courtesy of the Goff-Nelson Memorial (Tupper Lake) Library*

The tractor age has produced equally skillful road monkeys without whose assistance many a load would be lying at the foot of the hill.

Trucks. *While tractors were being developed on the Moose River and in several other areas, some operators were making experiments in the use of the truck. John E. Johnson of Port Leyden became a pioneer in using the truck to transport wood from the cutting operation directly to the mill. With the use of the newly developed bulldozers, circle roads were constructed through the entire operation. On large operations, scores of trucks could be used. In the years before World War II, trucking was done by men who owned their own trucks and hauled by the cord. With the scarcity of trucks, tires and gasoline during the war, most companies purchased fleets of trucks for this transportation.*

Circa 1890s. Huge sleigh loads of logs once moved along the Cold River tote road to frozen landings at Duck Hole, Moose Creek Landing and Big Dam. *Courtesy of the Goff-Nelson Memorial (Tupper Lake) Library*

The difficult task of loading large four-foot blocks onto trucks pro-
duced another invention, the loader. This is powered ordinarily by a
tractor with a conveyor to lift the wood from the ground to the truck.
Other types have also been invented.

The development of truck transportation opened many new areas of
timber land for lumbering, particularly in hardwood, which could
not be floated in the streams. Hardwood operations had been limited
to areas near the railroads or to those where railroads might be built.
Logs were skidded to the rail spurs by horses, using woods trails or slides
or occasionally with overhead skidders. Logs at greater distances were
hauled to the rail spurs by horse or tractor.

By 1948, the *Lumber Camp News* monthly newspaper had been reporting the highly developed and everyday use of truck transportation of hardwood logs, as Reed wrote in his "Operation at Jessup River Completed" column in September 1948. From the Jack Works[3] the logs moved from booms in Indian

In the days of real horsepower. Looking at pictures of large loads of logs being hauled by a single or four-horse team, today's questioners might ask, "How could those horses pull such a load?"

The answer lies in the effort that was put into preparing and maintaining the ice roads and in the construction of the sleighs. *Author's collection*

Lake to land, where they were transported by a fleet of trucks to the International Paper Company mill at Corinth, N.Y.

Reed continued:

> *Most every state road leading out of the Adirondacks forms an artery for these logs on the way to the mill. Much of it is done in winter but many operators also truck in the summer season.*

> ***River Driving.*** *In early years, the river furnished the cheapest and best method of transportation for pulpwood on its way to the mill. There were great drives on the Black River and its tributaries, on the Hudson, the Oswegatchie, the Raquette and other streams. Sometimes, as in the case of the Hudson, several companies used the same stream. Logs were driven under cooperative supervision and were sorted at sorting booms.*

Logs were unloaded at frozen landings from large ramps. Men dressed in heavy wool clothing held up with hefty suspenders worked logs into place with canthooks. Circa 1900. *Author's collection*

Adirondack Logging

Splash or flood dams were man-made impoundments built across Adirondack rivers. The dams held water in large basins or reservoirs behind the dam. When a gate in a splash dam was opened, water flushed logs through a spillway. These wooden sluiceways provided a jam-free passageway through rocky channels. *Courtesy of Pat Payne*

> *River driving has continued on several Adirondack streams including the Moose River, West Canada Creek, the Jessup, and the Hudson. However, in the spring of 1949 the Hudson and its tributaries probably will be the scene of the only drive in the Adirondacks, the Finch Pruyn drive to the mill at Glens Falls. Drives on other streams may be resumed at a later date. [But mechanical equipment continued to play a larger and more efficient and safer part in transporting wood out from the timberlands and in the continued decline of river drives. W.J.O.]*

In the years before and after Reed began his lumber camp ministry, many of the logs that were cut in the forests during fall and winter had to be floated on the smaller streams to the larger streams and rivers, where they were assembled into rafts and transported to market far down the river and closer to the centers of population and to the sea for shipment abroad.

Logging equipment of the 1940s like log loaders, bulldozers, chain saws and other, then-modern, equipment radically changed logging jobs, but the new gadgets probably created no more of a stir than did the advent of the gasoline buggy in the north woods some forty years earlier. *Courtesy of Paul Sykes*

The high waters of early spring were utilized to "drive" the logs. These flood waters usually lasted for only a few days and it required unceasing herculean efforts by all hands to float out the winter cut, even with the aid of a series of temporary log-cribbing dams that were built at shallow places in the streams.

Historically, "many interesting and exciting books have been written based on the hazards and back-breaking work involved in these spring drives," wrote W.A. August, a senior silviculturist in the June 1949 issue of the *Lumber Camp News*. "Log-jams would often result, which threatened the drive's success, and skilled dynamiters would be required to break them. It required a special breed of hard-working men to be able to withstand the rigors of life in a logging camp and the log drives that climaxed their winter's work. One can imagine the rigors of such a life and perhaps justify their rough and riotous actions when they were paid off and went to town."

In the portion of his remarks on lumber camp structures, Rev. Reed reflected on the thirty-plus years of changes he had witnessed that had brought beneficial improvements in lumber camp construction.

In earlier days, when transportation was more difficult, most camps were built of materials near at hand. The log camp was warm and comfortable in winter. The pole bunks with a little straw over them were not so comfortable. The board camp, with a covering of roofing, is probably easier and less expensive to construct, but it does not give the same degree of warmth in winter. Both types are used extensively in the Adirondacks, although the trend had been in the direction of board construction.

In most Adirondack camps the bunkhouse and cook camp are under the same roof, with an open shed between them which formerly was used to store stovewood in winter. Some operators have enclosed this open shed for a washroom and have equipped it with running water, showers and a washing machine.

Progress had been made in bunk construction. The early pole bunk was supplanted by the double board bunk which was built in double-decker

Adirondack hermit Noah John Rondeau standing on the log sluiceway at the site of Big Dam, Cold River. Rondeau's hermitage was the site of Santa Clara's abandoned Big Dam lumber camp. Circa mid-1940s. *Courtesy of the Goff-Nelson Memorial (Tupper Lake) Library*

style, and it gave way to the same type of bunk of metal construction. The most recent model is the single iron bunk in double-decker style.

Pennsylvania operators who moved into the Adirondacks used a somewhat different style of camp. In this style, a lobby was built at the end of the cook camp with sleeping quarters over both rooms. The ordinary double bed was used in this type of camp. The woodsman was awakened a little earlier than ordinarily by the pleasant odor of pancakes and sausage from the cook room below.

With the development of new equipment, a tracery shed and shop were added, along with the barn and blacksmith shop.

Woodsmen. Personnel in the lumber camps have also changed with the passing years. In 1918 Adirondack woodsmen could be divided into three major groups: (1). The American woodsmen who came from

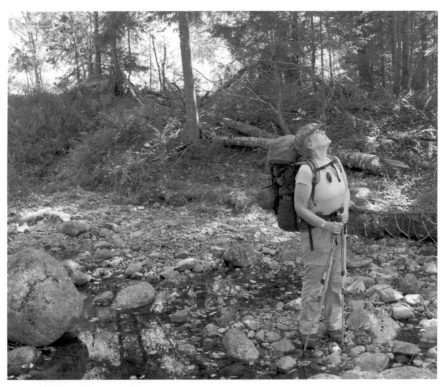

Bette O'Hern rests along the beaten Cold River tote road. Once used to haul supplies to logging camps, the route is now part of the Northville-Placid Trail. *Photo by the author*

*Adirondack villages or from the lumbering areas of Pennsylvania, West
Virginia or New England. (2). French Canadians who came to the states
previous to World War I or in the early days of the war. (3). Central
Europeans who had come over previous to World War I. These included
a large number of Poles and Russians with some Swedes and Lithuanians.
There were also a few Irish and Scotch.*

*Most of the French Canadians settled in northern New York and have
continued their lumbering activities, and some have become operators.
Many of their children have not followed the woods program. A large
percentage of the Central Europeans have continued in the lumber camps,
but most of them have not married.*

Reed stated, "American woodsmen have decreased in numbers. The men
from all three of these [early] groups have grown older and average around
fifty years of age. In twenty years they will have disappeared from the scene
of Adirondack lumbering."

*Bonded[4] French Canadians came to the Adirondacks early in World
War II to supplement American woodsmen who had joined the war effort.
These men have rendered real service in a time of scarcity. The quota
perhaps should be reduced somewhat, to avoid unemployment on the part
of American woodsmen.*

*Woodsmen of the future will undoubtedly be recruited, as previously,
from three possible sources: (1). American young men who are attracted
by opportunities to lumber jobs where there is more mechanized equipment,
better living conditions and the chance for advancement; (2). French
Canadians who may or may not be bonded; and (3). some displaced
persons from lumbering areas of Europe.*

Rev. Reed ended with a concluding thought that remains a concern today.
His drumbeat was the question of future timber supply.

*A greater appreciation of the forest has been evident in the past thirty
years. In earlier times when lumber and pulpwood were abundant,
few thought about the future supply. As forest resources became*

somewhat exhausted, men began to think in these terms and to plan perpetual lumbering programs. By selective cutting methods, better fire protection, better pest control, and a more effective program of reforestation, foresters are seeking to provide for an inexhaustible supply which will provide a lumbering program adequate to supply the needs of coming generations.

In Reed's editorial column in *The Northeastern Logger's* November 1952 issue he outlined what he believed was the best answer to the timber supply question.

1. *Better management of the private forest land in the area. The owner of the land is the Steward of the Forest. He must use it wisely for the welfare and happiness of himself and family, those who live around him and those of Coming Generations. Better management will include plans for a much thriftier stand of young trees...*

2. *The possible opening of some State Land for conservative and well-managed cutting. [This happened only through a special vote to allow timber removal following the 1950 Big Blow. Heavy rain and hurricane force winds in excess of 100 mph damaged more than 800,000 acres of timber land protected by the Forever Wild amendment. A historic suspension of the tree cutting provision of this clause allowed temporary logging. John Warren's "The Big Blowdown" is an excellent review of this historic provision. It can be found at: http://www.adirondackalmanack.com/2010/11/natures-wrath-the-big-blowdown-of-1950.html]*

3. *The limitation of manufacture and logging so that it will not exceed timber growth in the area. This could best be achieved through the cooperative effort of the land owners and forest industries, with such technical assistance as public agencies may be able to supply.*

4. *The Adirondack section is not peculiar except in the program on State Land. Similar conditions prevail in most forests of the Northeast. The improvement of the timber supply will undoubtedly require similar measures.*

CHAPTER 2

The Brown Company's
Creative Hauling Idea

Edited and with Commentary by William J. O'Hern

A clever and useful building development that Reverend Reed did not mention in his address at the Ranger School was that when the Woods Department of the Brown Company moved, they took their buildings with them.

Buildings up to 32 feet by 16 feet were moved because it was felt that the cost of such an operation would be much less than building a whole new camp. The buildings were loaded on special trailers, and taken over narrow and winding roads to be set up at a new site.

These buildings, when first constructed in 1943, were built to be moved—but not over the highway and certainly not for 60 miles. Each had been built on skids, so that they could be moved through the woods to new cutting sites. But you can't move a building on skids on the main highways. It would have been too hard on the paved surfaces and on the wooden skids.

So with clever ingenuity the members of the Mechanical Equipment Division of the Brown Company "went into a huddle and came up with plans for a specially-constructed trailer to carry the buildings," reported Louis Castello of the clever invention in "Brown Company Moves 15 Camp Buildings 60 Miles" in the January 1949 issue of the *Lumber Camp News*.

"To make an ordinary-type trailer strong enough to carry a building 32 feet long would have been quite a job.

There were always uses for the Linn, including towing portable bunk houses and Barnhardt loaders. *Courtesy of Ernest L. Portner*

"'Why not make the buildings a part of the trailer?'

"That was the question they asked. And the answer was: 'It can be done.'

"The trailer was composed of two long telescoping eye beams, which, with the correct bracing, became the foundation for each building.

"Low-boy trailer wheels were used. Power came from an all-wheel-drive, six-by-six trailer truck.

"In designing the trailer, there were more things to take into consideration.

"The trailer, of course, had to conform to the laws of two states. Bridges had to be measured. Woods roads had to be straightened in some places. [Why two states? What two states? The article did not provide information to these vexing questions. W.J.O.]

"It was found that the buildings were too high to pass under all overhead obstructions.

"So the 'V' roofs were collapsed like the folding covers on a box.

"To avoid any possible traffic snarls, a 'traffic man' rode about a half mile ahead of the trailer to stop any on-coming cars at wider areas in the road.

"The work went ahead without difficulty, and…the buildings [were] ready and waiting for the crews to move… ."

Another moveable building was the wanigan. It served as a home for the river driver when the annual log drive was on. Some companies fed and slept the 'jacks in these floating buildings, while other companies only used the wanigans for cooking. The men slept first along the river banks in makeshift quarters and later in established driving camps. This wanigan is on the Bog River near Tupper Lake. *Courtesy of Special Collections, Feinberg Library, SUNY College at Plattsburgh B-2-188*

Collection 2
The Gould Paper Company

The Gould Paper Company at the confluence of the Moose and Black Rivers, Lyons Falls, N.Y. Circa 1940s. *Courtesy of Harold Link*

CHAPTER 3

An Informal History of the Gould Paper Company

William J. O'Hern

I n the village of Lyons Falls, New York, alongside thundering seventy-foot
Lyons Falls—where the Moose and Black Rivers meet—once sprawled
the immense Gould paper mill. Aglow by day and ablaze by night, its high-
speed operations ran ceaselessly 24 hours a day (except Sunday), "but its
people were as warmhearted and friendly as village life itself," reported an
article in the 1948 *Lumber Camp News:*

> *[There is] A three-way bridge at the junction of the two rivers, one of the
> few such bridges in the world. Beneath it, where the logs float lazily down
> into the plant, fishermen cast their lines. Small boys dive from log booms
> and a horse-drawn gig moves idly over the bridge in the summer sun.*
>
> *In the spring when the log drive is on, it's a different story. Then the
> river is a roaring, tumbling mass of timber. Huge jams form, requiring
> all the skill of experienced woodsmen and, sometimes, even dynamite. A
> river driver's life often depends upon his ability to run over floating logs.*

The early history of Lyons Falls began with French refugees establishing a
settlement in 1794, on the east bank of the Black River, a short distance below
the present water-power site. The pioneering settlers could not endure the
harsh climate and physical hardships and soon returned to France. The
first permanent settlement in the region was the hamlet and post office of

Lyonsdale, founded by Caleb Lyon in 1823. Soon after, in 1829, Christopher Gould, patriarch of the renowned Gould family, arrived.

His grandson, Gordias Henry Plumb Gould, known as G.H.P. Gould, became one of the wealthiest men in New York State. In 1892, G.H.P. Gould formed a partnership in the paper business with Lowville's John E. Haberer and Charles W. Pratt[5], from Boonville. The men organized under the name the Gould Paper Company with G.H.P. as president. Following the formation of the partnership came the purchase of the water-power rights from the village, and in 1895, the company completed construction of a pulp and paper mill on the west bank of the Black River.

Emily Williams tells in "Good as Gould" that the firm that Gould, Haberer and Pratt formed continued to multiply "dramatically" over the following ten years: "In 1898 the Gould company bought a mill at Shuetown, upriver from Gouldtown. Two years later the company built a sulphite mill in Lyons Falls. In 1907 the company bought two International Paper Company pulp

Three-way Bridge, Lyons Falls, N.Y. Circa 1945. With the purchase of the Gould Paper Company by the Continental Can Company in 1945, a program of modernization began. The principal objective of the program was the installation of equipment for the production of high quality pulp and paper, retaining a maximum flexibility of operations so that grades of pulp could meet the future requirements, and the installation of equipment would place the Company in a strong position on manufacturing costs. *Courtesy of Harold Link*

Lyons Falls owed its existence to the initial investors who built the dam and pulp mill and harnessed the waterpower of two major rivers in the North Country.
Courtesy of Harold Link

mills in Kosterville, on the Moose River." In *The North Country*, historian Harry Landon writes that "G.H.P. Gould …built up one of the largest strings of paper mills in northern New York."

Williams continues:

> *During the first six years, the Gould Paper Company harvested all its timber on its own vast acres in the Adirondacks. Soon the expansion of its mills demanded an additional source of raw material. In December 1902, according to a diary kept by mill manager G. Williams, the company bought the 30,000-acre Tug Hill wilderness tract for $435,000. In succeeding years the company continued to buy Tug Hill land until its holdings there totaled 70,000 acres. A 17-mile standard-gauge railroad,*

The improvements made to the groundwood, sulphite, and paper mill, the finishing room, office buildings and new steam plant at the Gould Mill between 1945–1949 were accomplished without interruption to production and during a time when the mill operated at full capacity. *Photographic image from The Lumber Camp News, Volume 11; Number 2, June, 1948*

jointly owned by Gould and the Dexter Paper Company, carried supplies to the forest hamlet of Page and brought logs to the New York Central Railroad at Glenfield.

Gould's largest tract of timber in the Adirondack Park was in the central Adirondacks. The vast holdings encompassed the wild territory of the Moose and Black River headwaters.

"The Gould Paper Company cut its 100,000 acres near North Lake, in the area drained by the South Branch of the Moose River," Williams reported in her story of the life and times of the timber tycoon."

The company managed its timber carefully, with concern for a continuing supply of logs. Gould often went into the woods to supervise the logging. No trees under ten inches could be cut. On each acre, one tall tree was left for seeds. This method left young, growing timber to naturally reforest the area.

Ten lumber camps were scattered within the company's vast territory, and 150 teams of horses worked in the woods. In early summer, lumberjacks felled the big trees with crosscut saws and axes, and peeled the bark with sharp iron-bladed spuds. Logs were cut into thirteen-foot lengths and skidded with horses to collection points.

When good sledding conditions came, crews built roads over which the big teams pulled bobsleds stacked high with logs. Gould Paper Company's main haul road started at the base of Ice Cave Mountain and continued to a landing on the Moose River. There, hundreds of thousands of logs were piled on the ice in huge tiers. When the ice melted in the spring, the logs splashed into the water and tumbled downstream to Lyons Falls.

Although the determining factor in the defeat of the Axis Powers during World War II was the spirit of the men and women under the American, the British and the Soviet flags, the final victory was wrought by the stupendous mass production of American war material: Lumber furnished the paper, cartons and boxes, the superstructure of ships and landing barges, and the basic material for much of the equipment and supplies, and was truly one of the vital cogs in the victory machine. Northeastern operators such as Gould were proud of their contribution. *Courtesy of Lyons Falls History Association*

The Gould Paper Company's lumber camps were designated by numbers. This is the Headquarters, Camp 7 (1920–1930). Fred Worden said he remembered that the day he snapped this picture "the temperature was 40 degrees below zero." The camp was situated by the head of Ice Cave Creek, snugged in the valley between Ice Cave and Canachagala Mountains. *Courtesy of Fred Worden*

1940 Ford V-8 engine. Hardwood logs were trucked out of the woods. Gould foresters left their woodlots in a good, healthy condition from which other crops could be cut. The company's philosophy of logging with regulations guaranteed the chances that a future crop could be harvested in years to come. *Author's collection*

The pulp and paper mill property at the junction of Black and Moose Rivers at Lyons Falls was continuously operated by the Gould family until 1945, when it was acquired by Continental Can. The plant's doors permanently closed in 1995.

This Gould Paper Company manufacturing operation was a whole integrated mill owning its own forests, cutting its own pulpwood for both groundwood and sulphite pulps, and manufacturing groundwood papers for printing, converting, and for specialties from its own pulps. It had an enormous developed and undeveloped water-power system.

The whitewater man or "river pig" was a special man who possessed skill, courage and determination. He worked with danger every minute he was balancing on a rolling, tumbling log floating down a river. Any misstep caused by a hidden obstruction, failing to adjust to a capricious current, or losing his concentration could spell his demise. These "glory boys" were a marvel to watch. *Courtesy of Lyons Falls History Association*

It was necessary for the plant to operate continuously for six days because of the long and involved preparations necessary to start it up. Maintenance and repair work was done on Sunday, and late that night the boilers were fired. By Monday morning the plant was ready to hum again for another continuous stretch of 144 hours.

It's interesting to note that during this time period papermaking was the sixth largest industry in America and that New York was the leading paper-

First Linn tractor used by the Gould Paper Company in 1918. Note the bright Rome Turney radiator. Softwood logs were transported over haul roads to landings to await the spring thaw log drive. *Author's collection*

End of the spring river drive. Thousands of logs from miles away arrived at Gould's mill pond. *Courtesy of Lawton L. Williams*

making state. Eighty-one towns in New York were partially or completely dependent upon paper and pulp mills for their support.

Gould employees lived in an area that extended north to Lowville and south to Remsen, a distance of forty-five miles. Many of these people owned small farms and contributed not only to the industrial economy of the area, but also to the agricultural economy.

Hard at work in the mill, their weather-beaten faces wore ready smiles. *The Lumber Camp News* reported the workers seemed "to enjoy their work, whether it be outside handling logs or inside where the steam rises in a hot, white cloud. And, indeed, in this industry, perhaps more than in any other, they are the controlling factor—for though most of the operations are automatic or semi-automatic, it takes years of experience to know just when to turn the steam up or down, just when the texture of the pulp has reached its peak of perfection.

"After hours, you'll find them down by the river trolling for bass...over in the ball park rooting for the home team...out in the garden setting tomato plants...or just chatting across the fence with a neighbor."

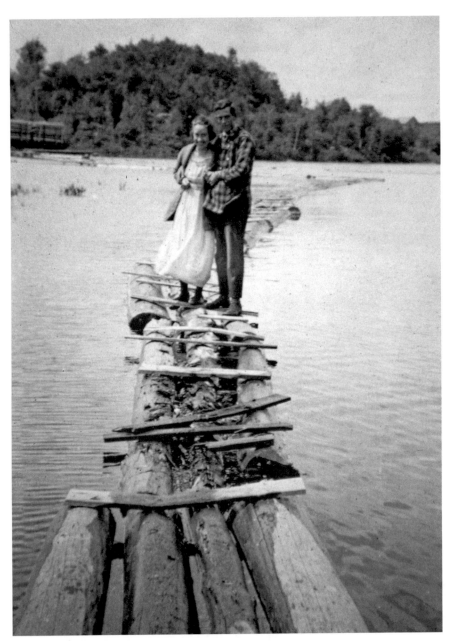

Eva Bishop and Dewitt Wiley standing on a log boom in 1920. Dewitt was a tough, experienced, callused-handed "wood tick" who worked in the woods and enjoyed the tales of those river drivers who rode logs to shore ahead of all the pulpwood. Eva cooked in the lumber camps during the last days of the ax and cross-cut saw and fell in love with playful, rugged Dewitt. *Courtesy of Ernest L. Portner*

Adirondack Logging

CHAPTER 4

Gould's Old-Time
Logging Operations

Rev. Frank A. Reed

The story of the old days in the Adirondack and Tug Hill logging camps is told in part by two old friends: the late William H. McCarthy[6] and C.W. Mason, both of whom played a vital part in the logging program of earlier days. Mr. McCarthy describes the logging experiences of former times in these terms:

> *During the last half century and more a great many changes have taken place in the lumbering business, and I have seen and experienced them all.*
>
> *The equipment used in my youth would be a curiosity today in the lumber woods. Our log sleighs were built solid with 3½-foot length runners, three 3½-foot wide beams and four-foot bunks connected together by a short neap. The loose-jointed sleigh with 8-foot runners and the 10- and 12-foot bunks used today have been developed during the years. About all the logs were moved on sleighs from the woods to the mills or streams where they could be floated to the mills. In the early days of logging, manpower and horses were the only power used.*
>
> *Most timber was cut by choppers or axe-men. There were few crosscut saws and the modern bucksaw and chain saw were not thought of.*
>
> *Bark peeling was the main job in the woods. The hemlock bark was taken to tanneries for the tanning of leather. In those days, tanneries*

were located in about every hamlet and town. The best hemlock logs were sometimes got out and sawed into lumber for local building. My father delivered hemlock logs to the sawmill for $4.00 per M[7] and thought he was getting a very good price.

Days were long, cold and wet during log hauling and driving season. There were no eight-hour days, and strikes in those days were not thought of. The average day was from 10 to 16 hours, but every man in the crew was a lumberjack and worked at no other trade, so didn't mind the long, tedious hours.

They were hard workers and hearty eaters. Oh, yes, they occasionally took a drink or went on a "bender" but they always returned to camp ready for work. If a buddy or a friend needed a helping hand they were always ready to help even though it may have meant giving their last dime. These men were all capable of doing any part of the work or taking over any particular job when necessary, and they did it with pride. While they weren't as good as Paul Bunyan they were next to him in power.

Health care changed dramatically during McCarthy's and Mason's days in the lumber woods. Injuries from crashing trees were common. In the early days a lumberjack tragically paralyzed from the chest down would have been given only a fair chance to live. By 1952, through the teamwork of physicians, nurses and hospital staff and an interested insurance carrier, a similarly-injured 'jack would receive vigorous treatment, testing and training. *Courtesy of John Donahue*

Adirondack Logging

1910 Cranberry Lake. Old-time "timber beasts" scarcely talked about black flies, mosquitoes, punkies, chiggers—in fact any pestiferous insects they encountered in the deep woods that raised painful welts. One stand-by for relief when "the 'bite' has been put on you," according to Earl Kreuzer, an old-fashioned lumberjack, was to apply a tannic acid solution in some form such as strong tea or pine tar-oil. *Courtesy of John Donahue*

Mr. Mason, who was said to be undoubtedly the greatest woodsman of Northern New York in his generation, describes life in the Tug Hill logging camps years ago:

> *Looking back over the years, it does seem as if deep snow came in the Tug Hill area much earlier than in these later times. The Gould Paper Company had pulpwood jobs both on Tug Hill and in the Moose River country and they frequently planned to haul the Tug Hill jobs first, and then move across and haul the Moose River jobs.*
>
> *One year not long after Christmas, I was on the Hill in Pete Loren's camp. I think snow came that year early in December and they had been*

Ernest Portner Sr. and Fred Portner used a crosscut saw to fell trees.
Courtesy of Lyons Falls History Association

Life in the woods is rugged at all seasons. 'Jacks worked long and laboriously and faced hazards and endured hardships daily. *Courtesy of Lyons Falls History Association*

Adirondack Logging

hauling right through the holidays. That was one of the snowy winters, which have helped to make the Tug Hill country famous. The snow when I was there was just about five feet deep on the level. After visiting Pete's camp, I crossed the woods on snowshoes to Barnes' Mills, where a crew was sawing lumber. I think that most of the crew were boarding at John Denison's house. That was the place known on the map as Hooker.

Sawing spruce trees into lengths with crosscut saws. *Courtesy of Edward Blankman (The Lloyd Blankman Collection)*

About two miles north of Hooker, Tom White had a pulpwood camp on what was known as the Plain Tree Road. I went and visited his camp. The next day I came back as far as the Denison House. There came up another blinding snowstorm. At the insistence of the residents of Hooker, I stayed over that day until the storm should be passed. On the next day I recrossed the woods to the Loren Camp, which I reached just as the crew was sitting down for supper.

Well, Loren's crew had finished their hauling job and were to move across into Moose River country the next day.

At 1 o'clock the next morning, breakfast was served and then all hands turned in to pack up the camp goods. Everything was packed up

Whether living in an Adirondack or Tug Hill lumber camp, the lumbermen cut trees in summer and piled the logs on skidways near the load roads so they could be drawn out by horse sleighs the following winter and delivered to the mill.
Courtesy of Edward Blankman (The Lloyd Blankman Collection)

except the stoves, the bed frames and the bed springs. Timbers were brought in to prop up the roofs, for believe it or not, the snow often reached a depth of eight or nine feet (or more).

I believe there were thirteen teams and the procession got started about 3 o'clock. Roads were good in the woods, but as soon as we left the woods we found the roads drifted full of hard-packed snow. Every man became a member of a road crew. A track was shoveled and tramped down ahead of the head team and the other teams followed.

Out in the clear, a bitter cold wind cut like a knife. I had with me a long double-wool blanket. We opened it full length and wound it snugly around the two women cooks and held it in place with large safety shawl pins. The outfit reached Turin about noon.

A telephone message was sent to a hotel in Lyons Falls that the gang was on the way and to have dinner ready when we arrived. We reached Lyons Falls at 1 o'clock and dinner was ready—and were we ready for

Adirondack Logging

it! It had been twelve hours since we had had breakfast and we had packed up the camp goods, broken roads and made the long trip in the biting cold wind. Well, we ate up about everything that was eatable in Lyons Falls.

I left the outfit at Lyons Falls—the crew went on and stayed at the McKeever camp that night and the next day reached the camp for the Moose River hauling job.

Frank A. Reed's first year in the Adirondack lumber woods was 1917. At that time, the Gould Paper Company had three major logging operations in the Adirondacks, which were under the supervision of John B. Todd.

Teamsters hauled loads of logs over winter roads to the Big Landing. Note the spring-pole binder used to tighten chains on the load. *Courtesy of the Maitland C. DeSormo Collection*

The Moose River operation was carried on by James Canaan as contractor. Mr. Canaan had two large camps on the Indian River with Gardiner Poore and Joseph Gordon as foremen. Two smaller camps were run by sub-contractors: Clinton and Walter Thompson at Stink Lake Mountain and Henry Hoe on Dead Man's Creek.

Lewis Joslin was the operator for the company in the Red River area with his son, Mort, as assistant superintendent. The large camp was located near the Upper Dam with Ward King as sub-contractor farther down the river.

Doug Purcell and Frank Murphy had two camps on North Lake under Mr. Compeau, who was general contractor.

In all of these extensive operations, felling and cutting were done with the cross-cut saw and the axe. The buck saw had not come to the Adirondacks at that time. The pulpwood was all felled and peeled in the early summer and cut into logs and skidded by horse in the late summer and fall.

As the winter season approached, it became apparent that Mr. Todd had a master plan to merge the results of these three separate log jobs into one big logging operation. A winter hauling road was constructed from North Lake over Ice Cave Mountain to the South Branch of the Moose River, where the logs were to be landed at the same big landing with the logs from the Moose River camps. The big hauling operation required the services of at least 150 teams.

The haul from North Lake to the Moose River was a one-trip haul, with several doubling teams stationed at strategic intervals on the upgrade.

The logs from the North Lake and Moose River camps were landed successfully that year at the Moose River landing. Mr. Joslin landed his logs on the Red River, where a system of three dams had been constructed.

With the coming of spring, Mr. Joslin drove his logs down the Red River into the Moose, where they joined the other logs at the Big Landing and moved down the river to the mill at Lyons Falls.

Mr. Fuller was the foreman on the Red River drive that spring, with William Mealus on the Upper Moose and James Haley on the Lower Moose. Skilled river drivers moved a tremendous log drive that year, sometimes through very rough water and in many dangerous places. At times they had narrow escapes, but the only fatal accident was at the Lower Dam on the Red River, where one man lost his life.

Adirondack Logging

In the fall of 1918, Mr. Todd entertained a visitor who was destined to exert a profound influence upon Adirondack logging. He was Mr. H.H. Linn, of Oneonta, New York, who had invented a gasoline tractor, propelled by tracks in the rear and guided on the road by steering runners in front.

After some discussion, Mr. Todd said, "If one of your tractors will haul as much pulp as twenty teams, I will buy some of them."

In answer to Mr. Todd's statement, Mr. Linn brought a tractor into the woods for experimentation. He proved that one tractor could do the work of twenty teams. Mr. Todd purchased three tractors for use on the North Lake and Moose River hauls that winter.

This was the beginning of an era of tractor transportation in the Adirondacks and much of the Northeast. As time went on, Mr. Todd replaced these tractors with new and more powerful ones, which had been made in the Linn factory. These powerful tractors, in the hands of skilled drivers, sometimes hauled as many as eighteen loaded sleighs at a trip.

1922 at Camp 7. Third from Lt. H.P. Gould, far Rt. H.H. Linn. The Linn tractor proved its worth and quickly became "the new kid on the block." *Courtesy of the Town of Webb Historical Association P5798*

The Linn tractor made its way onto the market following that successful 1918 trial on the steep slopes of Ice Cave Mountain in the central Adirondacks. The powerful machines had proved their value hauling trains of log sleds much like a muscular locomotive engine. According to Rev. Reed, "Surplus tanks after World War I had also laid the foundation for the use of crawler tractors, particularly for yarding the logs."

The introduction of Linn tractors totally changed the logging industry. For additional information about these extraordinary pulling, hauling, plowing and maneuvering machines that Holman Harry Linn demonstrated to anyone who showed an interest in his tractors, refer to Appendix A: *An Informal History of the Revolutionary Linn Tractor,* and Appendix B: *Leigh Portner's Logging Connection with Linn Tractors.*

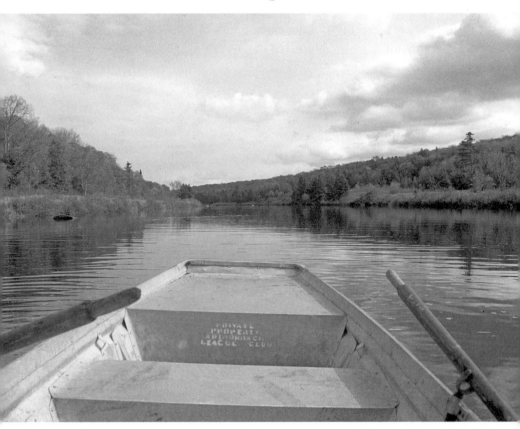

The Big Landing, in summer, on the South Branch of the Moose River is a long wide stillwater. *Photo by the author*

CHAPTER 5

Old-Time Logging Horses

William J. O'Hern

Prior to the coming of the Linn tractors, large, strong oxen and workhorses were as important to the logging operation as was a good lumberjack. J.C. Ryan began working in the lumber woods in 1918. He explained, "Good horses were like good men—if they were not worth good wages they were not worth feeding.

"A team of horses and one man would skid up to 150 logs per day. There was usually one 'swamper'[8] cutting trails for each skidding tram. Often, as many horses skidded as hauled logs in camp… the skidding was done early in January before the snow got deep. Most sleigh-haul logs were decked"— loaded on to a sleigh in the woods so a whole load of logs could be piled in one spot. It was a waste of time and energy to move a partially loaded sleigh several times.

Ryan pointed out, "The cost of log skidding was one of the factors a lumber camp foreman watched very closely. And he always tried to get a good straw-boss[9] to handle the crews."

The immense, one-ton Belgians the Gould Paper Company used hauled massive loads of pulp logs over the hardest of skid paths. Their work was heavy, taxing and dangerous. Iced haul roads were made by rolling the snow and then driving a big sprinkler or water box over it to build up several inches of solid ice. This allowed well-shod horse teams to haul log sleighs from the large skid ways to the river landing. Hauling over these iced roads often

Part of the George Colvin[10] stable, with veteran Jack Stewart in charge. Colvin was one of the larger and more progressive logging operators in the Adirondack and Tug Hill area. *Courtesy of Eric Johnson, Executive Editor at The Northeastern Logger*

involved steep inclines and downgrades where a snatch team was hitched to help get over a rise or hitched on the back runners to arrest a descent, but loads sometimes "got away." The horses seldom escaped these accidents alive. On the most damning descents, sleighs were held back by a Barrenger brake, a system of long cables wrapped around revolving drums at the rise, so that both load and horses would get down safely.

Clarence J. Strife[11] thinks it over. During C.J. Strife's logging career in northern New York his total cutting program included about 500,000 cords of pulp wood and 125,000,000 feet of hardwood. *Photograph by William Weedmark. Courtesy The Northeastern Logger, November, 1952*

The revolutionary methods of plowing, rolling and icing roads led to rapid and efficient hauling. Rev. Reed said it was so efficient that the old-time axmen had difficulty "felling and trimming enough trees to keep the expanded program in operation." Technology's answer was the crosscut saw.

Linn tractor driver Henry Ruber recalled that in 1917 the Moose River-North Lake area had more than one hundred teams of horses operating at Gould logging camps. Planning was required to keep them running smoothly in a regular hauling rotation.

The work animals were purchased in the late summer from any of the numerous sources of supply in and out of the North Country. The Sullivan

Colvin was a pioneer in using the beds of Tug Hill brooks as truck roads for the summer and early winter transportation of both pulpwood and hardwood logs. The nature of the rock made it easy to clear from the route of travel with a bulldozer. This method was also used on other Gould operations. Circa 1940s. *Courtesy of Harold Link*

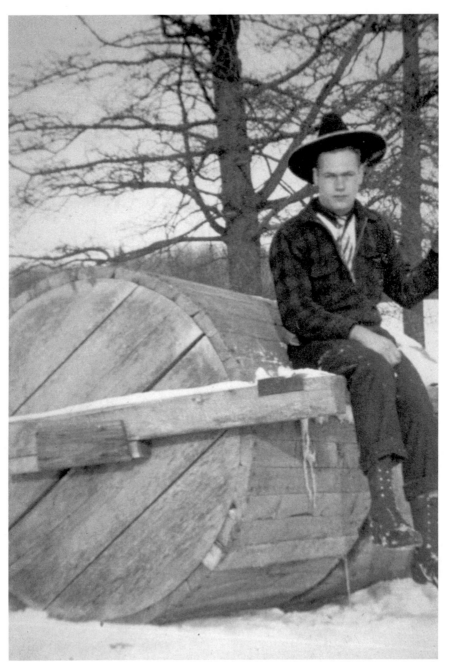

Howard Wieman sits on a horse-drawn wooden snow roller. Having a good ice road for hauling began with rolling the snow once the right-of-way was cut and the road was laid out for grade and drainage. *Courtesy of Howard Wieman*

Brothers in Utica and Aldous LaPlantney of Harrisville, New York, were two well-known dealers in logging horses. Some of the horses were experienced from several years of working in the woods, but many of them were fresh from the western farms where they were being superseded by the tractor. The logging contractors bought the harness-broken workhorses in the fall for around four hundred dollars per beast. In the spring they were sold for as little as twenty-five dollars. Some went to dealers who had enough pasturage to carry them over the summer; others went directly into dog food. It was economics as much as technology that caused their phasing out. A logging contractor could not usually afford to pay a man for the horses' daily care until they were again needed.

In earlier years of horse transportation, this recognized method of logging Tug Hill was done before Christmas because the Tug Hill is the greatest snow belt of New York State, with snow often reaching a depth of four to five feet. The horse teams were then transferred to the Adirondacks for other log hauls. *Author's collection*

With the advent of mechanization, J.B. Todd continued to keep some horses. The animals could do the kind of work no gasoline vehicle could conceivably achieve. On steep slopes in the woods, where no tractor could maneuver, a horse with only a margin of management (or perhaps none) could withdraw

A sprinkle box was drawn over snow roads by teams of older horses that could handle themselves in the dark and on the ice, or by tracked vehicle. A water tank conductor's job was one of the very special jobs in the haul camps. *Courtesy of Earl M. Kreuzer*

a log from a dogged stump or other barrier, winding and wheeling until the log was snaked in to the skidway landing.

In 1919, Stanley H. Sisson of the Raquette River Paper Company summed up his opinion of the use of Caterpillar tractors[12] that steered by means of a steer sled in front compared to the use of draft horses. His viewpoint appeared in section VI of the Empire State Forest Products Association.

Well-maintained roads of ice were essential to a logging operation. Water was sprayed on a road through holes in the bottom of the sprinkler box. The conductor could open and close the holes as needed. Tanks had heaters to keep the water from freezing.
Courtesy of Howard Wieman

Summary of Experience. There are 4 points which seem of particular importance in the use of tractors: (1). A machine of simplicity, sound construction and sufficiently rugged to stand the punishment of logging. (2). Warm garages and competent repair men. (3). A separate road on which tractors may return empty at full speed. (4). A dispatch system which will keep the machines moving and prohibits hold-ups for loading and unloading. For this purpose a driver's report card is possible, which will show where the machine has spent its time for each day and reasons.

Big loads earned bragging rights. 21 cords (298 logs) hauled by one team moved easily over a well-maintained iced road. *Courtesy of George R. Cataldo*

"Altho our costs records are not complete at this time, I feel safe in saying that it would have cost at least one third more to draw the same amount of logs with teams.

"I have roughly calculated the thing as follows in the case of the team versus the tractor—these factors are widely variable with different concerns and different localities, but are fairly indicative.

One Pair of Horses

Purchase price	...($500.00)
Interest 6%, 6 months	...$15.00
Depreciation prior to spring sale 10%	...$50.00
For capital charge dead horses 3%	...$15.00
Feed for sixty days in woods	...$141.00
Teamster for sixty days in woods	...$300.00
Horsemen at headquarters	...$54.00
Feed for horses at headquarters (100 days)	...$200.00
Total	...$775.00

Plus cost to work one team one day hauling logs ...$15.50

Double Headers to Landing—basis 9 cords—1 trip—cost $1.72 per cord.

One Tractor

Purchase price	...($5,000.00)
Depreciation 20%	...$1,000.00
Interest 6%	...$300.00
Summer repairs—labor	...$18.00
Winter repairs—labor	...$110.00
Annual renewal plus repair parts	...$50.00
Fuel cost plus lubricant	...$400.00
Driver—wages	...$275.00
Total	...$2,153.00

Plus cost to operate one tractor one day hauling logs ...$43.06

Double Headers to Landing—basis 30 cords—2 trips—60 cords—cost 71.7 cents per cord.

I can say also that we drew logs ten miles with tractors for 63 cents less per cord than we were able to do with teams on a 3 to 4 mile haul under the same general condition."

The horse was every bit as important as the lumberjack in getting out the logs from the vast virgin softwood timber stands of Upstate New York, but its days were numbered following the introduction of steam haulers and skidders, followed by the even more efficient Linn tractors.

CHAPTER 6

The Gould Paper Company's North Lake Operations

William J. O'Hern

When Rev. A.L. Byron-Curtiss came to the headwaters of the Black River, he was another witness to two logging ages: the early logging period of the "shanty boys," and the advent of mechanical equipment. His first exposure was during the tail end of the early period in the 1890s, when Gid Perry and James Canan, running small operations, were the principal jobbers around North Lake. It was the custom then to send a squad of men out to the place selected for the headquarters of each job during the early fall. There they would build rough logging camps. Once the camps were established, gangs of hard-working, hard-drinking choppers, the "shanty boys," came in and worked through the spring river drive.

The second phase brought the many innovations discussed in earlier chapters. During the early teens of the 1900s, the Gould Paper Company moved into the North Lake region, Byron-Curtiss's neighborhood.

It was during this period when Rev. Frank A. Reed recalled in his book *Lumberjack Sky Pilot* a 100-mile cross-country journey he took in May 1917 to visit "the Gould Paper Company camps up the Moose River from McKeever." Reed wrote, "A hike through the woods to North Lake led to a camp run by Frank Murphy and Doug Purcell of Lewis County for the Gould Paper Company. This job would later become a striking demonstration of careful planning and large-scale execution on the hauling phase of the operation. On this trip the "sky pilot" met Rev. Byron-Curtiss, who had a camp on North Lake and was the author of the well-known book, *Nat Foster.*

The Gould Paper Company was a big outfit by this time. They occupied two of Canan's original camp sites, expanding the affairs to fit their needs. They also chose sites for additional camps in central locations, each as close to the logging operation as possible. In the vicinity of North Lake, Gould operated Camp 5 near Horn Lake, Camp 7 in the deep, wide valley between Canachagala and Ice Cave mountains, and Camp 9 on a rise above the great stillwater on the South Branch of the Moose River and beyond the western end of Stink Lake Mountain. Camp 10 was set up along Elbow Creek, north of Honnedaga Lake.

Far off in the deep recesses of the forest beyond the eccentric Kettle Jones's old camp site, where Byron-Curtiss first vacationed in 1896, the minister would hear during late fall the echoing blows of the wood choppers' double-bitted axes from early morning until darkness. Spruce, pine, hemlock, balsam and cedar fell by the hundreds of thousands, timber that had grown over centuries in a vast expanse of primeval forest, standing in valleys, blanketing the hillsides, and darkening steep slopes whose colossal rock masses are the oldest of all rock formations in the world.

Byron-Curtiss couldn't help but be intrigued by the lumber camps and the lumber business all around him at North Lake. From his first glimpses of Forestport's mills in 1891, to transporting lumberjacks years later on his North Lake ferry, to his friendship with Scudder Todd, the "woods boss" of Gould's North Lake operations, Byron-Curtiss had been fascinated with the life of the lumbermen. Years earlier, Scudder's father John B., a superintendent at Gould's, offered him the opportunity to live and work at one of the camps through the winter should he ever be able to coordinate it with his clerical duties or when (or if) he ever retired.

OPPOSITE: Rev. Byron-Curtiss, circa 1930s. "B-C," as he referred to himself, and G.H.P. Gould shared a common condition: rheumatism, a common complaint around which they often started a conversation. Gould introduced B-C to his superintendent, John B. Todd. Todd, in turn introduced B-C to Frank Reed in 1918.

About this same time, logger J.E. Cannan of Tug Hill, who it has been reported once employed more than 500 men, designed Gould Paper Company's "10-camp logging system." This timber removal operation, which included the use of twelve Linn tractors, was designed to transport logs through the mountainous North Lake territory to the landing on the South Branch of the Moose River. *Courtesy of Thomas and Doris Kilbourn.* (*The Rev. A.L. Byron-Curtiss Collection*)

  *Adirondack Logging*

St. Catherine's Outdoor Chapel at Nat Foster Lodge. B-C's memorial chapel and camp were often a resting place for lumberjacks going into distant lumber camps. B-C was a wealth of stories about the 'jacks he had met. *Courtesy of Thomas and Doris Kilbourn. (The Rev. A.L. Byron-Curtiss Collection)*

Scarely beyond the surge of traffic darting
Cradled midst a chain, with lofty mountains parting,
Lies a lake of glistening steel; a gem set to grace.
The solemnity of what a Master hand once traced.
The myriad waters catch the shore's reflection
And thus reveal the man whose passion fashioned
A simple Lakeside Shrine, admist the stately trees.

In the sun's first rays, the cross gleams out across the lake
With but the canopy of sky, the glorious dawn breaks
Its light before an Altar no walls conceal.
And so the mossy earth's a kneeling bench
One wakes to lift up the soul with true reverence.
An offering of wild flowers told of someone blessed.
For here in God's simplicity, the soul's refreshed.
                    —Hazel Todd, Forestport, N.Y. July 4, 1935

The Reverend found the logging camps picturesque. No two were exactly alike, but they resembled each other so closely in architectural style and furnishings that a description of one serves as a description of all. By and large the buildings that constituted the camps were not built for many years of use; rather, they were temporary structures pinned, spiked and hammered together from a combination of green timber and rough-sawn wood. They consisted of an office (with space for the bookkeeper, time-keeper and the company store); stables and barns for animals, tack and related paraphernalia; a blacksmith and carpenter shop; and a main bunk house or men's camp complete with adjoining kitchen and dining area. A root cellar, too, was as common and necessary as was an icebox for the population at large outside the woods.

Emily Mitchell Wires stands on the porch of Gould's old Camp 5. Circa 1900. [*Author's note: This camp is distinguished by the adjective "old" from Gould's later-day Camp 5 that was located along Wolf Creek above the Indian River.*] Positioned along Gould's log road to the Indian River, sandwiched between the western base of Ice Cave Mountain and the North Branch of the Black River, old Camp 5 was a favorite stopover for anglers on their way to Horn Lake. *Courtesy Roy E. Wires (The Emily Mitchell Wires Collection)*

Howard Wieman loading logs. Howard felt in all the world there was no place more complete to be working than in the depth of winter in the Adirondack Mountains. Only those who had experienced it could fully appreciate what it meant to be working deep in the woods with the cold and deep snow in all kinds of weather conditions. He joked there were few men unaccustomed to it who could fight off its effects altogether, and it drove those men mad with spruce fever. *Courtesy of Howard Wieman*

The largest buildings were the men's camp and the stable. The latter was usually large enough to shelter a minimum of ten to twenty horses or oxen and sometimes as many as fifty head of stock. Camp buildings were long, low structures made from logs laid up cob-house style. The crevices between the peeled logs were packed with moss or clay chinking or, to save time, small straight saplings of a diameter slightly larger than the gaps between the outside walls were positioned over the cracks and nailed into the adjoining logs. The low, sloping roofs were clad with bark, hand-split wooden shingles or tar paper. The floor supports began as spruce poles hewn flat on the upper side and laid level. Rough planking for floor boards was then laid over the joists. A simple two-batten door hung from leather or iron hinges. If the carpenter was particularly skilled, he would fashion wooden hinges that turned on burl hangers. Small windows were usually fit into the gable ends. While not affording the refinements of a fine hotel, the cabins were snug and warm.

Adirondack Logging

The dormitory or men's bunkroom with its attached kitchen/dining room was the focal point of each camp. Lining the sides and ends of the men's room were built-in bunks, the lower and upper front rails of each range of bunks being fashioned from maple poles, while the bottom of the bunk, upon which the mattress of balsam boughs was placed, was made of small

Scudder Todd. *Courtesy of Fred Worden*

flexible spruce poles. Sheets were a luxury unknown in camp. Instead, "shanty boys" contented themselves with a couple of blankets for bedding while grain bags filled with pine needles formed their pillows. In those bunks the men would lie with heads and feet alternating. With a dozen sticks of seasoned hardwood blazing in the big box stove, they were rarely cold when they slept.

Gould's tractor driver's building at Camp 7. Circa 1924. Regardless of the feud between H.H. Linn and Alvin O. Lombard and the legal wrangle between Benjamin Holt and Clarence Best over patent rights and the trademark for the Caterpillar, the revolutionary mechanical workhorse was the single invention, according to Linn historian and collector Robert Smith, "that changed the face of the earth as much as the crawler tractor did." *Courtesy of Fred Worden*

Attached to the dormitory by a breezeway was the "cook shanty," a portion of which served as the dining room. Over the big wood-burning cooking range at one end of the building, the cook, the most important person in camp, would be found busy boiling, frying and baking for the crew of hearty boarders. He brewed tea and coffee in a pot that held nearly a barrel of either beverage. Lumberjacks liked their hot drinks "strong enough to float an

OPPOSITE: The author at Camp 9 (1930–1947), the Landing Camp. This was the only remaining building of Gould logging camps by 1989. The author was given permission from the Adirondack League Club to help Linn tractor collector Leigh Portner salvage usable pieces of logging machinery from the remains of Gould's tractor garage and yard. *Photo by the author*

iron wedge." Soup was prepared in a big tin wash boiler. In the early years it was usually bean soup, known in the camps as "swagger." Eating utensils consisted of an array of tin cups and plates, and steel knives and forks. The long tables, made of planks, were without tablecloths or napkins. Around them the crew would gather at 4:30 in the morning and at 6 at night, with their other two meals served hot to them in the woods.

Camp 9's office survived until 2002. The prevailing thought is that it burned to the ground at the hands of an arsonist. The aged building had showed its seventy years, but it was the single surviving structure that marked the location of Gould's later headquarters. Discernible beside the building's site is a depression where the root cellar's door once led to the cold storage area.

Rev. Frank Reed entering logging camp. *Courtesy of Lyons Falls History Association*

The route of the major haul road nearby—where hundreds of thousands of cords of wood passed on the way to the "Landing," the frozen surface of the stillwater on the South Branch of the Moose River— is barely visible, nearly a footpath in most places. The site of Camp 10—nothing more than a slight clearing in the forest—is near Adirondack League Club land. The locations of camps 5 and 7, mere clearings also, are on state land, too.

Very little first-hand information has survived from the lumbering operations of the Gould Paper Company at the headwaters of the Black River. Reverend Byron-Curtiss most often visited Camp 7. In Collection 5, Rev. Byron-Curtiss' story, "Flapjacks for Lumberjacks," describes the camp and tells of everyday life there.

CHAPTER 7

The Coming of the Linn Tractor

William J. O'Hern

Clarence W. Mason was a thirty-five-year veteran Christian "sky pilot" in the Adirondack Lumber Camp Parish when he decided he wanted to write "The Coming of the Tractor" for the May 1949 issue of the *Lumber Camp News*. The only thing Mason had published had been prayers and accounts of his travels in the woods to visit lumber camps. He wrote from personal experience when he came home after work, or in camp at night, but usually, he was too tired after a long snowshoe trek in very deep snow.

Rev. Reed said of Mason and his ministry as a sky pilot, "He became increasingly recognized by the men of the woods for a variety of achievements."

Mason was considered an outstanding woodsman. He knew, Reed went on, "the Adirondack wilderness better than any other man and traveled long distances through the forest as well as over tote roads and trails." Reed was not bragging about Mason but simply stating facts. Mason estimated that during his active lumber camp ministry, he had traveled "450,000 miles by automobile and 30,000 miles on foot, often walking as many as thirty miles in a day to reach some isolated camp."

The men in the camps were not only interested in the religious message he brought; they recognized Mason's love for his fellow man, his oratory skills and his deeds. One needs to remember that Mason journeyed to camps during the days before radios were handy, and communication was difficult.

Throughout the 1920s, Linn Manufacturing Corporation catalogs touted, "There is a definite swing toward LINN haulage! Contractors, loggers, mine and quarry owners, large industrials, and townships and counties, have standardized on LINNS for all heavy duty, as well as a wide variety of other haulage needs. The reasons are obvious. In design, construction and performance, the LINN is wholly unlike any other type of haulage equipment available. It combines the massive power of the crawler type tractor with the payload capacity, ease of operation and safety of the motor trucks. In addition, it has many exclusive features which enable it to do more, and earn more, on most hauling tasks. LINNS are furnished powered with rugged, high torque, 4 or 6 cylinder gas engines, and with the proved 6 cylinder LINN-Cummins Diesel engine."
Author's collection

Mason's stories in camp, his news and true tales of spending a winter night on Big Slide Mountain, experiences with big work horses, an escape from a falling rock, being lost in the woods and his wild rides and other adventures, according to Rev. Reed "laid the foundation for the creation of the *Lumber Camp News*," a publication Reed established in 1939 for the entertainment and education of men in the lumber camps.

By the time Mason's Linn tractor article appeared, the paper had grown in volume and news coverage as well as circulation.

We revere what has come before. Classic trains, trucks and cars, hand-crafted colonial furniture, the old masters' paintings, and the first caterpillar—a gasoline tractor propelled by tracks in the rear and guided on the road by steering runners in the front—the first of its kind.

Clarence Mason tells in his own words why he cared to document the coming of the Linn tractor to Adirondack logging operations in the fall of 1918.

> *I will tell the story just as it was told to me by Mr. John B. Todd. Mr. Todd was for many years Woods Superintendent for the Gould Paper Company of Lyons Falls, N.Y., and was still Superintendent at the time he told me this story.*
>
> *The Gould Paper Company bought the pulpwood stumpage of the Adirondack League Club and has lumbered over most of their pulpwood*

Sky pilot Mason spoke to loggers with passion about the Bible being the record of man's search for God and a higher way of life. The holy book contains a variety of literature. It traces the rise and fall of empires, the movements of people, the origin and growth of great ideas and particularly the story of the Hebrew people in their struggle upward. It is also the record of God's revelation of Himself to man. *Courtesy of the Goff-Nelson Memorial (Tupper Lake) Library*

holdings. At the time of which we write, the early part of the twentieth century, the Adirondack League Club owned a large amount of extra good pulpwood in the Black River watershed. That part of their holdings took in Horn Lake and Honnedaga Lake, on which one of their club-houses is located.

The LUMBER CAMP NEWS

VOLUME 10; NUMBER 3   PUBLISHED MONTHLY AT OLD FORGE, NEW YORK   JULY, 1948

Field Day Planned-Old Forge July 17

PROGRAM

Parade 12:30 P. M.—

Participating units: Town of Webb School Band, New York State Music School Band, Old Forge Fire Department, Covey-Pashley Legion Post 893, The Boy Scouts, The Girl Scouts.

Cross-Cut Saw Contest—

Each two-man team will roll logs onto the skids, saw them into short lengths and pile them between stakes. Contestants will be judged by the quantity sawed and piled in ten minutes. Prizes: 1st team, $50.00; 2nd team, $20.00.

Axe Chopping Contest—

Contestants will be judged by the quantity of blocks chopped and piled in fifteen minutes. Prizes: 1st place, $40.00; 2nd place, $15.00.

Bucksaw Contest—

Contestants will be judged by the quantity of blocks rolled onto skids, sawed and piled in fifteen minutes. Prizes: 1st place, $40.00; 2nd place, $15.00.

Tree Felling Contest—

Contestants will each chop down a tree and attempt to drive a stake by felling the tree onto it. Prizes: 1st place, $40.00; 2nd place, $15.00.

Chain Saw Contest

Two-man teams will roll logs onto skids, saw them into blocks and pile them. Contestants will be judged by the quantity piled in ten minutes. Prizes: 1st team, $50.00; 2nd team, $20.00.

Forest Fire Fighting Demonstration—

This demonstration is put on by the New York State Conservation Department.

Log Rolling Contest in Lake—

This will be an elimination contest with two river drivers to a log, each trying to roll the other off. The winners on each log will

A BUCKSAW CONTEST

CONSERVATION PLEDGE

I

Pledge as an American To save and faithfully to Defend from waste the Natural resources of My country—its soil And minerals, its Forests, waters, And Wildlife

Committee Planning Interesting Variety of Contests, Prizes

A Woodsmen's Field Day will be staged near the beach on Old Forge Lake on Saturday, July 17. On this occasion many woodsmen will match their skill and strength in a variety of events in which the axe and saw play a prominent role

The program will include contests with the bucksaw and the cross-cut as well as chopping contests and log rolling. The New York State Conservation Department will give a demonstration of forest fire fighting, and several distributors of woods tools and machinery will exhibit and demonstrate their latest equipment.

The list of judges includes John Curry of the U. S. Forest Service, H. V. Hart of the St. Regis Paper Company, Sid Lawson of the Atkins Saw Company, Mr. E. Blue of the New York State Conservation Dept., Prof. Edward F. McCarthy of the New York State College of Forestry and Perry Leary, State Forester of Vermont.

The Committee

The Field Day is being promoted by the Woodsmen's Club. It has been planned by a committee consisting of Louis Seheult of the Finch Pruyn Company as chairman, James E. Davis of the Gould Paper Company, Clarence Strife, Joseph Lindsay and Don Kiefer of the C. J. Strife Lumber Company, Roy Lavoy of the Oval Wood Dish Company and Philip W. Burdick, Supervisor of the Town of Webb.

Kinne Williams, Al Woodford and Ernest Blue of the New York State Conservation Department are the committee in charge of the Forest Fighting Demonstration.

A local committee composed of Leo Burke and Floyd Farmer of the Old Forge Fire Department, Jake

Frank McCormack Dies at Bangor, Maine

Frank McCormack passed away suddenly at the E.M.G. Hospital, Bangor, Maine, Saturday, May 22, 1948.

Frank was formerly employed by the Parker Young Co., Lincoln, N. H., and the Houlton Plywood, Houlton, Maine. For the past two years he worked for the Atlas Plywood Corp., Howland, Maine.

Rev. Reed, part of a small force of Presbyterian ministers who traveled to the lumber camps providing religious services and support for any men who needed help battling the addictions common to many lumberjacks, gambling and alcoholism, was the founder and editor of *The Lumber Camp News*. It was at Reed's suggestion that Rev. Byron-Curtiss wrote a series of articles for the newspaper about North Lake's hermit, Atwell Martin, and other North Woods characters. *Author's collection*

Road monkey Louie along his sand hill inspecting a sleigh of logs that overturned on the steep slope after some of the bull-bows (the logs set between the loads to keep the sleds from running into each other and the train from buckling) broke. *Courtesy Fred Worden*

As far as I know, pulpwood logs have never been driven on the Black River between Forestport and Lyons Falls. The Moose River and the Black River meet at Lyons Falls and the Gould Paper Company wanted the pulpwood from the Black River Valley hauled over the divide and landed at what was called No. 9 so the logs would come down to their paper mill with the Moose River Drive. The Gould Paper Company made a contract with Murphy and Compeau to cut and deliver 25,000 cords of pulpwood to No. 9.

When I first began to visit the lumber camps in 1914 and for many years after that, all the work of skidding logs, breaking out log roads during the winter and hauling the logs to the landings was done with horses. A cord of peeled logs will weigh not far from 3,000 pounds. A set of bobs ironed up with long, heavy hardwood bunks will weigh well up towards a ton. If you build a load of five cords of logs you may figure for yourself about how much weight you have.

Logs being unloaded into neat rows on a frozen landing. Most of Gould's outfit of working lumberjacks never worked at anything else. They were of four or five nationalities, but they were all alike in one thing—they were all 'jacks who liked the work, or couldn't get away from it. *Author's collection*

The weakest available place in the ridge between the Black River and the Moose was a road up what was called Ice Cave Mountain. It was about four miles of steady, stiff grade from the bottom to the summit. I have seen many teams in the woods where each horse would weigh eighteen hundred pounds. Strong, young horses.

A C-cab (without a windshield) Linn tractor demonstrating Mr. Linn's claim that the tracked vehicle had the ability to deliver heavy payloads over Ice Cave Mountain. Circa 1918. *Courtesy of Ernest L. Portner*

It is one thing to haul a load of five cords of logs on a downgrade, well-iced road, and it is quite a different thing to haul the same load for miles up a steep grade. The horses did their best, but they didn't begin to get all of the 25,000 cords to the landing at No. 9.

H.H. Linn (far right) in front of one of his early tractors. Circa winter of 1918–19.
Courtesy of Ernest L. Portner

Mr. Todd said Gould told him to go look the road over. He walked the whole length of the road, up one side and down the other, and went back to the office, and said, "There is no use talking; it is simply out of the question to think of hauling any amount of wood over such a road with horses."

About that time Mr. Gould received word from a man by the name of Linn that he would like to meet Mr. Gould in Utica. Mr. Gould sent Mr. Todd to Utica and he met Mr. Linn at Bagg's Hotel. That was a famous hostelry that stood near the New York Central Railroad station.

After a word of greeting, Mr. Linn said, "I understand you are having trouble getting your pulpwood hauled over to the landing." Mr. Todd admitted that the horses had found it hard to haul heavy loads up-grade. Mr. Linn said, "I have a machine that will haul your loads up-grade." Mr. Todd replied, "Have you ever hauled loads of logs with your machine over winter roads?" Mr. Linn replied, "No, but I am sure my machine would haul any load you could put on." What was the price of the tractor? $6,000. Mr. Todd said, "I turned it down; it seemed to me to be too much money to put into something that had never been tried out."

The first Linn tractor purchased by The Gould Paper Company.
Courtesy of Lyons Falls Pulp and Paper Company's archives

Before they parted, Mr. Linn said, "Would you be willing to have me drive one of my tractors up into the woods and show what it would do at my own expense?" Mr. Todd replied, "I would be very glad to have you do so." So they drove on the tote road to old No. 8, reaching the camp about dark. Bill Mealus was foreman at No. 8. Bill was a good foreman and he had a good load of about five cords standing in the yard ready to hitch onto in the morning.

In the morning they hitched the tractor onto the load and started up the log road to the summit. They overtook one of Murphy's teams on the road hauling a load by short hitches. They yelled at the driver to get out of the road. He pulled off as far as he could and the tractor with the load pulled off the road the other way and they crowded past. Then they hitched a chain onto Murphy's load and hauled tram and load back into the road, unhitched the chain and went on to the summit. There they left the load and came back for another, but the second trip they hauled up two loads, one behind the other. And the third trip they took three loads.

Mr. Todd said, "That convinced me, and I told Compeau to write a check for $6,000 to pay for the tractor. Before that night they were hauling four loads at a trip and I told Compeau to write checks for two more tractors."

Compeau had a little impediment in his speech. He began to swing his arms and said, "I...I ain't got it in the bank." "Never mind," Mr. Todd replied, "write the check. The money will be in the bank before the check arrives." Compeau began to be scared about it and he said, "Well, if-if you w-want to d-do business th-that way, y-you do it. I d-don't want to."

So the company took over the job of hauling. I have seen as many as fifteen loads of logs go in a string from the summit down to No. 9. The company built a garage large enough to hold ten or twelve tractors at No. 7. They heated the garage with steam and kept mechanics at work on the tractors through the night to have them ready for the next day's hauling. They also did all the breaking out of new roads with a five-ton Holt Caterpillar. It was altogether a great relief for the horses.

CHAPTER 8

Gould's Freight Hauling Arrangement with the North Lake Navigation Company

William J. O'Hern

"Bucksaws and *BIG* fish," that's the way Byron-Curtiss once described his connection with John B. Todd. "We hit it off right away," he wrote. The men shared many interests and grew to be fast friends. It was Todd who took the Reverend around to see the pulpwood being felled, peeled, and cut into logs in the early summer. He was also the person who authorized the transfer of freight-hauling contracts from Charley Brown, North Lake reservoir's gate keeper, to Byron-Curtiss.

The North Lake Navigation Company began on April 25, 1917. Up to that time Byron-Curtiss had been lending a helping hand to his friend, Charley Brown, who had made a freighting arrangement with the lumber company. Following supper one evening, Byron-Curtiss and Charley Brown began playing checkers. During the evening Charley disclosed that he was tiring of the freighting. Byron-Curtiss was acquainted with what the job entailed. Charley viewed it as a "nuisance" that "sapped" his energy and "cut into his time."

Brown suggested that if the Reverend's son Joseph could be persuaded to leave New York City to help his father, this might be the perfect opportunity for father and son to enjoy more time together.

Logging contractors Sherwood Purcell and Frank Murphy, Pratt, Joslin and the Gould Paper Company were in the process of building, or had recently completed, new lumber camps in the wide range between Golden

Stair and Ice Cave mountains, and in the virgin forests southeast of North Lake. The logging companies needed someone to transport supplies and personnel back and forth from the foot of the lake. Charley had never considered how deeply the work would cut into his life. He had "bigger fish to fry" than loading all sorts of supplies on to the small scow he had christened the *White Swan.*

North Lake, spring 2014, the headwaters of the Black River. Its basin embraces a wide-ranging system of lakes, ponds and extensive swampy areas that through their turbulent outlets drain the regions bordering the West Canada Creek and Moose River watersheds. Once named Lake Sophia, a tiny jewel lying on the floor of a long, narrow valley walled in by sweeps of mountain, the lake was dammed and the reservoir gates closed in November, 1855.

Today North Lake reflects an aspect no less serene than that which greeted Rev. Byron-Curtiss and John B. Todd a century ago. *Photo by the author*

Brown proposed that Byron-Curtiss rent the *White Swan* and take over his contracts with the lumber bosses. "I entrust my boat to your safekeeping," he urged. "Besides, your semi-retirement pocketbook has fewer dollars and coins in it than mine. You don't know how long that skimpy sum will have to last before more ready cash comes your way."

Byron-Curtiss seized the opportunity. John B. Todd was pleased. Byron-Curtiss was dependable and was familiar with the drop points for the lumber

The skipper of the scow was a colorful North Country character. He has been described as being in many ways "an Everyman, displaying good traits and bad." A talented preacher, a master storyteller with a consuming curiosity, a woodsman, an excellent writer, a social activist, a tippler, an avid hunter and fisherman, a man who brought humor to all his endeavors, and an occasional scamp. His life story is told in *Under an Adirondack Influence: The Life of A.L. Byron Curtiss 1871–1959.*
Courtesy of Thomas and Doris Kilbourn. (The Rev. A.L. Byron-Curtiss Collection)

  *Adirondack Logging*

camps. The camps needed a continual replenishing of supplies for the workers as well as new teams of horses and extra equipment. The many lumber operations arranged to have goods delivered by truck to the State House or to Joslin's warehouse at the west end of the "Baby Dam" along the road to South Lake. (This building was eventually moved across the road and is today Burton C. Sperry's camp.)

Within a few days Byron-Curtiss had ordered a rubber stamp. He wanted to give what paperwork was generated an official look. The stamp read:

North Lake Navigation Company
Atwell, N.Y.

On May 20, 1917, Byron-Curtiss wrote in his camp journal after a long day of slowly towing a well-loaded barge of lumber camp supplies: "Took up a load of freight to Murphy's [logging camp] in late p.m." The barge was loaded with "food provisions, lumber, tar paper, a bag of sugar, and five half-drunk lumberjacks headed to Purcell's camp. I landed them at the foot of Sugar Loaf Mountain." There the preacher told them to "hit the trail the rest of the way."

North Lake Navigation's White Swan barge loaded with passengers and cargo.
Courtesy of Dorothy Payton

By ferrying workmen and freighting supplies, Byron-Curtiss became acquainted with the men and the timber operations from woods to pulp mill, where newsprint is manufactured. He observed trees being felled with axes and crosscut saws, saw how the bark was peeled with sharp iron-bladed spuds and cut into thirteen-foot lengths, then drawn from the woods by horses to collection points where the logs were loaded on sleds to be taken to the frozen river landing, where they would eventually be driven downstream to Gould's mill at Lyons Falls.

Purcell, Murphy, Pratt and Joslin's camps were typical small jobber buildings in the woods, built from logs and boards, the roofs covered with tarpaper, with an outhouse out back. The bunkhouse was simple, warm and made as comfortable as possible. A sink was made of boards where several wash basins sat. Towels and a mirror completed the basic washroom. In all Gould camps, food was always far above the average bill of fare. *Courtesy of Thomas and Doris Kilbourn. (The Rev. A.L. Byron-Curtiss Collection)*

On June 2, 1917, while B-C was returning from transporting meat and other food supplies, Joseph arrived from New York City. During 1917 and 1918, father and son established a routine that required them to be on the water almost every day. Single-handedly (unless friends or B-C's daughters were in camp) they operated the White Swan. B-C recorded, "The Gould Paper Company was my one and only reliable client. I did however ferry, for hire, recreational

A "boiling-up shed" was in close proximity to a camp. There were large iron kettles, and supplies of wood, water and soap were available. A boiling kettle could be anything from a 50-pound lard can to a large cast iron kettle to a galvanized wash tub. Laundered clothing was hung to dry on lines stretched between trees. The boiling was done to kill any lice that may have been in the clothing. Lumberjacks knew clean woolen mackinaws, stag pants and socks were warmer than soiled wool. *Courtesy of George Shaughnessy*

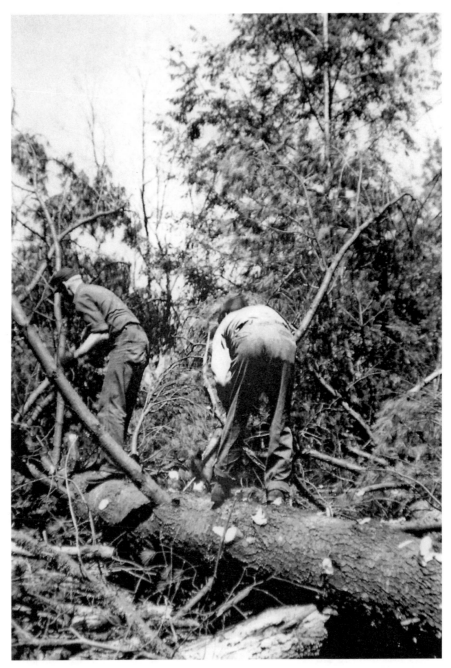

The limbers followed the saw-gang. All phases of logging were back-breaking work. It took a tough breed of men to stand up without whining to the challenges they typically faced to get the wood out. *Courtesy of Eric Johnson, Executive Editor at The Northeastern Logger*

Adirondack Logging

Supplies for the logging camps were trucked in over the North Lake road past Reed's Mill. The mill pond and Addie and Henry Hull's cellar hole, on the hill opposite the pond, are the only traces that remain of the complex that stood along the roadway that winds through thirteen curves that twist like a cork-screw over Railroad Hills. The history of Reed's Mill is told in *Adirondack Stories of the Black River Country*. *Courtesy Fred Worden*

campers, fishermen and hunters around the lake." It was during this tenure that Todd gave him an open invitation to stay at the lumber camps whenever he went into the backwoods.

From June to November, B-C's Nat Foster journal is dotted with short entries. The samplings tell little about the work, illustrating only that he made numerous weekly deliveries.

The Cobweb, Byron-Curtiss's sleek rowboat. "May 11, 1917. 5-o'c. Temperature 34°. A cold, damp snowstorm all day. It has scarcely been above 40°. Discouraging has been the Navigation business. The Evinrude motor on the White Swan scow could not be made to go, so B-C rowed the supplies to the Murphy Camp. Wet to the hide from the damp, heavy snow." —From Byron-Curtiss' Nat Foster Lodge log book.
Courtesy of Thomas and Doris Kilbourn. (The Rev. A.L. Byron-Curtiss Collection)

"Up lake in p.m. With freight." "Back today from a trip to Murphy's and Purcell's landing. Vile weather. Cold and misty rain." "Rather happy day for B-C. All of a.m. to himself; tho busy with transportation in p.m. A big load at 1:30 o'clock and another at 4:45 p.m. A total of over four tons." "B-C on job of transportation almost continuously from 9 a.m. to 7:30 tonight. Three freight trips." "Rivett's truck broke down today at Reeds [Mill], so he did not get in until 5:30 p.m. B-C made two commercial trips with launch and cobbled a pair of woods shoes [boots]. The latter proceeding probably saving $1.50." "Messieurs Gould and Todd along for a ride. Pleasant weather." "A freight trip in early p.m. And a launch trip at 5 o'clock." "Took two Roman Catholic sisters up to Murphy's camp. They are to collect money for a hospital in Ogdensburg."

Byron-Curtiss' car along the North Lake road. In 1915, highway superintendent Will Ano tacked a sign at each end of the Reed's Mill property line where the road ran between the buildings. The sign read: "North Lake, 5 miles. Please close the gates and slow down to 75 miles an hour." It was a joke, of course, for the "Railroad Hills" that extended beyond could never be driven at breakneck speeds. *Courtesy of Thomas and Doris Kilbourn. (The Rev. A.L. Byron-Curtiss Collection)*

Adirondack Logging

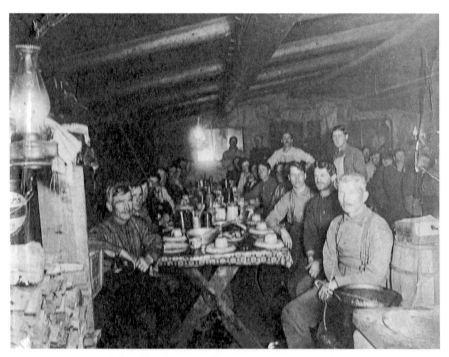

"We're proud of the food here. As you see, we even bring in green vegetables over nineteen miles of snow. But the cook's masterpiece is apple pie. Everybody can have all he wants of anything," G.H.P. Gould proudly boasted to Carl Carmer on the occasion of the author's visit to his logging operations. —From *Listen For A Lonesome Drum*, by Carl Carmer. *Courtesy of the Goff-Nelson Memorial (Tupper Lake) Library*

B-C recorded, "Todd told me it was not unusual for 'HP' [Gould] to be seen in the woods, supervising the logging. He was a hands-on president, having come up the hard way. He was interested in what went on." To Gould, efficiency and conservation were important.

The 1918 freighting season began on May 6.

> *June 5: Closed contract with Mr. Alex Compeau to transport his freight on the lake at $3.00 a ton. No mail. But Mr. Compo gladly took out a letter to mail to Joe telling him to hustle in. Got a small trout off dock tonight. Weather pleasant.*

With Joseph's full-time commitment once again, Byron-Curtiss worked at his navigational enterprise. The company's work took the greater part of almost every day throughout the year. Tons of supplies and equipment (cabbages, potatoes, hay and oats, and building materials, to name a few) were transported to the camps at the head of the lake. The previous year, Rev. Frank A. Reed had made his first trip to the Purcell and Murphy camps to deliver a religious service. He was whisked from one to another in B-C's launch "pushed by a balky outboard."

June 18—A "lucky" p.m. for the North Lake Navigation Company… marooned by a stalled and bound engine at the head of the lake. Mr. Compo's sport fishing motor being then requested and made use of. On arrival at the foot of the lake, Joe prepared to take it out to Forestport for repairs when Fred White intervened and speedily fixed the Evinrude.

September 10—Alex Compo and two Government officials to register the men at the lumber camps for the military service taken up lake. Compo's small boat with four men taken up in good time.

November 8—…made one freight trip in p.m. Also bailed out the White Swan *scow, preparing to use in hauling oats…*

The Cottage, Camp 7. *Courtesy of Fred Worden*

Adirondack Logging

November 21—Achievements in the commercial line this day. 8½ ton
of freight taken up the lake. Alex *the motorboat employed to aid pulling*
the barge.

November 23—Up lake this p.m. … Afterwards to the Head Camp
and settled up, for all accounts of the season. Altogether it has been a
satisfactory season. We made a little money…Winter has set in for sure.
Cloudy, cold and snow today. Ice is forming at head of lake.

The North Lake Navigation Company folded at the end of this year. The Bob Jones Trail that ran along the side of the lake was widened. Culverts were placed under the woods road, and gravel was brought in for hardening soft spots. Trucks and Linn tractors took over the job of hauling freight. Murphy's operation shut down. The remaining lumber camps could be accessed via the new road.

The Reverend found the work and contact with the camp personnel "dynamic" and "adventurous." He explained why: "The work [of the lumberjacks] was physically demanding and dangerous. The men lived in small, roughly built, unpolished quarters, but I found the food to be first-rate, prepared by cooks with imagination."

Throughout the North Lake Navigation Company's tenure, Camp 7 was Gould's headquarters. Byron-Curtiss recalled in his memoirs, "It was on Ice Cave Creek at the base of Ice Cave Mountain, 26 miles from Forestport. The main haul road passed through the camp. Camp 10 was about ten miles southeast of Camp 7. These two camps were the largest, and a large percentage of the men working the woods lived at one or the other.

"The buildings were big and long, made of peeled logs and tarpaper. I well remember the prune pies, candy, sugar cookies, and so forth, and lots of coffee. After working 10–12 hours in the cold air even stale bread would taste good to those 'jacks."

Camp 7 was not a romantic log complex set in a picturesque setting, but it sported a major advantage over earlier camps: it was illuminated by a Delco electric lighting system. Byron-Curtiss said the most interesting structure was a long rectangular building with a roof-covered open space that connected the bunkhouse to the cookhouse. Firewood was piled in the space under the roof.

The benches were all the furniture the men needed to gather together in the bunkroom. There they read or relaxed for the short time between supper and lights out. Overhead hung drying racks. There they draped their wet leather boots, woolen jackets, caps, mittens, socks, shirts and pants. The nauseating odor of human perspiration and drying wool from the assorted apparel did not keep the men from a good night's sleep.

Another building was a root house, where the vegetables and canned goods were kept. This log-constructed cool cellar was built into the side of the mountain. There was the horse barn where the horses were stabled and a storage barn for hay and feed grain. Also included were a company office and store, a woodworking shop equipped with whatever machinery was needed and a blacksmith shop where any metal repair could be handled. There were two tractor houses. One accommodated eight Linn tractors; the other contained four. Near the tractor houses was the bunkhouse for the mechanics and shop-workers. Near the "Cottage" office was the storehouse where tools and supplies were kept for the camps.

The Cottage perched on a rise above the camp on the side of the mountain. It was where the superintendent lived and where visiting officials of the company were quartered. This is where Byron-Curtiss bunked. Directly in front of the office was the gas pump. An oil house was positioned near the gasoline pump. Each day a 700-gallon tank filled with gasoline was hauled in by tractor from Forestport. Linn tractors used in hauling the logs consumed more than 500 gallons a day.

There was a small commissary where general provisions could be purchased. Playing cards and alcohol were not sold. The nearest place a lumberjack could "get a jigger" was miles away in Forestport. A saloon destination was off-limits until the end of the season—as was poker or any other form of gambling.

Undoubtedly the experiences clung to Byron-Curtiss long after the navigation business folded.

These are some of the true stories he recorded.

I had just walked out of the cook house in the company of two camp cooks when we came on to a 'jack looking at a stump that needed to be taken out. Ed [Wheeler, the head cook] asked the French Canadian how much powder he was fixing to put under that stump. The feller

scratched the back of his head a bit before responding, "Jest one." We all continued up the road a piece, not thinking any more about that 'jack, when all of a sudden there was this huge KA-RA-RA-RA-BOOM! We turned and looked up and saw a stump circling around and around as it continued to lift higher into the air. Soon after it swirled upward, it turned earthward and plunged into the shanty's dining room. And as fast as that happened, that Frenchie, with nerves more than a bit jangled, bolted right past us down the trail. There was no doubt he was heading straight out without collecting his time he had coming.

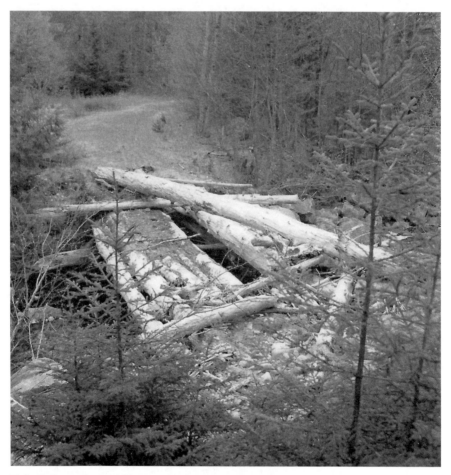

Twin Falls on the Middle Branch stream was a favorite trout fishing spot of B-C and J.B. Remains of Gould's road and the log bridges spanning the Middle Branch and Jock's Brook have fallen into disrepair. *Photo by the author*

One story I'm told he repeated over the years was about one of log jobber Sherwood Purcell's men. Back then there were no radios. As a result, there was no way to keep up with the local news, so the loggers used to lie a lot. But he swears Doug Purcell claims this event was true.

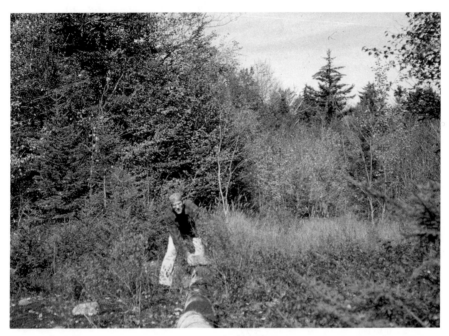

The author at the clearing of the former Camp 7. Old logging camp sites make excellent wildlife habitat and places to pick berries. The opening shown here has adequate cover around the outer edge, which provides good homes for wildlife. *Photo by the author*

One 'jack who had been out of the woods for a couple of weeks for rest and drinking came back into the woods and informed everyone in camp that old Bill Kinney, a retired lumberjack who made moonshine for everyone, had passed away. Bill was reported to have hanged himself. That was all the talk about Forestport for weeks. Some said they knew Bill and that he'd never kill himself. Others said he was killed for his money and hung up to make it look like suicide.

But one of the first things one of the loggers saw when he came out of the woods and went into town was old man Kinney. He went up to him and said, "I heard you hanged yourself, Bill Kinney."

"Yep, that's what I hear too," replied Bill, "but s'pose I jest didn't do it."

Adirondack Logging

Then there was this story about George, the lumberjack who years earlier had run an axe blade into the fore part of his foot. The lumberjack had grown old and hard of hearing and had gotten quite sick, so his wife took him to the doctor. She went right into the examination room with him. When Doc Kilbourn got all done with the examination, he said, "Well now, I want a sample of your stool, a specimen of your urine and a specimen of your semen. The old 'jack turned to his wife with a puzzled look and asked, "He wants a what?" She turned and shouted into his ear, "He wants your underwear."

And what was the worst thing about being a logger?

"The outhouses," Byron-Curtiss said old-time lumberjacks claimed. "They were unconventional. Not your regular variety. There were no individual seats but instead a peeled pole stretching across a dug trench where ten to fifteen men could sit together across it."

Whether everything the Reverend recorded was true can be questioned. J.B. Todd's grandson and great-grandson, John and Scott Todd, admitted a bit of exaggeration might have slipped in over the years.

Byron-Curtiss and J.B. were known to have held quite a few sawing contests for the Atwell Fish and Game Club. Once the club had a man go up against a one-man chain saw with a buck saw, on a nine-inch piece of frozen rock maple. The logger beat the chain saw by 2½ seconds!

At the club, they also ran something else that drew a lot of attention, and that was a liar's contest. All lies had to be about fishing or hunting. Byron-Curtiss and John B. heard some pretty good ones.

One trout fishing experience Byron-Curtiss recalled over and over to many visitors was of a day of angling in the waning years of the 1920s.

His partner was Scudder Todd. Scudder managed his duties so that Byron-Curtiss and he were able to spend part of a day enjoying the total silence in the deep woods of the Black River headwaters and fishing the streams in the vicinity of Camp 7.

Pushing through a thick growth of bushes, crowded witchhopple and alders that lined the banks of a stream they had earmarked for fishing, both found the intertwined plant thicket a difficult stand to penetrate. "We were forced to look for ways out over the water or wade in," recalled Byron-Curtiss.

Spying a large three-foot-diameter pine leaning out over the stream, Scudder struggled over to it, mounted the log and began an unsteady creep—

careful to recognize the slippery green patches of moss, and navigating through the tangle of broken and half-rotten branches that were not at all reliable handholds. About four feet out on the log the shoulder strap of his creel became tangled with an upright branch. As he twisted sideways to untangle it, his pole caught another branch. In one unexpected instant he lost his balance and slipped off. B-C related, "First came a great shout, followed by a loud splash. He landed in waist-deep water." B-C was concerned, but the tone of his voice showed that the happening was a very funny scene.

Byron-Curtiss continued his remembrance. "Stumbling, falling, laughing, bumping into a rock I never saw, and dragging a long branch I planned to poke out over the water as a retrieval pole, I worked my way as best I could to the edge of the bank to help him. Reaching land, I kicked the ground to make a good foothold, leaned backwards, stood immobile to steady myself against Todd's pull, and outstretched the pole in my arms."

Scudder couldn't help noticing Byron's grin. Grabbing hold of the pole his partner had extended to help him haul himself out of his cold bath, Todd yanked hard enough to tip B-C forward and into the stream. Then, looking at B-C, he cursed: "Sorry Reverend, but damn your comic rippling and a footbridge anyways!"

"We were wet anyway, so we proceeded to fish by standing waist deep in the water. In no time the trout began responding well to our attractive offering of 'garden bait,'" B-C said.

Eventually the chill and discomfort became too great. B-C shouted over to Todd, who was working downstream but within earshot, "Todd, I love the forest as much as you value the precious timber. I'm going to start a fire." He clambered out of the water as he called a warning that was meant to be a parting salvo: "Stay off the bridges."

Byron-Curtiss had a fire going in no time. Soon Scudder, with chattering teeth, joined him, holding out his shaky hands to the heat.

The close friends laughed about the day's experience. Todd nominated the Reverend for "Hero of the Day," and their little fishing adventure became fodder for amusement in their many chats in later years.

CHAPTER 9

In the Heyday of Gould's Paper-Making Days at Lyons Falls

Edited and with Commentary by William J. O'Hern

When Adirondack author and editor, Neal Burdick wrote an article on the now-defunct Newton Falls paper mill for Adirondack Life *magazine a few years ago, one of the workers told him he could explain paper-making in one sentence: "You take a bunch of wood chips, add water, then subtract the water." The following description provides an interesting and easy to follow explanation of how a dilute suspension of fibers in water is drained through a screen, so that a mat of randomly interwoven fibers is laid down to produce paper.*

In 1949, the "miracle" of paper-making at the Gould Paper Company's Lyons Falls plant developed in the midst of the company's heydays. I didn't work at the Gould plant, but I have talked extensively with Lawton Williams, Dorothy Payton, Irene F. Rogers, Fred Worden, Howard Wieman, Ed Kornmeyer, Harold Link, Leigh Portner and a number of other people who shared their knowledge and photos of Gould's operations from the woods to the mill. I also have first-hand hand experience at the Hammermill Paper Company in Oswego, where I worked as a trouble-shooter.

From my first steps inside, I recognized that the puzzling mass of machinery created both an interesting and a dangerous place to work. Papermaking is an exceedingly complicated process. Completely unacquainted with it, I was immediately warned by the foreman that my job required working within the complicated-looking maze of working parts that I swore had to be as long as a football field. At one end was the liquid pulp; at the other end were gargantuan rolls of paper. The transformation process was interesting, but what I found alarming was the number of workmen who were missing fingers. "When you hear a sound like the **CRACK** of a .45 pistol going off," the foreman warned, "immediately drop to the deck. V-belts snap all the time. They go flying at a high rate of speed. They'll kill you."

I was also warned that part of my job involved jamming hot semi-liquid paper into massive beaters to be turned back into pulp when the papermaking line broke. My crewmen cautioned that it was forbidden to put our legs over the protective railings around the immense spiraling beaters but everyone had done it at some point because the mammoth sheet of broken, hot semi-liquid paper fed over the rollers that vomited into the machine so quickly that it tangled and engulfed the crew, who worked to kick it back into the beaters.

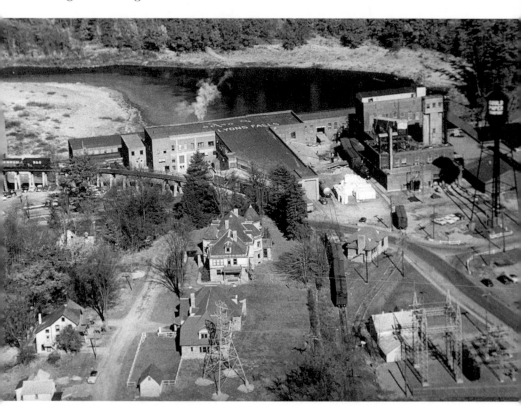

Aerial view of Gould's plant at Lyons Falls. Circa 1945. *Courtesy Harold Link*

Adirondack Logging

"Lyons Falls had a three-way bridge from 1849–1964. The Three-Way Bridge was built in 1849 and connected the Greig Road, Laura Street, and Franklin Street. The original wooden bridge was refurbished in 1916 and was turned into a steel bridge. The Three-Way Bridge at Lyons Falls was the only one in the United States. The bridge was torn down in 1964, and separate bridges were built over the Black River and Moose River." Circa 1945. —Lyons Falls History Association. *Courtesy Harold Link*

Setting the dangers of the workplace aside, what follows is an intelligible explanation of the papermaking process. It is a brief and elementary explanation, furnished by various personnel who worked at the Gould Paper Company of Lyons Falls. My attempt to make this "miracle" of transformation a little less of a miracle and somewhat more understandable is accompanied by photos that show paper in the making.

☆ ☆ ☆ ☆

The following account of paper-making at Lyons Falls appeared in the Fall 1949 issue of North Country Life *magazine.*

The wood used in the manufacture of paper at the Gould Paper Company plant is principally spruce, though hemlock and balsam are used, too, and an increasingly large amount of hardwood. The wood is delivered to the mill by trucks or, especially in the past, by log drives down the Moose River. In either case, the wood finally arrives at the foot of the "jack-works," where it is poled onto the "jack-ladder," which carries it through the saws. The wood is sawed into 32-inch lengths, principally because this is the size necessary to fit the equipment.

After the wood leaves the saws, it travels onto the conveyor, which takes it into the wood room or wood preparation department. If the wood is not needed immediately in the mill, it is guided to another conveyor, which carries it to a storage yard.

In the wood room, the wood is prepared by being barked, split if too large, and cleaned. Every particle of bark and dirt must be removed. The most select wood is conveyed to the ground wood mill for the manufacture of ground wood pulp while the poorer grade goes to the "chipper," a powerful machine equipped with sharp knives mounted on a large revolving disc. These knives "chip" the wood into chips about an inch square. After being sorted by a system of screens, these chips are conveyed to the sulphite mill to be made into "chemical" or sulphite pulp.

In the sulphite mill, the wood chips are cooked under steam pressure in an acid. The cooking process destroys the non-fibrous material but not the wood fibers, which contribute strength to the paper. After the cooking process the sulphite pulp is discharged into machines that wash the acid from the pulp.

In the sulphite screen room, the sulphite pulp goes through screens to remove all impurities and foreign matter. Some of the screens rotate, some vibrate up and down, and others vibrate sideways. Before it can leave this room, the pulp must pass through screen plates, which have openings approximately .008 inch in diameter. Then it flows to large tile storage tanks, where it is kept in constant agitation until it is needed in the paper mill.

The more select wood from the wood room is made into "mechanical" or ground wood pulp in the ground wood mill. Here, large, ponderous machines grind the wood into dust or pulp. This pulp, because the wood fibers are greatly reduced in length and size, does not have the strength which sulphite pulp has. The ground wood pulp is passed through a screening process and then is pumped to storage tanks, where it is kept under agitation until it is used on the paper machines.

Ground wood pulp and sulphite pulp are the principal ingredients of the ground wood specialty paper manufactured at Lyons Falls, but several other ingredients are added. Principal among these are clay, alum, and size.[13] In the tank room, they are mixed mechanically, and this solution is piped to the paper mill.

Machine shop, Gould Paper Company. Circa 1945. *Courtesy Harold Link*

All the ingredients are now ready for use. In the beater room, the predetermined amounts of sulphite pulp, ground wood pulp, and other ingredients are thoroughly mixed into "stock" in machines called beaters. The stock, is pumped to the "wet end" of each paper machine, where it is reduced in consistency to over 90% water and 10% stock. This greatly thinned mixture is poured out onto a fast-moving, endless bronze wire screen. Much of the water passes through the wire; but that which stays on the wire is carried over vacuum suction boxes.

Beater room, Gould Paper Company. Circa 1945. *Courtesy Harold Link*

It is here that the sheet of paper first assumes definite form. It is transferred from the wire to a wood felt, which carries it through the presses. The presses literally press the sheet both to decrease the amount of water and also to help form it into a uniform sheet of paper. As the sheet leaves the presses, it resembles wet paper toweling. The paper then travels through a series of dryers, where the rest of the moisture is removed. After leaving the dryers, it goes through a "calendar stack," which puts a glossy finish on the paper. It is then wound to guarantee uniformity and cut to required widths. The paper rolls are ready to be prepared for shipment.

The rolls arrive in the finishing room from the paper mill via an elevator. The foreman, who has all the shipping and packing instructions, sees that the paper for each order is properly wrapped, labeled, and packed in railroad freight cars. Approximately five carloads of paper were shipped each day by the Gould Paper Company.

To summarize the papermaking process, I use the crisp words of reporter David Beetle, who once described this process in the Utica *Observer-Dispatch*.

> *To make paper the Lyons Falls way, you pressure cook some of your logs in sulphurous acid. This gets rid of the noncellulose and keeps the wood fibers. It also gives you sulphite pulp—a white fibrous mass that looks like warm, shredded codfish.*
>
> *Other logs you simply chew up by grinding them. This gives you ground wood pulp.*
>
> *Then—as though you were making a huge cake—you whip up a batter of ground wood pulp, sulphite pulp, and such chemicals as clay, alum, and rosin size.*
>
> *After that you pour your batter on a screen at one end of a papermaking machine, squeeze out water, lock the fibers under pressure, steam dry, iron to a smooth finish, and take off a roll of paper for the customers.*

As interesting as the process of paper-making was for me, I didn't work long at the Hammermill Paper Company. I had lost some toes and a finger in earlier industrial accidents. The loss of appendages, listening to "war" stories of long-time employees, and considering their safety warnings about the machinery, I decided I'd leave to experience a six-month stint at Crockett's Saw Mill. When I left the paper mill I felt happy not to have been killed by a flying V-belt, to still have nine fingers, and to be able to explain an interesting process of which most people are unaware.

Collection 3
Life in the Lumber Camps

"Oui, I mak' heem full. Dey eat her all up!" —Pierre, Camp 7's cook's enthusiastic endorsement of Gould's forester's wife, Barbara Bird, who shared her flapjack recipe.

Recipe **BARBARA'S FAMILY-SIZE FLAPJACKS**

Pancakes were a staple breakfast dish in a logging camp.

1 qt. wheat flour
2 tablespoons corn meal
½ can condensed milk
3 eggs
3 Tablespoons baking powder
1 Tablespoon salt
Water

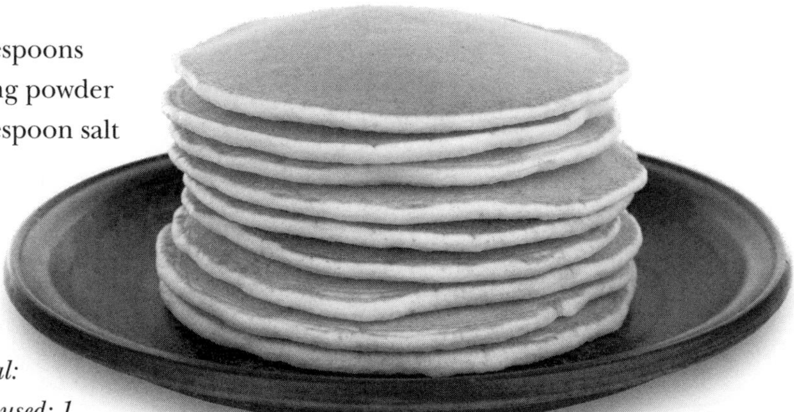

Photograph by Africa Studio/Dollar Photo Club

Optional:
May be used: 1 heaping Tablespoon soda
2 heaping Tablespoons cream of tartar

OPPOSITE: Lt. to Rt. Barbara Bird and Hazel Todd. Circa 1924.
Courtesy of Dorothy Payton

CHAPTER 10

A Dream Realized

William J. O'Hern

Ever since coming to the North Country, the urge to intimately mix with Gould's lumbering operation on a day-to-day basis had been on Rev. Byron-Curtiss's "bucket list." The invitation to spend a few days at Camp 7 to deer hunt around Ice Cave Mountain only served to intensify that desire.

He wrote:

> *October 26, 1927—S.B. & J.B. Todd called in A.M. and invited me to go to Camp VII to hunt and etc. So set aside my work and after getting mail, went to head of the lake in my row boat and on to Camp VII, arriving about four o'clock. Weather, pleasant and mild.*

> *October 28, 1927—Back from Camp VII in A.M. Hunted yesterday both A.M. and P.M. but no success for any of us. But, had a good time, with a pleasant break in the inventory of life...*

The first snow of the winter of 1927–28 arrived November 4 at North Lake. Signs of oncoming winter had been anticipated since the hard freeze under an October 9 hunter's moon. Three days after Christmas he recorded, "plump white flakes the size of communion wafers" began to fall and "settled fast."

The Reverend enjoyed winter at Atwell. A blanket of snow draped roofs and tree branches, decorated the landscape and made the entire territory look, as he put it, "as if God had painted a fresh, calm scene." Charley and Anna Brown and Byron-Curtiss were the sole occupants along the lake.

Nat Foster Lodge, North Lake. Circa 2006. The author's family had the privilege of renting Rev. Byron-Curtiss's camp for one year. *Photo by the author*

The Todds had made it clear B-C had an open invitation to live and work at a lumber camp. He figured the itch had gotten under his skin since his first days in the territory when he would pack into Gid Perry's and the Brooks abandoned lumber camps, using the shelters as a hunting base. The only way to cure the itch was to follow that dream. Now that he was retired, he could finally do it.

Camp 10, Circa 1928. Upon reaching Camp 10, Wells was given the grand tour and admitted "There were much pleasanter places..." to be. It was during that initial spin about camp that the reporter met Rev. Byron-Curtiss, whom he described as "...a retired Episcopal minister...who acts as bookkeeper and helps about the cookhouse."
Courtesy of John Todd (The John B. & Scudder Todd Collection)

It was dusk when he pulled out his camp log book to record, "spent a good season" in camp and "much to be thankful for."

On December 28, with duffle packed, B-C waited for a snow taxi to carry him into the tall timber where he planned to stay, "alternating," he wrote, "between Todd's cottage at Camp VII and Camp X" where countless 'jacks labored in the timber woods.

Most people knew very little about how lumbering operations were carried out from the timber woods to the pulp mill, where newsprint is manufactured. How were the trees cut and hauled? Just how did they make their way to the mills? And even more important, were the men who worked in the lumber woods really the rough-and-tough hard-drinking Goliaths that legend would have us believe?

Not only would B-C learn those answers but so too would Robert Wells, a *Watertown Daily Times* newspaper reporter who experienced logging first-hand the winter of 1927–28. B-C and Wells met at Camp 10, and "the Rev. Mr. Curtiss" is described in one of Wells's articles. B-C was hired to carry out clerical duties and help in the cookhouse. Wells was there to write a story for his readers.

Camp 10's bunkhouse offered few comforts following a rugged day of killing cold and dangerous snow and ice of winter. *Courtesy of Lyons Falls History Association*

According to Scudder B. Todd's 1930 Map of Adirondack League Club Preserve, Camp 10 was located at the 2,400 ft. contour line along a secondary road above the source of Elbow Creek, north of Honnedaga Lake. It was not built for many years of use. It was a temporary cluster of structures pinned, spiked and hammered together from a combination of green timber and rough-sawn wood. The main building was a long, low structure made from logs laid up cob-house style.

The camp consisted of an office with space for the bookkeeper, time-keeper and the company's van (store); stables and barns, tack and related paraphernalia; a black-smith and carpenter shop; and a main bunkhouse complete with adjoining kitchen and dining area. A root cellar, too, was common and necessary. Byron-Curtiss found the rough camps picturesque. "No two were exactly alike, but they resembled each other so closely in style of architecture and furnishings that a description of one serves as a description of all." —*Under an Adirondack Influence, The Life of A.L. Byron-Curtiss 1871–1959*, by William J. O'Hern. *Inset courtesy of John Todd (The John B. & Scudder Todd Collection)*

Byron-Curtiss ended his stay before the spring thaw when the Moose River moved the logs from the landing to the mill. He recorded on February 23, 1928:

> *B-C, owner, stopped at camp, to pick up his duffle, on way to State House, from the lumber camps. Was at Camp X, at Todd's cottage at Camp VII alternating from Dec. 28, 1927. Found Nat Foster Lodge O.K. A spruce tree near front door, only winter damage discerned. Made trip from Camp VII in Linn tractor No. 1. Weather cloudy and mild, and a bit of rain. We saw a deer with a broken leg this side of North Branch [of the Black River].*

There was no phase of Gould's logging operation that was as colorful or as exciting as the log drive. By the time the logs reached the McKeever bridge that spring of '28, B-C was among the crowd that gathered to watch the river drivers work the logs downstream toward their final goal.[14] His long-time dream had been realized, and both he and Robert Wells had experienced an extraordinary few months in the winter lumber woods.

The logs arrive at McKeever Dam. Circa 1928. The original McKeever Dam was constructed by the Moose River Lumber Company in 1891. *Courtesy of Dorothy Payton*

Adirondack Logging

CHAPTER 11

A Reporter's Adventurous
1928 Winter Lumber Camp Trip

William J. O'Hern

A bit of good luck came to *Watertown Daily Times* reporter Robert Wells during the winter of 1927–28. The newspaper columnist was given the opportunity to spend a week in the heart of a central Adirondacks lumber camp, and thus to enjoy and later report to his newspaper's readership the very novel experience of winter life among Gould Paper Company lumberjacks.

From the hour Wells arrived, he took brief notes. His many trips beyond the camp familiarized him with the ordinary incidents of logging life, from mixing with the men in their bunkhouse to hitching a ride on a Linn tractor as it pulled a load of logs to the Moose River landing.

Wells did not say what he expected to see or learn, but from his writings it is clear he enjoyed many new experiences and relished every moment.

When the adventure was first proposed he might well have anticipated a twinge of trepidation due to the very cold temperatures. During the week he covered many miles, often tramping with the mercury seesawing above and below zero, and through feet of deep snow. If he had ever thought his blood would be too thin or feet too tender, his fears proved groundless. To be sure, he was warmly clad and found the bright clear air of the mountains satisfying; the snow glistened and sparkled in the bright sunlight as though strewn with myriad diamonds. And the snow proved its artistry as it transformed ugly cut-over landscape into beautiful scenes. The stump-dotted clearings, with

Eating was a serious business in a lumber camp for both men and guests. This white-tailed deer might have thought the handout from the cook was the best, guaranteeing her daily return to get more from Camp 7's messhouse. Circa 1924. *Courtesy of Dorothy Payton*

brush and log heaps, ordinarily hideous disfigurements, were blanketed with arched white caps and side trimmings. Brush heaps were a symphony of pretty rounded hillocks; the unrefined log and board shanties, with billows of rising smoke from wood fires heating the interior, rose through pitted smoke pipes as a fresco of icicles adorning the eaves turned buildings into Swiss chalets as picturesque as could be.

Wells's outing might have seemed quaint to the many who lived far removed from the lumber woods where men worked from before daylight to dark and ate their meals in large mess halls, whose long tables were arrayed in dull utensils and grey tinware—all as clean as a whistle—ready for meals prepared for hungry, hearty men.

Whether or not Wells actually pondered the beauty of the logging camp life, he did share in the enjoyment of the bounty of food—one of the few amenities offered in Gould's lumber camps. And, from his six daily installments it's clear he gained a real measure of respect for the men and the labor during that winter week in 1928.

  *Adirondack Logging*

CHAPTER 12

Big Tracts in 3 Counties

First Installment, February 13, 1928, Watertown Daily Times
Robert A. Wells

Headline: *Scores of Hardy Workers Busy in Forests of Adirondacks during bleak Winter months cutting timber and hauling it to rivers to be floated to paper mills in spring— operations at headwaters of Black River Extensive.*

This is the first of a series of articles on lumbering operations, written by a *Times* staff correspondent who visited the camps of the Gould Paper Company, located in the North Lake section of the Adirondack Mountains at the headwaters of the Black River.

The lumbering industry is one of the most important industries of northern New York and one of the important factors in the industrial growth of this section, yet the average layman knows little about the actual lumbering operations. He knows little about how the trees are cut, hauled out of the woods to the rivers and driven to the mills. He knows little about the men who are engaged in this great industry except that popular fancy has them pictured as rough, hardy giants who fight at the drop of a hat and drink "hard liquor."

Realizing that the average layman knew little about the lumbering industry, H.P. Gould, head of the Gould Paper Company of Lyons Falls, invited *The Times* to send a member of the editorial staff to the lumber camps on the North Lake operation of the Gould Company and to describe the actual operations.

The timberlands of the Gould Paper Company in the North Lake section are located in the watershed of the Black River and extend through three counties, Herkimer, Hamilton and Lewis. There are approximately 100,000 acres of timberland in this section. Besides lumbering these 100,000 acres, the Gould Company works the Adirondack League Club reserve, buying timber from the club by stumpage. The preserve is located in the same section as the Gould timberlands and the soft wood is easily available. Besides the North Lake timber lands, the Gould Paper Company owns about 70,000 acres in the Tug Hill country, west of Glenfield. Tug Hill is famous for its deep snow and Irish lumberjacks. It is said that snow eight feet deep has fallen there. No lumbering operations are being carried on by the Gould Paper Company in the Tug Hill section this winter.

Gould Lumber Holdings. The Gould holdings in the North Lake section are divided as follows: 24,000 acres in township five in Hamilton and Herkimer Counties—some of the country lumbered; 30,000 acres of virgin timber in two townships, each numbered four, in Hamilton County; 20,000 acres of lumbered timberland in township three in Herkimer and Hamilton Counties; 10,000 acres of lumbered timberland in township one in Herkimer and Lewis Counties in the Nelson Lake and Bisby Lake sections. The Gould Paper Company also owns 15,000 acres of virgin timber on Seventh Lake Mountain, near Seventh Lake in the Fulton Chain.

In the Tug Hill section, the company owns in one section 43,000 acres of timberland, which has been lumbered over. This is known as the Michigan Mills and Littlejohn tract. It also owns on Tug Hill 20,000 acres in the White tract and 7,000 acres in the Swanscott tract.

It is planned that lumbering operations will be renewed in these tracts of virgin timber in two or three years. Lumbering on Tug Hill was suspended last year when the 43,000-acre tract was finished.

The Gould Paper Company is doing its own lumbering in the North Lake section. On Tug Hill they have always let the job by contract, William H. McCarthy, lumber jobber of Lowville, doing the work there for many years. John B. Todd, 18 years in the employ of the Gould Paper Company, is the superintendent of the North Lake operation and is personally in charge of the work.

Six paper mills of the Gould Paper Company are supplied with pulp from these timberlands of the company. Three of the mills are located east of Lyons Falls on the Moose River, one on the Black River at Lyons Falls, one at Port Leyden on the Black River and one at McKeever on the Moose River. These mills specialize in the production of newsprint.

Nearly 20,000 cords of pulp, cut in 13 foot lengths, will be sent down the Moose River to the mills down river. Camp Seven is located at the base of Ice Cave Mountain, 26 miles from Forestport on the Adirondack division of the New York Central. The camp is on Ice Cave Creek in Ice Cave Valley. Through this camp passes the main hauling road. In a southeasterly direction from

Lumbering, like other American industries, was engulfed by a rapid-moving civilization which in a comparatively short time turned the nation from a vast forest into a land of farms and manufactories. Lumberjacks wanted nothing more than a chance to work, enjoy good grub and take an occasional trip out to the bright lights. *Courtesy of Eric Johnson, Executive Editor at The Northeastern Logger*

Camp 7 at a distance of about ten miles is located Camp 10, where the loading of the logs is done. These are the two largest camps and here about 75 percent of the men at these two (largest) of the four camps on the North Lake operations on the entire job are quartered clad in winter garb. Four thousand four hundred cords have already been cut and piled on the banks of the Indian River by the Joslin lumbering crew working under contract with the Gould Company. The Indian River flows into the Moose River and it is by this route that these logs will go to the paper mills nearly 75 miles distant. Several thousand cords are already at the landing on the Moose River.

The younger lumberjacks of Wells' day were not the old-hand, swaggering, hell-roaring, fierce-fighting, hard-drinking 'jacks of years past. When Wells visited, men were not continuing the stereotypical tradition. Still, it was obvious that lumberjacks old and new formed a fraternity of their own. *Courtesy of Pat Payne*

The North Lake operation has four camps. Camp 7 was the headquarters camp in 1928, with Camp 10 ten miles alway where the loading of logs was done. Camp 9, 5 miles north of Camp 7, quarters 25 men, the "landing crew." Camp 5, the remaining camp, not yet operational on a big scale, is about 5 miles northeasterly and on the opposite of Ice Cave Mtn. from Camp 7. About 150 men in all.

Adirondack Logging

CHAPTER 13

Snow Taxi Follows Forest Trail
to Lumbering Camp

Second Installment, February 14, 1928, Watertown Daily Times
Robert A. Wells

Headline: *Vehicle pitches and slides through mountain region along ice-covered lake to domain of the Hardy Lumberjack—main camp of Gould Paper Co., consisting of twelve buildings, situated at base of Ice Cave Mountain.*

This is the second of a series of articles on lumbering operations written by a *Times* staff correspondent who visited the camps of the Gould Paper Company, located in the North Lake section of the Adirondack mountains at the headwaters of the Black River.

The inaccessibility of the lumber camp to the layman may be assigned as one reason why he has little knowledge of the lumber industry. A lumber camp in the wintertime is certainly a hard place to reach. The writer can readily testify to that after an arduous trip from Forestport into the head-quarters camp at the foot of Ice Cave Mountain and an almost unbearable trip out on a snow tractor.

After arrangements were completed with the Gould Paper Company, the writer went to Lowville where he was met by William H. McCarthy, lumber jobber who for many years has handled operations on Tug Hill for the Gould Paper Company. "Bill," as he is known to many, proved to be an excellent and entertaining guide. The next morning the writer in company with Mr. McCarthy boarded the train to Alder Creek. At Alder Creek, we were met

It was easier to guess the age of a skid horse or make of a tractor than it was to estimate that of a woods worker. "Lumberjacks have no specific age. They are active, or they are inexperienced, or they are old-timers. Years do not seem to figure much." —Barbara Kephart Bird. *Courtesy of the Town of Webb Historical Association P3849*

by a taxi driver who snapped us in rapid fashion across the four miles that intervene between the railroad station and Forestport. At that place the real trip began. From a comfortable sedan, we shifted to a novel form of a taxi, a snowmobile with an enclosed box-like cabin built on the back. The snowmobile has a tractor tread, the front wheels being replaced by runners. It had a fitting name, the "snowball taxi."

John B. Todd, superintendent for the Gould Company, was at Forestport but was unable to make the trip in with the "snowball taxi." The first few miles were not bad, the taxi following a level road past scattered farms, but when the woods were reached it was a different story. The machine swayed from side to side as it struggled up the steep grades. The cab in which the passengers ride is covered with sheet iron and permits little view of the surrounding territory, and even less light. After moving into the seat beside the driver, it was possible to enjoy the ride to a certain extent. The woods are particularly

Adirondack Logging

beautiful this time of the year with the green of the balsam and spruce out-lined against the snow and in clear weather a background of blue sky.

Reaching North Lake we took the winter road around the edge of that body of water. The road we had passed over previous to this time was as smooth as glass in comparison to the road which we then traveled. Pitch holes, spring holes, 60 degree grades, and sharp turns were the road's most noteworthy features. We were tossed about the cab from one side to another for many miles. It was impossible for the driver to make over a few miles an hour with the machine, but finally the "snowball taxi" rolled out onto the ice-covered log road. It was only a few minutes then until we arrived at Camp 7, slightly more than two hours from the time when we left Forestport.

Camp 7 with its twelve buildings is at the base of Ice Cave Mountain. It is decidedly different from most lumber camps, in that it is lighted by electric lights, the current being generated by a Delco system. The "main haul," as

A familiar sight on the road from McKeever to the Gould Paper Company's lumber camps on and near the Moose River was this snowmobile, Joe Gordon's woods taxi. Equipped with runners in front and caterpillar tracks in the rear, this machine pro-vided a ride that made you think you were on a ship in heavy seas, but it got you places no matter how deep the snow. *Courtesy of Lawton Williams*

the main highway for drawing logs from the woods to the river is called, passes through the center of the camp. On one side of the main haul is located the company office and store where the lumberjack obtains his cigarettes, chewing tobacco, heavy woolen socks, feather-faced mitts, heavy shoes and what few other things that he needs. Here is stored the medicine and first aid equipment. Above the office are the quarters for the office clerk and his assistants.

Near the office is the storehouse where tools and supplies are kept for the camps. Directly in front of the office is the gas pump, with a 2,000-gallon tank buried in the ground. The tank is always kept full, a 700-gallon tank filled with gasoline being hauled in by tractor from Forestport every day. The tractors used in hauling the logs consume more than 500 gallons a day, it is said. An oil house is near the gasoline pump.

The hauling roads on which the loaded log sleighs are drawn are ice-covered in many places, particularly on the up-grades. The water for the roads

Tough characters of the best kind, deep in the woods, clad in checkered wool shirts and woolen britches, battered hats, and heavy leather croghans. Rugged lumberjacks' noon meal was often warmed over an open fire. Most of the food was already prepared and brought from camp in pack baskets each day. *Courtesy of the Maitland C. DeSormo Collection*

Adirondack Logging

is obtained at Camp 7, where the big pump-house with its 40,000-gallon water tank is located. The water is pumped with a gasoline pump from Ice Cave creek up into the tank. The Gould Company also have several portable Metz pumps which may be put into any stream and which can fill the sprinkling tank at a rate of 400 gallons a minute. The sprinkling tank, which is hauled by the tractor, holds about 2,000 gallons.

On the same side of the road as the company office and store are the workshop and two tractor houses. The workshop is completely equipped with wood working machinery and also houses a blacksmith shop. Here any repairs that the equipment needs can be made. One of the tractor houses accommodates eight tractors and the other four. Near the tractor houses is the bunkhouse for the mechanics and shop-workers. Across the main haul from these buildings four more buildings are perched on a hillside. The largest of these is the combined bunkhouse for the lumberjacks and the cookhouse. Between 65 and 70 men are located at Camp 7, and all of these are fed in this cookhouse. Near the cookhouse is the log root house where the vegetables and canned goods are kept. This building is built into the side of the hill and is covered with two feet of dirt. At the farther end of the camp is the cottage where the superintendent lives and where visiting officials of the company are quartered. On the other side of the cookhouse at the opposite end of the camp is the horse barn where twelve teams are stabled. All of the buildings except the combined cookhouse and bunkhouse and the company office are of log construction. These two buildings are built of planed lumber.

Perhaps the most interesting building at the camp is the cookhouse. This building is divided into two portions by a roof-covered open space where firewood is piled. The interior of the bunkhouse was visited first. Double tiers of bunks line both sides of the long room. The bunks are of wooden construction and are as clean as lumberjacks' bunks usually are. The room has somewhat of a dismal atmosphere despite the feeble attempts of the electric lights to brighten the gloom. All the colors of the room are dull from the dark blankets to the dark wooden walls, but this means nothing to the lumberjacks, for they have no thought of atmosphere when they reach the bunkhouse at the close of day. Tired when they come in from their long hard work in the woods, they are soon asleep after their evening meal.

The cookhouse is a much brighter place. Long windows permit an unobstructed view of both sides of the camp and permit the entrance of plenty of light. Along one side of the room are long oilcloth-covered tables with wooden benches. Here the men receive their meals. There is no formality at mealtime in the lumber camp. The food is served heaped high in great bowls and is eaten off of metal plates with tin cutlery. On the opposite side of the long room, "Ed" Wheeler holds forth. "Ed" is the "boiler," which in the language of the lumberjacks means cook. In front of one of the long windows on the side opposite the tables is a long sink where dishes are washed; in front of the other window on the same side is the table where pastries are

Linn snowplows provided sure-footed traction, full ground contact at all times and tremendous power whether snow conditions were heavy or light.

The V plow was a Frink design with paneled moldboard to break up crusted snow; generous riser boards lifted snow being removed above adjoining snow before carrying it to the sides. *Courtesy of Howard Wieman*

Adirondack Logging

prepared. "Ed" works his magic on a great cook stove, which occupies a central position on the same side of the room. For pies and other pastries, he has a special oven, which is so large that more than 20 pies may be baked at one time. Several assistants aid the cook at Camp 7 in feeding the always-hungry crew.

After visiting all of the buildings at the camp we made our way to the storage space near the "main haul," where the log sleighs are left for inspection. Camp 7 is located about a mile and a half from the "summit," where the tractors that have hauled the logs from the loading places leave the logs. Other tractors haul them down the other side of the slope to the Moose River where they are piled ready for the drive. After leaving the loaded log sleighs at the "summit," the tractors bring empty log sleighs back down to Camp 7. Here in this open space, the empty log sleighs are left and a man goes over them carefully and inspects them and sees that they are in first-class condition. This prevents a breakdown of the sleighs during the hauling. If a broken part is found on one of the sleighs, the sleigh is taken out of the string. It is taken to the workshop and repaired.

The Gould Paper Company on its North Lake operation uses 225 pairs of log sleighs. The sleighs are of sturdy construction and are fitted with wooden runners. To haul the great loads of logs, Linn tractors are used. One of the tractors is capable of developing more than a hundred horsepower and the other nine are rated at 60 horsepower. The nine 60-horsepower tractors have been used for the past nine years and are now drawing more logs than when they were first put in use. Without tractors it would be impossible to lumber on the present great scale lumbermen maintain. The tractors do work that would be impossible where it is necessary to use horses. Teams are used only in the woods where they haul the logs sleighs from the "skid piles" to the tractor yards where the tractors take them to draw them to the river. The tractors are equipped with sleigh runners in place of the front wheels and make from 6 to 8 miles per hour when light. With loads their speed is much slower. Only 16 teams of horses are in use on the North Lake operation this winter.

To keep the hauling roads open, four Michigan plows are used. These plows, drawn by tractors, throw the snow from the center of the roads and make ruts for the runners to follow. All of this equipment, with the exception of most of the teams, is kept at Camp 7.

CHAPTER 14

Many Difficulties Face Men Driving Tractor Log Trains

Third Installment, February 15, 1928, Watertown Daily Times
Robert A. Wells

Headline: *Six to eight sleigh loads of huge logs pulled through deep snow of forest trails by single tractor—men called "Road Monkeys" stationed on hills to throw sand and straw on road to prevent laden tractor-trains from running away—cooks provide plenty of food for hungry lumberjacks.*

This is the third of a series of articles on lumbering operations, written by a *Times* staff correspondent who visited the lumbering operations of the Gould Paper Company at the headwaters of the Black River.

The lumberjack's working day begins at about 4 in the morning, long before dawn, while most of the world is still asleep. He gets up many mornings when the mercury is hovering around the bottom of the thermometer but he never complains.

The insistent clang of a hammer on an iron sleigh runner is the alarm clock of Camp 7, and it is certainly an effective one. The cook or his assistant wields the hammer. He gives it three or four …blows and then beats on the sleigh runner rapidly. It is impossible to sleep through the clamor.

After spending the first day at the camp inspecting the buildings and equipment, we retired early. A lumber camp is usually sound asleep by 6:30 with the exception of the …workers and mechanics who repair tractors and equipment during the night if it is necessary. Our first day in the woods was Wednesday. Wednesday night, the superintendent came into the camp with the company snowmobile. Gordon H.P. Gould, son of the president of the Gould Paper Company, was in the woods on an inspection trip with a party of friends.

Gould's party, Joseph McDermott, the forester for the Gould Company, Superintendent Todd, William H. McCarthy and the writer made up the party of seven that was quartered at the cottage. McCarthy tended the fire all through the first night and kept the cottage warm while a snowstorm raged outside.

Thursday morning at 4, the camp alarm clock was sounded. We dressed and hurried over to the cookhouse, for Superintendent Todd wanted us to see the lumberjacks at their breakfast. A few minutes after we were seated at one of the long tables, the clamor of the gong commenced again and a stream of lumberjacks poured through the door from the bunkhouse almost instantly. The men hurried to their places with hardly a sound.

One of the strangest things we noticed was the absence of conversation during the meal. The men hardly spoke, but hurried through the meal and rushed out the door. The tractor men were first to leave the table.

Wells spent the first day at Camp 7 sightseeing. *Courtesy of Fred Worden*

It was certainly a real meal. There were no breakfast foods. Instead the cook's helper set on the table great platters of pork chops, bowls of steaming potatoes, flapjacks, coffee, cakes, cookies, and other hearty foods. The lumberjacks stacked the food in a determined manner and after stuffing themselves full in a few minutes they were on their way to their work.

During the night ten inches of snow had fallen and the hauling roads were filled. With the mercury around the zero mark, the plows were hooked to the tractors and taken out onto the roads to clear them of the snow. A heavy snowstorm causes a loss of 20 loads in the day's hauling record. The tractors were on their way by 4:40 and in a short time Camp 7 was quiet again.

Howard Wieman saw plenty of accidents during the years he worked for Gould. This Linn overturned where the main haul road crossed Indian River Bridge at the second stillwater. *Courtesy of Howard Wieman*

At 5:30, even before it was daylight, the seven of us started for Camp 10, seven miles away. Camp 10 is one of the loading camps from where the loaded sleighs are drawn to the river. The trip to Camp 10 was made in two snowmobiles, one owned by the Gould Paper Company and the other the property

Adirondack Logging

of Gordon Gould. It was one of the most interesting trips made despite the fact that unpleasant weather conditions prevailed. The snow had cloaked the evergreen trees in the woods with a ten-inch soft white mantle, and in the darkness before the dawn the lights of the snowmobiles outlined the scene and emphasized its beauty.

On the hills along the road were stationed men to care for the road and to brake the speed of the log trains with sand and straw. Their flickering oil lights made an eerie scene. These men are termed "road monkeys" in the vernacular of the lumberman. The "road monkey" has a hole in the bank beside the road where he gets his sand and heats it. When the runners of the sleighs hit the burnt sand they stop dead still. On some of the hills straw is employed by the "road monkey" to prevent the log trains from running away.

The "road monkey" is usually one of the old time lumberjacks who is unfit for the heavy work. There are some interesting characters among them. Each takes considerable pride in the condition of his road and often gets angry and sometimes profane when the snowmobiles pass over his stretch of road just after he has prepared it with sand and straw for a log train.

When within a mile of the camp, we caught up with the tractor hauling the empty sleighs. From then until we reached the tractor yard, it was necessary for the snowmobile to crawl along at a slow rate of speed. It was daylight when the tractor yard was reached and that great open space was swept by cold winds. The tractor yard is an open space located at the end of the hauling road. Here, the tractors got their loaded log trains. The yard is usually located within a reasonable distance of the scene of the cutting operations. From the tractor yard in all directions run roads to the "skidways." The "skidways" are great piles of pulp logs. Horses draw the log sleighs to these piles. There the loads are about two-thirds loaded. The team then hauls this partly loaded sleigh to what is known as the "double header," which is located in the tractor yard. Here another load of logs has been drawn, and part of this other load is placed onto the top of the first load. This method is used where it is some distance from the piles of pulp wood to the tractor yard so that horses are able to draw the sleighs. If the entire load was placed on the sleighs at the pile, it would be almost impossible for the horses to pull it.

From the "double header" the load is hauled by the team to the train at the head of the tractor yard. There the sleigh is hooked into the train with chains. The loads are held apart by "bull poles." On each tractor besides the driver there is a "Whistle Punk," the lumberjacks' term for assistant. This man is assigned the task of hooking up the sleighs, putting the "bull poles" in place and while the train is in motion to keep careful watch of the sleighs and chains and see that everything is all right. If anything goes wrong with the train, he notifies the driver and the train is brought to a stop.

While at the tractor yard, a number of trains were loaded and hauled away. Two of them were stuck just out of the yard when the tractor struck a pitch hole, digging itself down into the soft snow. Logs were put under the tracks of the machine, and with another tractor pushing on the back of the train it finally got under way. This was just an example of the difficulties that are experienced by timbermen.

The log trains drawn from Camp 10 were made up of from six to eight loads. The train weighed from 65 to 70 tons loaded and carried 30 to 35 cords of pulp logs. After the snowfall, the number of loads was cut down on each train.

From the tractor yard the party walked over the hill a short distance to the camp itself, where we successfully attempted to get a "hand-out" from the cook. This was the second meal of the day. When we walked over the hill from the tractor yard to Camp 10, we passed from the watershed of the middle branch of the Black River into the watershed of West Canada Creek, which flows into the Mohawk River in the central part of the state.

Camp 10 is located in Township 7, a short distance north of Honnedaga Lake. The camp itself was built on the Adirondack League Club preserve and quarters 65 men. Scudder Todd, son of the superintendent of the operation, is the "woods boss" at Camp 10 and has charge of the loading and work previous to the hauling. Hugh Dowling, "the walking boss," which signifies that he is second in charge under the superintendent with supervision over all of the camps of the Gould Paper Company, is foreman of the camp.

Assisting the cook, "Bill" Youngs, at Camp 10, is Rev. Byron A. Curtiss retired Episcopal minister. Rev. Mr. Curtiss acts as bookkeeper at the camp and helps about the cookhouse. During the summer Rev. Mr. Curtiss has a summer camp on North Lake and conducts an outdoor chapel. This winter he decided to spend the season in the woods and so entered the employ of the Gould Company. He was a quiet figure about the camp when we made our visit, never making a remark while we were there but continuing at his work, which at that time happened to be peeling potatoes.

On our way from Camp 10 to Camp 7, we met a tractor with a string of empty sleighs on the narrow hauling road and were forced to take the ditch. We were near a "go back" road, which is a road used by the tractors in making return trips so that they may pass the out-going loaded tractors. Gordon Gould in his snowmobile ahead was not so fortunate. He pulled out into the ditch at the side of the road. The ten inches of snow, which had fallen the previous night, made that total depth about three feet. When an attempt was made to get back in the road, the machine dug its way down into the snow and got firmly stuck. The machine was finally pushed back onto the roadway.

'Jacks working in the tractor yard. *Courtesy of Howard Wieman*

Going back to Camp 10, the writer and a member of Gould's party rode on the back of the snowmobile. There were much pleasanter places, we discovered. The tractor treads throw snow up into the back of the machine when the snowmobile is run at any great speed and by the time we reached the camp we looked like snowmen.

We made the trip back in slightly more than an hour, despite the delays. The road from Camp 10 to Camp 7 crosses two branches of Black River. It crosses the middle branch near Camp 10 and crosses over the north branch at a point near North Lake.

CHAPTER 15

Thousands of Logs Piled on Ice
Awaiting Spring Drive

Fourth Installment, February 16, 1928, Watertown Daily Times
Robert A. Wells

Headline: *Tractor-trains haul forest Giant from Mountain Sides to bleak ice covered river—timbers piled on ice during winter months and rushed 50 miles downriver to mills when thaws come—lumber camps contain many interesting characters whose past life is shrouded in mystery.*

This is the fourth of a series of articles on lumbering, written by a *Times* staff correspondent who visited the lumbering operations of the Gould Paper Company at the headwaters of the Black River

Lumbering operations in the wintertime concern the hauling of the logs from the woods to the landing at the river where they are piled to await the spring floods. Having witnessed the operations in the woods when we made our visit to Camp 10, McCarthy and the forester, McDermott, took the writer in the snowmobile to the banks of the Moose River to watch the unloading of the logs.

Upon our return from Camp 10, we found the foreman of the landing camp, Gardiner Poore, at the company store after supplies. Lacking many supplies, the cook was complaining, and Poore made the trip to get the needed things. The supplies were piled in the back of the snowmobile and we started our second trip of the day.

It is a distance of about six miles to Camp 9 from headquarters camp. The road climbs almost steadily from the camp at the base of Ice Cave Mountain until it reaches a point known as the "summit" on the side of the mountain. At this point there is a large clearing where the tractors hauling from the lumber camps back in the woods leave their log trains for another tractor to haul them to the river. It is entirely down grade from the summit to the landing and the log trains sometimes contain as many as 16 loads of logs.

Linn driver Henry Ruber said drivers were required to make two eighteen-mile-hauls a day to earn a day's pay. He stressed that might not sound hard, but it wasn't as easy as it sounded. Breakdowns occurred, "blocking trains behind and everybody loses." Sometimes Ruber's runs took eighteen hours and he might not finish his second until it was almost time for breakfast on the next day's work! *Courtesy of Howard Wieman*

There had been no wagon or machine over the road from the "main haul" to the camp and it was necessary for us to break a road with the snowmobile. The machine went through the snow without any hesitation, pushing the snow in a drift six feet ahead of it. McDermott, the forester, and Poore were riding on the back of the machine. They got off just before getting to the "tote road" into the camp and only Poore was able to get back on. The machine had gained some speed and McDermott held on the back. The flying snow forced him finally to give up and walk the remaining short distance. When he reached the camp he was covered with snow from head to foot.

Empties (sleds) lined up outside the repair shed. In the logging days of old, there was no shortage of equipment breakdowns. Maintenance was not a matter of a simple call to the nearest equipment dealership before driving out to pick up the needed part. Repairs were made on site by the camp blacksmiths and carpenters. *Courtesy of Fred Worden*

Camp 9, the landing camp, is one of the Gould operations. It is located a short distance from the landing at Moose River and accommodates about 25 men. About that many men were quartered at the camp when we made our visit. It was about 11 when we reached Camp 9 and we thought it time to have another meal. Roy Crandall is the "boiler" at the camp and he served us with salt pork, squash, potatoes, soup, pickles, the best bread yet sampled at the camps, pie and tea.

After our meal we took to the road again and made our way back to the main hauling road. From Camp 9 to the river, the road goes down a steep hill. On this steep hill is one of the most picturesque figures of the lumber camps in the section. He is the "road monkey" in charge of the hill, and an old-time lumberjack. His past is shrouded in mystery, for he speaks but little English and he goes by the name of "Louie" Polish.

There is an interesting story in how he got that name. When he came into the woods many years ago, he said his name was "Louie." No one could discover what his other name was if he had one, so being a Pole, they called him "Louie the Polack." As time progressed, the name was shortened to Louie Polish, and that is the way it is recorded on the company payroll.

"Louie" has his sand hole in the side of the roadway boarded up and covered with tarpaper. He has been at this same spot for many years and takes considerable pride in the condition of the road that he cares for. There is no easier way to incur his wrath than to drive over the road after he has it sanded and covered with straw. The only words I heard him speak were, "Got a cigarette?"

It is only a short distance from "Louie's" hill to the riverbank. For nearly a half a mile the river presents a bleak open expanse and down this space sweep piercing cold winds that make the landing the coldest spot on the operation. During the snow storms that swept with blizzard-like proportions through northern New York several weeks ago, it was impossible for the men working at the landing to see each other if they were more than 15 feet apart.

Five bridges of pulp logs, 200 feet long, about 15 feet high and 150 feet apart, are built across the river. In each of these bridges there are about 200 cords of pulp logs. The log trains are brought down onto the landing and then hauled out onto the bridges. The logs on the sleighs are then dumped down over the side of the bridge and put into the space between the bridges. When the weight of the logs on the ice becomes great enough, they break down through the ice. This continues until the space between the bridges is choked with logs. It is estimated that 14,000 cords will be placed in the river and along the banks at this landing this winter.

These logs will choke the river until spring. Then when the river thaws and high water comes, they will rise up slowly and finally start down the river. Unless a jam forms, the great mass of logs will be on its way down the river to the mills 50 miles away in less than two hours after the first movement.

Across the river from the landing is Higley Mountain. Not far away to the eastward is the Higley Mountain dam site, where the state plans a great dam. In the opposite direction is the Panther Mountain dam site, where another great dam is planned.[15] At the point where the landing is located, the Moose River forms a natural stillwater and provides an excellent place to begin a log drive.

From the time the logs start coming down to the landing until the last load is in, the men stationed at that point have a very busy time. With most of the loads, it is possible to dump all of the logs at one time, the logs rolling with a roar to the ice below. In some cases it is necessary for the landing workers to use their "peavies," a short-handled pole with attached iron hook arrangement used as a lever in logging, to roll the logs to their places on the ice below the log bridge.

There is of course some danger to the workmen stationed here, but they go about their work with no thought of serious consequences. Their greatest trouble is from exposure to the severe cold, but they seem to notice even that but little.

After we had been at the landing for about ten minutes, we were more than ready to seek shelter from the cold wind. Joe and "Bill" were pleased when I concluded my wanderings about the landing and had finished taking several pictures of the scene.

By 2:30 we were back at headquarters camp. While we were at the landing, Gould and his party had left to return to their homes. When we had thawed out and rested for a while it was suggested that it was time to eat again. The idea was extremely welcome despite the fact that it was the fourth meal of the day.

After we had finished our evening meal we had little to do. The card game that flourished the previous evening had suffered with the loss of Gould's party. However, the writer was introduced to a lot of new games during the first evening in the camp.

Popular legend has it that the lumberjack is a great gambler. At the Gould Company camps, poker and any other forms of gambling are taboo. This eliminates any possibility of dissension arising among the men. According to stories of lumbering camps of the old days, many a fight started from a poker game.

As we hovered around the stove in the cottage at Camp 7, tales of personal experiences began to flow and in conjunction with these stories, "Bill" and

Adirondack Logging

"John B" staged their political argument. "Bill" is an ardent Democrat and "John B" is a steadfast Republican, and you can be assured that it was an interesting and entertaining debate that they staged. Tammany hall was raked over the coals in the course of the evening while the G.O.P. was the recipient of its share of caustic remarks before the two finished.

Log sleighs on the main haul road along Natural Hatchery Brook.
Courtesy of Lawton Williams

The political issues having been taken care of, the conversation turned to hunting and fishing stories. "Bill" had a wealth of stories to recount and kept us listening attentively, although "John B" scoffed at some of the stories he told.

In the cozy cottage the box stove radiated heat to all corners of the room, but outside the thermometer was creeping slowly downward. During the early part of the evening, the mercury stood at 15 below and gave no indications of discontinuing its downward course. Through the windows of the cottage we could see the star-lit sky above the mountain on the other side of Ice Cave valley, while close at hand the other buildings of the camp were outlined in the moonlight. The windows of the tractor houses and the workshop were squares of yellow, which showed that the mechanics were at work on the machines, although the rest of the workmen of the camp were asleep.

Tired after our wanderings about the job during the day, the warmth of the box stove soon had us all nodding. It wasn't long until we gave it up as a bad job and went to the floor above and crawled into our beds.

Canachagala Stillwater at the place known as Moose River Landing. In January of 1928, Gardiner Poore was the foreman in charge of Camp 9 and the landing camp. "In preparing for the haul down the Moose River, five bridges of logs, 15 feet high, 200 feet long and 150 feet apart had been built on the river ice. Each bridge consisted of about 200 cords of pulp logs. Additional logs were being dumped daily over the sides of these bridges. About 14,000 cords would be stationed in this manner for the spring drive, starting them on their 60-mile trip to Gould's Mill at Lyons Falls," reported Matthew J. "Joe" Conway in *Port Leyden: The Iron City, A Passing Glance. Courtesy of Lawton Williams*

CHAPTER 16

Veteran Woodsmen Describe Entire Lumbering Operation

Fifth installment, February 17, 1928, Watertown Daily Times
Robert A. Wells

Headline: *Roads brushed out and skidways built early in May while forester and his crew mark out trees for cutting later in month—Work of cutting and peeling starts in August and is followed by hauling logs to river as soon as cold weather comes—Lumbermen burrow under blankets as mercury falls to 30 below.*

This is the fifth of a series of articles written by a *Times* staff correspondent who visited the lumbering operations of the Gould Paper from the headwaters of the Black River.

The second night in Camp 7 at the foot of Ice Cave Mountain proved that lumber camps are cold places in the wintertime. The mercury on that night started on a downward journey that did not end until it reached 30 below zero, lumberjacks reported the next day. Camp 7 is located on Ice Cave Creek in Ice Cave Valley at the base of Ice Cave Mountain. The place is certainly appropriately named.

When the cook pounded on the sleigh shoe to awaken the camp that morning, we just turned over and ignored him. Buried under our blankets, we were far too comfortable to venture out. Finally the camp quieted down after the tractors made their trip out and we slept on until about 7 when the cook informed us that if we wanted breakfast we would have to come and get it then. When we got downstairs we found that it had been so cold the night before that the water in the water pail sitting inside the cabin doors had frozen over even with the fire blazing away in the stove. The weather warmed up fast and after we had finished our breakfast we went to the office, where we discovered a thermometer which registered 15 below. Even then that afternoon, we were forced to wait at the cottage before going to Camp 5. During the morning a tractor from Camp 5 came in with the driver gassed by the carbon monoxide fumes of the motor after the exhaust pipe had broken off under the cab. The man recovered soon after he was brought into the office. To get a picture of the camp, the writer climbed to the top of the horse stable where he waded through more than two feet of snow.

Whoever Wells visited, he was hailed with long halloos by foresters, foremen, cat skinners, whistle punks, loaders, sand hill men, road monkeys, swampers, and bunkhouse historians. In any kind of weather, these men attacked the most difficult jobs without complaint or whimper. *Courtesy of Lawton Williams*

W.H. McCarthy, who served as guide to the writer during his stay in the lumber camp, carries on the lumbering operations at Camp 5 through a contract with the Gould Paper Company. His contract called for the cutting and peeling of the logs and the hauling to the tractor yards. McCarthy has been associated with the Gould Paper Company for nearly ten years. Previous to that he had been employed with the Sulphite Pulp and Paper Company.

Breakfast at 3:30 in the morning. Reporter Wells learned from one 'jack named Bert that once, when the thermometer hit a deeply disturbing subzero temperature, Ben Snyder lit four dozen candles. When the flames froze, Ben broke off the colorful cones and packed them twelve to a box to be sold as Adirondack strawberries. Snyder claimed he made about four hundred dollars. Eating and storytelling were serious business in a lumber camp. *Courtesy of Lawton Williams*

At noon Friday McCarthy and the writer, together with McDermott[16] the forester, who had to visit a lumber camp on the Indian River, started on foot to follow the road over the shoulder of Ice Cave Mountain to McCarthy's camp. Wagons and a roller had broken a road through from the camp in the morning and it was comparatively easy going. Signs of wild life were evident on all sides. Although no deer were seen, their tracks crossed the road in every direction. Once the path of a hedgehog, where he had half-tunneled his way along, crossed the road. Fox tracks were noticed several times but squirrels were the only wildlife visible.

According to information available, deer are wintering well in that section. The snow is not deep enough to bother them seriously. The deer have moved from the high ridges and the mountain tops down into the low timber lands and are in many cases yarded together in virgin timber.

Robert Wells, Bill McCarthy and Joe McDermott followed this snow road over Ice Cave Mountain. Circa 1924. *Courtesy of Fred Worden*

Camp 5, where we arrived after a little more than an hour's hike, lay at the foot of Ice Cave Mountain on the opposite side from Camp 7. The route over the mountain from Camp 7 to Camp 5 is about three and a half miles long. The camp is not far from the headwaters of the Black River. The foreman at the camp is William Mealus, who has been associated with McCarthy for a long period of time. All of the lumberjacks at the camp have been in McCarthy's service for many years. The camp was not yet working on a big scale when we made our visit, with only eight men and two teams being employed, but expected to be well under way in a few weeks.

Another interesting feature of Camp 5 was that the cook was a woman, Mrs. George Maxwell of Adams Center. Her husband is her assistant. This is the only camp in that section that has a woman for a cook. The Maxwells have been 20 years cooking in lumber camps and on construction jobs and have been employed by McCarthy for a number of years. Jack Hurley, another old McCarthy employee, is in charge of the camp office and store.

Adirondack Logging

We looked about the camp, which is made up of four buildings—the camp office and quarters for McCarthy and the foreman, the combined cookhouse and bunkhouse, the horse barn and the store house for vegetables and supplies. "Bill"[17] and the writer started to make a trip to the North Branch of Black River and the virgin timber just beyond. After a 20-minute walk along the "tote road" and the hauling road, we left the roadway and took to the snowdrifts. We waded through snow to our waist and finally reached the river itself at a point just above a beaver dam.

We walked along the frozen surface of the river for some distance, taking great care to see that the ice was good. "Bill" walked ahead of the writer and as he passed over one dubious looking spot, remarked that it didn't look very good. He had hardly got the words out of his mouth when the ice gave way and the writer was in the water up to his waist. Half-crawling and half-pulled by "Bill," the writer got out of the water but not before being thoroughly soaked from the hip down. We started back to camp without going any further. The episode furnished the camp with considerable amusement.

The cookhouse [Rt.] Old Camp 5, Ice Cave Mountain. Circa 1900. The few visible remains of this camp that had survived have been obliterated by recent logging operations in the area. *Courtesy of John Todd (The John B. & Scudder Todd Collection)*

"Bill" outfitted the writer with an outfit made up from his clothes. A pair of heavy woolen pants was only half way to the ankles, displaying a pair of bright blue heavy woolen socks that were picked out of a pack basket. The final picture was an entertaining sight.

The swimming party prevented any further investigation during the afternoon and after our supper we prepared to spend the evening. The atmosphere at Camp 5 was considerably different than that at Camp 7, for instead of electric lighting the only illumination was furnished by kerosene lamps and lanterns and by the glow of the fire in the box stove.

An explanation of the process of lumbering from the time the operation is begun in spring until the drive is over was given that evening by the lumbermen at the camp for the benefit of the writer.

The lumbering operations start about the first of May when roads are "brushed out" and "skidways" are built. A small crew of men is engaged in doing this work. Later in the month the forester with a crew of men goes through and marks the trees to be cut, indicating only those that are over ten inches in diameter and leaving a good seed tree in each acre. Between the 15th and 18th of May, cutting and peeling is started. This continues until the first of August, when the peeling and cutting season is over. By peeling, it is meant that the bark is removed, leaving a smooth, even surface. Crews working in pairs perform this operation. After the first of August when the peeling season is completed, the lumberjacks start cutting the trees into 13 foot logs and turn them and clean off the knots and remaining bark. Three-man crews do this work, two men cutting and one cleaning the logs.

After this is completed the "swampers" and "rollers" clear the roads to the "skidways," and then the teamsters commence hauling the logs to these great piles. Three "skidpiles" hold from 30 to 90 cords. A "double header" to put the top layer of logs on the lead is then built in the tractor yard. After the logs have been "skidded," the roads are completed and the "corduroy" replaced if it is in poor condition.

Then the lumbermen sit down and wait for the snow. When the snow comes, the roads are ploughed out, rolled and then iced. The "road monkeys" improve the condition of the surface of the road, filling up pitch holes and spring holes and cutting off high places on one side and building up the other side where it is low to make the road...so that the loads will not tip dangerously.

With this completed, the drawing of the logs from the "skidways" to the yards is started. Many men are employed in this operation. There are the loaders who work at the "skidways" putting the logs on the loads; the men working on the double headers known as the "top loaders"; and the coupling

Adirondack Logging

North Branch of the Black River. Circa 1924. Fishing along this picturesque rock-strewn stream was impressive. Between May 9 and August 31, 1928, Rev. Byron-Curtiss recorded catching 67 legal-size trout. *Courtesy of Roy E. Wires (The Emily Mitchell Wires Collection)*

crew of two men who hook up the loads in the yard under the inspection of the assistant on the tractor train or whistle punk. The tractor drivers and pumphouse men and the bosses make up the balance of the workers. At the landing on the river is the landing crew, who pile the logs in the river and on the banks for the drive.

After completing the hauling operation the lumbermen again sit down, this time to wait for the spring thaws and floods when the great log drive begins and the pulp wood is swept down the rivers to the mills. The men working on this operation are known as the drivers.

Saturday morning we were aroused early. A visit to a loading operation back in the woods at the "skidways" was made after we had our breakfast. When we reached the tractor yard, the foreman of the camp was at work there preparing the log loads. He told us that three deer had been browsing about in the evergreen trees near him until just a few minutes before our arrival. The deer had paid little or no attention to him, going about their feeding not over ten or 15 feet from him.

The "skid piles" where the loading was being carried on at Camp 5 were back in the woods quite a distance, being connected to the tractor yard with a narrow, hilly road. Three men were at work there loading the logs on the sleigh while two teams were engaged in hauling the loaded sleighs to the tractor yard. The loaders slid the logs onto the loads over smooth poles. The big logs required the exercising of considerable energy.

Rain began to fall about noon. To the lumberman rain is a Godsend if it occurs when there is plenty of snow and is followed by freezing weather. We waited until late in the afternoon, hoping that the rain would stop, but it continued to fall in a drizzle. At about 3:30 we started our trip across the shoulder of the mountain back to Camp 7. The rain swept in a mist against us all the way to the camp. During the last half-mile to the camp, we found deer tracks that had been made but a short time before crossing the road about us in all directions. Despite the recent signs, we failed to catch even a glimpse of one deer.

The rain had the lumbermen worried, and time after time Superintendent Todd would go to the door to see if it was turning colder. When it finally did turn colder, relief was apparent on his face. A cold spell after a rain freezes the roads and speeds up the hauling operation to a great extent.

CHAPTER 17

Colorful French-Canadian Lumbermen Disappearing

Sixth Instalement, February 18, 1928, Watertown Daily Times
Robert A. Wells

Headline: *Wild, carefree worker of forests rapidly being displaced by common laborers and occasional hobo—shifting of pulp logging industry to Canada one of chief reasons for change in personnel of lumbering camp—camps are rich in quaint legends of the past.*

The lumberjacks of yesterday. *Courtesy of Eric Johnson, Executive Editor at* The Northeastern Logger

T his is the last of a series of articles on lumbering written by a *Times* staff correspondent who visited the lumbering operations of the Gould Paper Company in the Adirondack Mountains at the headwaters of the Black River.

The "modern" lumberjacks Robert Wells talked about enjoyed their employers' total confidence, and they in turn had the respect of the woodsmen who knew by experience that they stood inflexibly by their word and would do what they asked. They were utterly American in spirit, honest to a fault, and commanded the regard of all who became acquainted with them. *Courtesy of the Goff-Nelson Memorial (Tupper Lake) Library*

The lumberjack of yesterday, that colorful figure, whose carefree life and wild escapades have won him a place in lumbering history, is vanishing from the Adirondacks. Where 25 years ago there was a throng of this representative type of woods workers, there is scarcely a handful now. These few that are left are the French-Canadian lumberjacks, long connected with the

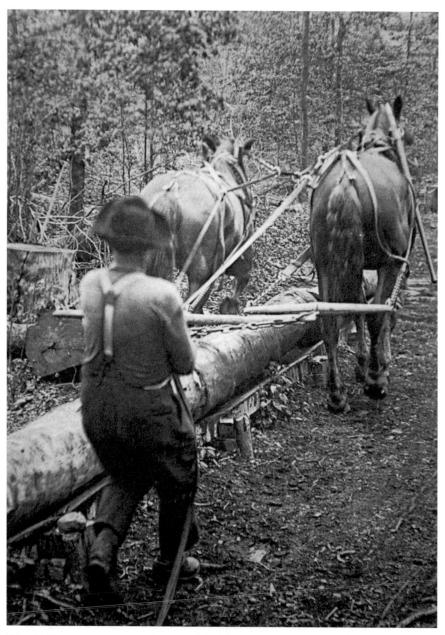

The skid-horse trained to drag a log through the woods was the only one not replaced by a motor in Gould's operation. The *Watertown Daily Times* series brought to its readers' attention the land of the virgin timber and the work involved in getting out the wood. In the process, Robert Wells learned the transformation that had taken place from the days of real horse power to mechanical horsepower. *Courtesy of the Carlton J. Sykes Family*

industry, but there are few of them in comparison with the past. In the place of the old-time lumberjack we find farm labor, in the woods for the winter season: common laborers driven from the cities by unemployment, in rare cases the wandering hobo. These workers go into the woods only in the winter season and never think of working there during the summertime. Besides these workers we find a few Poles, Hungarians and occasionally an Italian. These, with the French-Canadian lumberjack and a few old-timers, make up the workers in the lumbering operations of the Adirondacks today.

Deer were a common sight around all of Gould's camps. J.B. Todd is shown at the far left. Circa 1924. *Courtesy of John Todd (The John B. & Scudder Todd Collection)*

Various reasons are assigned for the passing of the old-time lumberjack. The main reason is an economic one. Wage scales are better outside and there are few young men breaking into the game. Then the motorization of the lumbering industry has brought a new class of labor into the woods, gradually replacing the familiar figure of the rough and ready "woods beast" of the past. "Woods beast" is the term lumbermen apply to themselves, claiming that they have spent so much of their lives in the woods their senses are developed and made as keen as an animal's. Then the shifting of much of the pulp logging industry from the United States to Canada has affected the personnel of the lumber camp.

Adirondack Logging

Linn tractor at Camp 9. Wells' series revealed to his readers much more about the Adirondacks than what they might have known. Many considered the region as purely a recreational area. *Courtesy of Ernest L. Portner*

Gone with the old-time lumberjack are the fights and brawls in which he entered. Those who have ridden the C and A division from Carthage to Newton Falls during the old days know what these are. At every station the lumberjacks would go out of the train and walk from the back platform to the smoker where they had their seats, cheering, singing and waving bottles of liquor, according to the stories of those who rode the trains 25 years or more ago. When the lumberjack got his pay in the past, he headed for the nearest village, there to "paint the town red" and enjoy himself thoroughly. He usually had three or four fights before he got back to camp.

Final look at Headquarters veiled in ice and snow. All that look of a wild, wonderful lumber camp with Ice Cave Mountain rising in the backdrop. Circa 1924. *Courtesy of John Todd (The John B. & Scudder Todd Collection)*

His reputation as a fighter was widely known. In the Tug Hill section, it was customary for newcomers to be invited to "fight or wrastle," according to legend. The story is told that one time many years ago, a Tug Hill girl married a miner from Pennsylvania and the couple came back to that section to live. The Tug Hill men, who were mostly of Irish descent, sought to find out if the newcomer could fight. The couple went to church the first Sunday they were there. A number of the "Tug Hillers" in the congregation could

Adirondack Logging

Robert Wells' winter exit on a Linn tractor was a wild, wooly ride.
Courtesy of John Todd (The John B. & Scudder Todd Collection)

stand it no longer so when the newcomer made his way outside, they managed to force a fight. He proved to be considerably more than they expected and it took three of their number to whip him.

Another interesting story is related about Tug Hill lumbermen. It appears that at one of the lumber camps there was a lumberjack, newly arrived at the camp, who found nothing to his taste. He was very bitter about the food, the beds and everything in general and on a number of occasions declared that he would like to blow up the camp. One of the lumberjacks finally conceived the idea to take a broomstick, drill a hole in the end of it and insert a fuse so that it would resemble a stick of dynamite. The other workers, with the exception of the lumberman whose "kicking" had aroused the camp, were called in. They were informed that the ....was false and told to run when the proper moment came. That night the "kicker" began his tale of woe. Finally, the lumberjack, who conceived the idea stood up and declared that he thought that "kicker" was right and that he was going to blow up the camp. All the men, including the "kicker," fled from the building as he lit the end and dropped the stick in the stove. It was a dismal night outside and the rain was pouring down in torrents. The informed lumbermen stepped just…outside the camp and then …back into the warm room. The "kicker" ran about a half mile. When he came back about an hour later, soaked through to the skin, he was greeted with roaring disdainful laughter. There was not more kicking in the camp that season and the next morning the "kicker" was missing.

There is quite a comparison between the modern lumberjack and the one that figured in these episodes in the past. The modern lumberjack strays but little from path of sobriety and one seldom hears of him in fights and brawls.

Upon entering the small hamlet of Buffalo Head, the tractor driver pointed out Gould's main office for the company's extensive logging operation. He called the long rambling building "the last port-of-call for the lumberjacks." The building, once known as the Forestport House, had been an old hotel. By 1928 it served three separate purposes: a business office, temporary living quarters for the superintendent, and a public lobby with rooms in the rear for the woodmen. It was there that the 'jacks came to sober up after their "Big Spree," and to wait for a company truck to transport them to the foot of North Lake and back to camp. *Courtesy of John Todd (The John B. & Scudder Todd Collection)*

Liquor and poker are taboo in the modern lumber camp. These two rules may be assigned as reasons for some change. The modern foreman has come to the conclusion he can't afford to allow either of these two things to exist in camp if he is to eliminate accidents. If a foreman finds liquor in a camp, the possessor is quite liable to lose his job while the liquor is destroyed at once. To eliminate dissension among the men, gambling is likewise banned.

Adirondack Logging

The mentality of the old time lumberjack on the average was that of a child from 12 to 14 years. Thrown into the woods when young and forced to fight nature, his mind had little opportunity to develop, although his body became a mass of brawn and steel-like muscle. His mind was given no opportunity to expand, for he was usually unable to read or write and the activities of the world seldom touched his sphere.

An improvement is noted in the mentality of the average modern lumberjack in comparison with the old timer.

From among these lumberjacks have emerged many colorful figures. One of the most famous of the Glenfield and North Lake country was "Roving Joe" Flannagan, singing lumberjack. Flannagan would wander from camp to camp in the course of employment and while at work and during the evening would sing for the enjoyment of the men. There are still some in the woods who remember "Roving Joe" and his harmony.

In addition, the lumberjack has contributed to American folklore with his Paul Bunyan stories. Paul Bunyan is a mythical character, whom the stories describe as a giant lumberman. One legend that they recount tells of Paul Bunyan and his blue ox which was "nine axe helves broad between the eyes." This story describes the formation of the Great Lakes by the blue ox getting stuck in the mud and digging the great cavities as he struggled to move on. According to one story, Paul Bunyan's flapjack griddle was as big as a lake and to grease it 40 French-Canadians with hams strapped to their feet skated about the surface.

The trip out of the woods to Forestport was far more eventful than the trip into the camp. The cold snap which had come after the rain of Saturday had iced the surface of the roads excellently and had it not been Sunday, the camp would have been drawing logs at a great rate. In the camps of the North Lake operation, work is carried on only six days a week. Some camps work seven days because of the shortness of the hauling season. This year the Gould Paper Company was not able to start its hauling activities until Jan. 18 in comparison with the latter part of December in the previous year.

On Sunday morning, another trip was made to the landing to secure several more pictures under better conditions and to take supplies to Camp 9. When we reached the summit we found a very interesting sight. About 60 loads of logs were standing there waiting for the tractors to begin hauling them to the landing Monday morning. We found the landing was an extremely cold place but bright sunshine made it possible to get several good pictures.

It was necessary to wait until afternoon before being able to leave camp, the only tractor out leaving at about 2:15. It had been planned that the writer would make the trip out by the same means of transportation used coming in. However, to avoid any possibility of missing train connections it was thought advisable to take the tractor and if the snowmobile taxi caught up with it, to transfer to that means of transportation for the remaining miles into Forestport.

Hauling a log sleigh and the empty 700-gallon gasoline tank behind it, the tractor began the trip. This tractor is used in hauling supplies from Forestport to the headquarters camp and makes a trip in and out each day. We had hardly left the main hauling road and started on the rough "tote" road when we saw a big doe standing in a clump of evergreens at the side of the road. It was the first deer seen on the trip. She did not seem to mind our noisy passing and, standing motionless, watched the tractor go by.

Riding in a log tractor is far from pleasant, especially over rough "tote" roads. You are thrown from one side to another in the driver's cab as the machine crawls along up and down the short steep hills, tipping crazily sideways as it crosses rough spots. The "whistle punk" stood in the cab doorway and hung on precariously as the machine tipped about. Gasoline fumes filled the place almost unbearably. The machine cannot travel any faster than six miles an hour and the trip seems almost unbearable as the tractor slowly crawls along. Several delays were experienced as planks came loose on the sleigh behind. A number of times the tractor stopped to allow the driver and the "whistle punk" to get a drink of water. Near the shore of Black Lake we paused as two small deer raced across before us.

It seemed as though we were getting nowhere. The afternoon passed and the sun set in the western sky. A full moon came up behind us and outlined

OPPOSITE: Having missed the last train to Watertown, Wells left the Adirondack forest on his way to Boonville and watched the moon rise as he crossed the Black River. Here the road entered a wooded section that followed along the Black River canal, where branches of dark evergreens reached toward the car, nearly brushing against its side. *Courtesy of the Town of Webb Historical Association P1521*

the landscape in silver. No snowmobile overtook us and there was no choice but to remain in the cab of the "porpoise." When we finally arrived at Forest-port it was dark and just a few minutes too late to get to Alder Creek to catch the only train north to Watertown that night.

There was no place to stay in the village and it was necessary to taxi to Boonville. The taxi never exceeded 35 miles an hour during the trip to that village, but it seemed that it was racing onward at break-neck speed after the ride of the afternoon. It was solid comfort to sit back in the cushions of the big sedan and feel it roll smoothly over the even surface of the macadam after having been tossed from side to side in a fume-filled cab of a tractor that lurched over the roughest of rough woods roads.

—The End—

Logging camp life with the Gould employees was eye-opening and informative. Robert Wells and Rev. Byron-Curtiss both learned the paper company played a historic role in the pioneer movements toward the mechanization of logging.

Rugged loggers position a horse-powered sleigh to receive a load of logs.
Courtesy of Lyons Falls History Association

Collection 4
Frank A. Reed, Sky Pilot

An unidentified lumber camp in the central Adirondacks that Rev. Reed visited. Religious activity was much more a part of the logging camp than might generally be believed. *Courtesy of the Town of Webb Historical Association*

CHAPTER 18

Sky-Pilot:
An Important Job in the Lumber Woods

William J. O'Hern

W hy were ministers who traveled from one lumber camp to another called "sky pilots"? They certainly didn't arrive in camp by plane or helicopter. Their mission was to "pilot" lumberjacks in a spiritually heavenward direction.

The term "sky pilot" is more focused, deeply thought-provoking and easily understood by reading a few lines Rev. Frank A. Reed asked loggers to ponder at one of his deep-woods logging camp church services.

> *Keep us, O God, from all complaining and self-pity.*
> *When our work is hard,*
>   *give us the strength we need to do our best.*
> *When our hearts are heavy,*
>   *give us a sense of Thy many blessings now and always.*
> *May our efforts and our hopes make us cheerful and serene*
>   *that others may take new vigor and joy from us.*
>
> *—Amen*

Rev. Reed was an Adirondack sky pilot—a preacher who traveled from logging camp to logging camp either on foot or by riding on whatever means he could find. He was at home in in the back woods. Axemen and others like Ken Sprague, who wrote about Reed in the "History & Heritage" column of the

Adirondack Express newspaper on December 18, 2003, said Reed would "take the opposite end of a cross cut or push a buck saw with the best lumberjacks."

Religion and the sky pilot were much more a part of the logging camp life than one might expect. A majority of Gould's camp crews were comprised of Americans and French Canadians—but no matter what denomination, like most early Americans, most came from families with religious backgrounds and training at home. They had profound respect for any man of the cloth. Ministers were well received when they visited camp. Lumberjacks had their favorites, but all were welcomed into the bunkhouse.

On April 16, 1917, Rev. Frank Reed joined sky pilots Aaron Maddox and Clarence Mason for his first lumber camp visit and bunkhouse worship service. The sky pilot's service during good weather that brought the "good news" was conducted outdoors. The men in Donahue's grandfather's camp, as in other lumber camps, welcomed and had great respect for the ministers of the gospel. *Courtesy of John Donahue*

Sky pilots commanded such respect that they were often entrusted to hold on to a 'jacks "stake" while he whooped it up in town; they also helped those who had spent their pay in town to get back on their feet.

Rev. Reed, like other traveling preachers, was an engaging speaker and fine singer. He was known to have an entire bunkhouse ring in joyful sound. He also generously distributed hymnals, Bibles and reading material to the men.

An example of his thought-provoking sermons can be gleaned from one Reed delivered "at an open spot in the forest near the headwaters of the Ausable River."

Across the river one looks upon several rugged peaks including Haystack, Saddleback, Gothic and Marcy, which are only a short distance away. A transport plane is heard in the distance approaching from the south. It flies over Marcy and is lost to view as it approaches the Lake Clear Airport.

The experience raises the question, 'How shall we view the mountains?' One man in a neighboring camp who worked on the steep hillside cutting and skidding pulp dropped the remark that the Creator must have been absent when that mountain was formed. Any man who shared his

In time Reed became a familiar figure in the logging areas of the central Adirondacks, as his influence and reputation extended far beyond the borders of the Adirondack Park. *Courtesy of the Town of Webb Historical Association, P3878*

experience is bound to have respect for his point of view. However one of the tests of life is found in our ability to find the spiritual values in the things among which we work day after day.

One day on the top of Mt. Marcy I met a family who spent their vacations climbing mountains. To those people, the mountains were a constant challenge and the source of many thrills.

One mountain climber, who was a poet, expressed the inspiration of the mountains in these lines:

'God meets me in the mountains when I climb alone and high.
Up where the tapered spruce will guide
My glances to the sky.'

This man had a deep appreciation of the hills among which he lived and the eye to see their spiritual values.

Camp collections were often taken care of by the payroll clerk, who made out checks for the men's donations if the 'jacks wished to contribute but had no ready cash. The Gould Paper Company itself donated funds to the Adirondack Lumberjack Parish in Tupper Lake and McKeever so they could send sky pilots into the woods.

In his *Lumberjack Sky Pilot* autobiography, Rev. Reed wrote about his initial introduction as a young sky pilot headquartered in the lumbering village of McKeever during the winter of 1916–17.

McKeever was a thriving village at the time with a pulp mill operated by the Iroquois Paper Company and a big hardwood sawmill operated by the Moose River Lumber Company. Former Governor John A. Dix was active in the leadership of both mills. The Gould Paper Company of Lyons Falls had its wood headquarters at McKeever for extensive operations on the South Branch of the Moose River and neighboring areas.

McKeever was an excellent place for the on-the-job training of a new sky pilot. Logging activities were vigorous, and manufacturing operated round the clock. Several men helped with information and other forms of assistance. ...

Religious services were held on Sunday morning at the schoolhouse…
and on Sunday afternoons at the schoolhouse in Moose River which
was five miles down the road…and for an evening service in the rural
church at Pinney Settlement…

In his "An Adirondack Sky Pilot" chapter, Reed wrote:

It is 24 years since I had my first service in a lumber camp. That was
in the camp of Pete Gumlaw and he was jobbing for the Rogers Company
of Ausable Forks. His camp was on the west branch of the Ausable River,
not far from Lake Placid.
It is a far cry and many a long mile from that camp on the Ausable
where I had my first service, until I had my last one in March 1949.

Following the sky pilot's retirement, he envisioned a newspaper that would benefit the logging industry. The first issue of his *Lumber Camp News* was published in 1939. Ken Sprague described it as a "historic publication."

"And his literary interests extended in other directions, too, both as a writer and a publisher," Sprague continued, "He founded North Country Books, which has become a key literary stronghold in documenting and preserving regional history and heritage. His book, *Lumberjack Sky Pilot*, was among his first successful releases.

"After 11 years as the sky pilot minister, he came back to Old Forge and Niccolls Memorial Church in 1949. He died on December 10, 1980 and is buried here in Old Forge."

"He seemed to live his life without limits and accomplished so much, not least of which was his work as a minister," reflected Sprague. "Those who knew him said that few people had so much influence on the personal lives of so many individuals. He would hike miles into the woods in minus 40 degree temperatures with only a flashlight to reach the remote lumber camps where he would conduct services and would carry on his back 50 pounds of Christian literature for the loggers. He recorded that he walked 75,000 miles, rode 1.6 million miles and flew many air miles for his mission. His ministry was not heavy-handed, and he succeeded most through the example of his own life."

Adirondack Logging

CHAPTER 19

Lumber Camp News
Senior Editor Reed Speaks Out

Frank A. Reed

R ev. Reed made many contributions to help the cause of the lumbermen during their active and retired lives. He cared about the woodsmen both spiritually and in their earthly lives. His editorials and columns in "The Sky Pilot's Page" of his paper reflect the passion he had to lead people to follow the righteous path in life as evidenced in this April 1953 editorial:

Two years after accepting a post in the Adirondack Lumber Camp Parish, Frank Reed married Mary Posson Reed. This photo was taken on their wedding day in 1919.
Courtesy of the Town of Webb Historical Association

*As an eloquent speaker brought his interesting address to a close he
remarked, "If you are going to steal, don't steal a goose. Steal a railroad or a bank. Your punishment will be lighter and the possibility
of escape better."*

*Very late on a recent evening, the writer was sleeping in the back seat
of his car while one of his sons was driving home. A Utica motorcycle
cop drove alongside, baited us and said, "You went through a red light,
drive back to the police station."*

*At the police station, the lieutenant asked a few questions and said
politely, "Your fine will be $15.00."*

*During the conversation, the lieutenant revealed that accidents had been
on the increase and the city was becoming more strict on law enforcement.*

Hitching a ride with tote team or riding a retuning tractor would be a plus for a
traveling preacher. *Courtesy of Special Collections, Feinberg Library, SUNY College at Plattsburgh, C-2-68*

*The writer began to reflect a bit on "Law Enforcement" in the city of
Utica. During the last few years, he had conducted funeral services for a
few woodsmen who had died in hotels and saloons in the city. In most
cases these hotels and saloons had sold liquor to men who were intoxicated.
In some cases there might have been foul play. Yet the death of these
woodsmen seems to have been of little interest in the police department.*

Adirondack Logging

For many years, saloons in some areas of Utica, as well as other cities, have thrived on the hard-earned money of the woodsmen. The policy has been to relieve a man quickly of his stake and to give little in return.

It was not unusual for Reed to hike through the woods, sometimes in sub-zero temperatures with only a flashlight to reach a remote camp where he would conduct services. This early camp was located on Third Lake in the central Adirondacks. *Courtesy of the Town of Webb Historical Association, P3881*

The writer has no particular argument against "strict law enforcement" or the $15.00 fine for driving through a red light. He does think, however, that the driver who passes a red light should get as good a break as the man who operates a saloon in the 'Red Light District'; who thinks only of a man's money, with very little concern for the man; who sells to men who are already intoxicated and has little regard for human welfare or the good of the community.

In reflecting on such situations one is reminded of the statement of an ancient teacher: "They strain at a gnat and swallow a camel."

CHAPTER 20

Influential Ministerial Service

William J. O'Hern

rank Higgins of Minnesota was the pioneering sky pilot. Aaron W. Maddox, Charles Atwood and Clarence W. Mason followed Higgins' service as ground-breaking lumber camp sky pilots in the Adirondacks. During their tenures, Frank A. Reed was pastoring at Niccolls Memorial Church in Old Forge. *Adirondack Express* newspaper columnist Ken Sprague said, "The parish flourished with the new pastor, and then the churches in Inlet and Raquette Lake asked him to serve them, too. This was the founding of the Central Adirondack Larger Parish, headed by Reverend Reed, who stayed in Old Forge until 1938.

With the retirement of Clarence Mason on March 11, 1938, and at Mason's invitation and the urging of lumberjacks far and wide, Reed stepped in to fill Mason's lumber camp parish position.

The appeal of all the sky pilots was their knack of imparting a reverence for Christian ideals while respecting the honest toil of hard-working men. They respected and inspired their parishioners while devoting themselves to improving the "spiritual welfare of those whose environment is too often far removed from spiritual experiences," said Sherman Adams. The sky pilots were unusual men with an uncanny ability to bring religion and spirituality into the lives of the men they worked so hard to reach.

Sky pilots championed loggers in their quest to bring religion to the Central Adirondacks. "Mr. Mason spent a quarter of a century in Adirondack lumber camps during the period from 1915 to 1939," said Reed. "In winter, he travelled on snowshoes from one logging operation to another. He might enter the woods near Lake Placid after Christmas and emerge in the spring at Forestport or Dodgeville, after a journey of several hundred miles with visits to many lumber camps along the way."

Reed was a strapping strong man. He had no problems toting for miles a 50-pound backpack that contained, besides personal belongings, religious literature for distribution to the loggers. He was accustomed to the toil and hardships of life in the woods. Reed gained the lumberjacks' confidence. His powerful physique and background of hard manual labor put him on the men's own level and made him very approachable. *Courtesy of the Town of Webb Historical Association, P3880*

The following articles provide a sample of the guidance Reed and fellow Christians provided to readers in the *Lumber Camp News*. Their decades-old words continue to this day to carry the same weight.

Reed offered Clarence Mason "The Sky Pilot's Page" in the July 1952 issue of *The Northeastern Logger* to recall his working days. Mason titled his memories "A Good Ending."

When I began my work in the lumber camps in 1915, there were thirty-two log drives on the rivers and streams in the Adirondack area. With the coming of the gasoline truck, now most if not all the pulp wood is hauled to the mills on wheels.

Thousands of cords of logs have been driven down the Hudson River and its tributaries. Fishing Brook, the Newcomb River, and East River unite at Newcomb to form the Hudson River. It is more than a hundred miles from the log landings at Little Bay near Glens Falls, where the Finch, Pruyn Co. has a large mill.

During all the time I was in the lumber camps, I never but once was denied the privilege of speaking to the men at camp. The foreman was pleasant enough and cordial but he had an idea that a church was the only proper place for the preacher to exercise his talents.

I did not argue the question with him. It was his camp and he had a right to run it as he saw fit; but, when I bade him good-bye the next morning, I said, "I will be around again in a couple of months and I will come in and see how you are getting along." "Sure," he said, "come in any time you are in these parts. You will be welcome."

So the next time I came into his camp, I said to him, "Now if you do not want to have me hold a religious service in the camp, I might tell the men what is going on in other camps and some of the news of the outside world and maybe give them a little temperance talk." He said, "How long do you speak to the men?" I told him, "Not a very long time. The men are tired from their hard work in the woods. Probably not over twenty-five minutes."

"Well, if you want to address them, go ahead." I thanked him and told him I should like to have him come to the service. He said to let him know when I was ready. So when the men had finished the chores around camp, I told him we were ready and he came. After that I was in his camp a good many times and always spoke to the men the same as in other camps.

Adirondack Logging

Reed kept detailed notes of his travels. Those records became the basis of his *Lumber-jack Sky Pilot* book. *Courtesy of the Town of Webb Historical Association*

One year the camp foreman who had refused to let me hold a service in his camp was foreman on the Hudson River drive and I was on my way, by auto, to meet the log drivers. It was near the last of May. I did not know where the crew might be, at the Glen, or at the Fish Hatchery, or at Thurman Flats, or they might be going through Moulton Bars. I found them at the Fish Hatchery, near Warrensburg.

I was a little late; the crew had had supper and some of the boys had gone over to the village to see the movies. The foreman welcomed me into the camp. He said it was a little late and some of the boys were gone, but added, 'We are going to move tomorrow down to Thurman Flats. You stay over until tomorrow night and we will all be together down there.' I thanked him and bunked that night in the foreman's tent. The next day was Memorial Day and as fine a May day as ever was. We used to move camp in those days with horses and lumber wagons. I found I could make myself quite useful in the camp moving operations. Everything was in order and supper was ready by the time the men came off the river at night.

The foreman came around to me and said, "Now this is a holiday and there are a good many strangers here who have stopped to see the log drive. When you get ready to speak, give them the works." After supper I mounted a wood pile and "gave them the works" to the best of my ability.

It was not the first time I had met the Hudson River drive at the Fish Hatchery. I met them once at the same time of the year when Mike Buckley was foreman and Dyer Daniels was cook. He cooked on the Hudson River drive 32 years. He could bake as good cake or biscuits in a reflector as ever came out of an oven. That Memorial Day was also a fine one, but frosty. Ice half an inch thick formed on a basin of water just outside the door of our tent.

Hauling pine in the Adirondacks. *Courtesy of the Lewis County Historical Society, Larry J. Myers Collection*

Adirondack Logging

CHAPTER 21

Planning One's Life

Rev. Frank A. Reed

In his travels through the Adirondack woods, the writer often observes a striking contrast in the way lumber jobs are carried on. At one camp, the hauling program was far behind schedule. Men seemed to be working with great energy but achieving little. Suitable roads had not been laid out in the summer and fall. Machinery was broken down. With a heavy blanket of snow covering the area, it was impossible to open roads to the stump piles which were scattered here and there in the forest.

On another job, the writer observed that machinery for winter hauling was carefully repaired in summer. Roads were laid out during the cutting season. Even in the deep snow of mid-winter, the job moved smoothly and hauling was completed by March 1st. The difference in the two jobs lay in the planning.

What one observes in lumber jobs, he may also observe in human lives.

Some people plan well. In the time of opportunity, they develop the spiritual resources which will carry them through the period of emergency. Others plan poorly or not at all. Their lives are guided by appetites or by circumstances. When emergencies arise, they have neither the material nor the spiritual resources to withstand the storm.

The most striking example of a well-planned life is to be found in the life story of Jesus who was, at the same time, the great architect of human life and the example of noble living.

Life Objectives. Jesus had certain great objectives for which he was constantly striving. One of these is evident in the story of his boyhood. When his parents found him in the temple after a long search, his mother said, "Son, why have you dealt with us this way? Your father and I were searching for you sorrowfully." Jesus replied, "Didn't you know that I must be about my father's business?" The doing of God's will was a dominant life motive in the life of a boy of 12. It continued to be dominant throughout the days of his ministry and to the very end of his life. He accepted the way of the Cross as God's will for his life.

Free from the distractions of the logging woods, the bunkhouse served as the lumberjacks' church on occasion. The informal service was held at a convenient time in the evening when men were all in from the barn, and included news from other camps, the reading of scripture, a short sermon and a closing prayer. *Courtesy of the Town of Webb Historical Association*

Jesus urged his disciples to strive for perfection, to build lives which were strong and beautiful. His own daily life furnished the world's most striking example of a person who not only strove for this objective but who actually achieved it.

Jesus planned his life in terms of the enrichment of the lives of other people. In stating his purpose on one occasion, he said, "I came that they might have life and have it more abundantly." His life was spent in achieving that goal, in making blind men see, lame men walk and sick people well again,

Adirondack Logging

in giving to people great ideas and ideals. He worked not only for the enrichment of the lives of individuals but for a better social order, the Kingdom of God.

Reed wrote that the old-time lumberjack's bunkhouse was his home. "It was where he slept, visited on winter's evenings, sometimes played a game of cards on the table and wrote letters." *Courtesy of Pat Payne*

Major Activities. Jesus worked toward the achievement of these great goals through three major activities. As a young man he worked in the carpenter shop, where he made many useful things including yokes for oxen, and learned that a well-fitted yoke was the best way for the ox to carry his burden.

He became the great healer of his generation, at least, and perhaps the greatest of all time. Inspired by an ardent desire to make men well, to alleviate human suffering, he brought new life and hope into the lives of thousands through his healing ministry.

But Jesus was primarily a teacher. Most people recognize him as the greatest teacher of all time. He gave to the people of his generation many new and revolutionary ideas which changed the currents of thought and the stream of human life. Those ideas were expressed with great clarity, force and beauty. They were enduring truths which still stand as a challenge to our thinking and living.

In these ways Jesus furnishes us the example and the dynamic for well-planned lives in our generation, lives whose energies and talents are devoted to these same great Christian goals, lives which are well-planned and which have spiritual resources sufficient for every emergency.

CHAPTER 22

A Christmas Wish to Dear Friends
of the Adirondack Lumber Woods

Clarence W. Mason

Rev. Mason had been retired for thirteen years when he wrote the following Christmas
wish. Twenty-three years of ministry as a sky pilot in the Adirondack lumber camps
had taught him there was little seasonal entertainment in the camps. It was not the
business of logging camps to offer entertainment. Especially in the early days, most
'jacks spent the entire winter in the camps. A rare break in the day-to-day routine
consisted of resting up, washing clothes and sharpening tools. A rare holiday ritual
following an extra-good Thanksgiving or Christmas meal might be for some of the
younger men to build a snowman clad in lumberman clothing. Old timers would tell
of their experiences; younger 'jacks might relive their youthful family holidays, and
engage in games of strength like wrist-wrestling and bending horseshoes. Some tal-
ented 'jack would play a violin, harmonica or Jew's harp. And of course there was
the steady stream of conversation around a large load of logs, a team of horses that
broke through the ice, poor food or good food furnished by some other camp and tales
about some of the ladies a 'jack had fun with while spending his stake in the city.

Mason remembered previous Christmases in his 1951 wish for those he knew were
spending theirs in the lumber woods.

Dear Friends,

Granting that Jesus was born in December, the temperature was different
in Bethlehem of Judea from what it usually is in the Adirondacks at that time
of year. In fact it is different up there from what it is in Tompkins County

178 *Adirondack Logging*

[in the Southern Tier] where I now live. Often as cold weather as we get all winter comes in Northeastern New York in December.

Fortunately I was able to get home always for Christmas, though many times it involved long trips through rough stormy weather and over icy roads.

A lumberjack's home in winter. Camp 9's cookhouse and sleeping quarters. Circa 1930s.
Courtesy of Fred Worden

I recall many occasions when we had severe cold weather in the lumber camp area just before Christmas. I always carried a thermometer with me. Once on Tug Hill, in the McCarthy Camp, I hung it outside the office. The next morning I looked at it and came in and said that it was 25 below zero. Mart McCarthy spoke up and said "Don't tell the men how cold it is. We would lose a trip." When the men came in to breakfast, they were rubbing their hands and saying that it was a cold morning. "Yes," said Mart, "It must be down to zero anyway."

On that occasion I had with me several of the little comfort kits which the Women's Societies of the churches made up for us. I gave one of them to the chore boy, saying I would make him a Christmas present of one of them. He took it and untied the ribbon that was around it, unrolled it and looked over the contents: sewing needles, darning needles, thread and yarn, buttons, pins and safety pins, a large shawl pin and a copy of one of the Gospels. When he had looked everything over, he drew a long breath and looked up at me and said, "Do you know that is the first time in my life that I have ever had anything given to me?"

Camp 9's mess hall. Circa 1930s. Rev. Reed, following the lead of his earlier sky pilot counterparts Frank Higgins, Aaron Maddox, Charles Atwood, Clarence Mason and William Burger, Jr. all spoke the lumberjacks' language and were concerned with the loggers' welfare. It was not uncommon for lumberjacks "thirsty for diversion" to turn over their money to the sky pilots for safekeeping before swarming into the numerous saloons where "whiskey, women, and the wheel" offered mental release from the privations and risks of life in the camps. *Courtesy of Fred Worden*

It is to be hoped that he found in the Gospel story the meaning of it all—the great Gift within reach of all of us, and the cause of His coming. Said He, "I am come that they might have life and that they might have it more abundantly."

This life is my wish for you all.

CHAPTER 23

God's Work

Rev. Frank A. Reed

"I must work the work of him that sent me while it is day." Rev. Reed was known to quote these words of a young man who had achieved much. He died at the early age of thirty but had already changed the lives of thousands of people. His influence has changed the history of the world.

Jesus spent his energies in three particular fields of endeavor: as a carpenter in the shop of Joseph, as a healer and as a teacher. By the Master's teaching and his life, he inspired men to seek the best in thought and action.

"Jesus looked upon all of these activities as his opportunity to do the work of God and to serve his fellow men," said Rev. Reed in his February 1949 column, 'God's Work.'

There are at least two ways in which we may do the work of God. We do it through our daily tasks. The woodsmen of the Northeast have been doing the work of God in getting out 1,000,000,000 feet of hardwood and 2,000,000 cords of pulpwood. These products enter the homes and business places of people and make an important contribution to their daily lives.

Of course we do God's work better when the cutting of these forest products is planned also in terms of coming generations.

We do the work of God by words of cheer and deeds of kindness along the way. This may be expressed in little things. A man at the table is considerate of his neighbor to the right or left and sees that he is supplied with food. The truckman halts to see whether the man he meets on the way is stuck in

One sky pilot "told that once while he was speaking a lumberjack called out in fervent tones, 'You're damn right!' This unusual 'amen' surprised the speaker considerably, but he recovered his poise and appreciated fully the earnest approval of the listener." —Floy S. Hyde, *Adirondack Forests, Fields, and Mines*

Occasionally in his later years, Rev. Reed flew in a float-equipped Piper Cub with his son as pilot, but it was not why he was called a "sky pilot." *Courtesy of Fred Worden*

a bad turnout. The workman makes another man's task easier by lending a hand in time of need. A neighbor gives a word of encouragement to one who is facing a difficult situation or has met with reverses.

> *Take my life and let it be*
> *Consecrated, Lord to Thee;*
> *Take my moments and my days,*
> *Let them flow in ceaseless praise.*

OPPOSITE: Often homeless and migratory, lumberjacks walking the Bob Jones tote road that winds along North Lake's shoreline toward Gould's numerous camps tucked back in the Black River headwaters passed Rev. Byron-Curtiss' outdoor chapel. The sanctuary was a welcome place to rest and relax, pray, and if B-C was home, mix with the camp owner who joined the men in smoking, telling yarns and, in his relaxed way, intermingling theological opportunities. *Courtesy of Thomas and Doris Kilbourn. (The Rev. A.L. Byron-Curtiss Collection)*

PART TWO

Stories and Recipes

Lt. to Rt. Byron and Lea Moyer at Moyer's McKeever logging camp, 1913. Irene arrived in a cutter at her grandfather's camp, just in time for supper at the big oilcloth-covered table. The kerosene lamp was lit. She remembered talking to her gram and gramp and how warm and relaxed she felt by the chunk stove. *Courtesy of Irene F. Rogers*

Collection 4

Cookhouse Chronicles and
Lumber Camp Memories

Central to the success and happiness of any lumber camp was the cook. While the men, horses and machines were the muscle of the woods, the log-jobber knew to take his crew's well-being into consideration and feed and house them well while they were on the job. *Courtesy of John Donahue*

CHAPTER 24

A Good Chef Makes
a Good Lumber Camp

William J. O'Hern

B y the 1880s, lumber camps were springing up throughout the Tug Hill
and Adirondack Mountains. Mary Rita Gadway's grandfather, along with
many other men, mostly of French Canadian descent, went to work in these
lumber woods. She said, "Grandfather worked for a company which operated
a string of camps. In one camp were 120 men who paired up and cut logs by
the month. In the woods, physical prowess was indispensable because the
men were paid not in proportion to the time spent, but rather for the specific
number of logs cut. For example, $20 a month would be paid to two men
who could consistently cut 100 logs a day, $18 for 90 logs, or $15 for 80 logs."

Mary Rita Gadway's grandfather's logging camp life was one of the mainstays
of employment for men in the 19th and early 20th centuries. During that
period the Adirondacks led the nation in lumber production. Some estimates
report New York had over 4,000 sawmills in operation.

Logging camps blanketed the mountains. They employed hundreds of
hard-working men—including some women "cookies," helpers to the chief
cook. Often an elderly man worked as "bull cook." It was his job to keep a
good supply of dry wood on hand and to keep the water barrels full.

Men came from a diversity of backgrounds "and from every corner of the country and the world," Ken Sprague reported in his "History & Heritage" column in the *Adirondack Express* weekly newspaper. "There were unemployed drifters, farmers supplementing their incomes, and even professional men who came to the woods looking for a new life and perhaps leaving personal and professional problems behind." Many of the men were single, others had few family ties, and others were married with families. A majority of recruits in Adirondack camps came from ethnic groups including Russians, Poles and French Canadians.

Molasses and beans, potatoes, two meats and several kinds of vegetables, loaves of bread, cookies, cakes and pies, puddings and doughnuts at every meal "and always gallons of steaming coffee" spelled the recipe for success, according to former lumber camp co-cooks Harriet and Carl Sweeney. According to the couple, logging-jobbers preferred to hire husband and wife teams. Harriet told her Glenfield, N.Y. neighbor and writer Louis Mihalyi that couples, "were rocks of stability, working seven days a week at isolated, remote logging sites." *Courtesy of the Carlton J. Sykes Family*

Camp food was one of the few amenities in early lumber camps. A vast variety of bean dishes and prune cake surfaced in older 'jacks' memories of their younger years, when they sat silently eating at long plank tables where the hard-working men consumed countless calories. (There was one cardinal rule: No talking. You sat down, ate your fill and got out of the dining room.) No one counted calories, nor were they concerned about a balanced diet in those days. "The coffee was hot and wetted your whistle and those beans sure kept your belly from rubbing against your backbone," said Edward R. Raymond of his first-hand lumber camp experiences.

Harriet Sweeney was 23 years old when "she and her husband Carl, with two infants, took their first job supplying three squares a day for 25 eternally hungry lumberjacks. Harriet Sweeney followed in the path of her family, which counted five other cooking teams among its members. But this was Carl's first venture into the business, and he had reservations. 'There were the little ones,'" he said. —Louis Mihalyi "Lumber Camp Cooks," *Adirondack Life* magazine, May/June 1988. *Courtesy of Dorothy Payton*

Bambi Norman is a friend of our family. She grew up on a farm. Bambi knows all about hard work. She also knows about good food and how it can fuel one's body. We bring a huge pan of her special baked bean recipe to almost every bring-a-dish-to-pass-around function we attend. The pan almost always returns home empty. An early river driver would have willingly traded his favorite pike pole for her tasty formula.

| Recipe | **BAMBI'S BAKED BEANS** |

Ingredients:

1 pound ground beef and ½ pound bacon

2 teaspoons Worcestershire sauce

1 cup chopped onion

1 can kidney beans (drained)

1 can butter beans (drained)

1 can pork & beans

1 can black beans (drained)

1 cup ketchup

2 teaspoons salt

2 teaspoons prepared mustard

1½ cups brown sugar

1 teaspoon cider vinegar

Directions: brown bacon until crisp. Break into bits. Add beef and onion (break up meat). Add remaining ingredients. Mix well. Bake at 350°F. for 1 hour. (Ground venison and pork can be substituted.)

4,000 cords of pulpwood in a pile in Carter, New York. *Courtesy of the Lewis County Historical Society, from Larry J. Myers Collection*

CHAPTER 25

How Mrs. William Warner Fed the "Timber Beasts" in a Rough Backwoods Camp

William J. O'Hern and Silas C. Kimm

Although they are often stereotyped, loggers are not all the same. Their backgrounds, education, and experiences all vary. Their families, their lifestyles, and their needs are no more identical than anyone else's.

On the other hand, some generalities do characterize most loggers, both past and present.

All loggers burn a lot of energy.

It was not only the incredible exertion of old-time, muscle-power and logging. There were also the caloric demands of the bitter winter cold and deep snow that were physiologically almost as exacting as the long hours of work.

There's an old and common superstition among loggers that if they see a fat man in the woods it is time to blow the whistle. There would be three accidents in quick succession.

Loggers always ate plenty of food. And, in many camps the men were eating a variety of fresh, wholesome, and well-prepared foods.

'Timber beasts' before the beginning of the 20th century were "not typically remembered for their lives of comfort," wrote Joseph R. Conlin in "Oh Boy, Did You Get Enough of Pie" in the October 1979 issue of the *Journal of Forest History*.

Wages were not good, well into the twentieth century. Employment was unsteady; job security did not exist. Bunkhouse conditions appalled the roughest of outsiders. (Sled drivers delivering supplies to the camps often preferred to sleep in the snow.) Lumberjacks were despised and feared by much of conventional society. During the years of the First World War and just afterwards, employer-employee relations in the logging industry in general across the United States were among the worst in the country. The Industrial Workers of the World—the Wobblies— the union of last resort, won thousands of adherents among woodsmen of the Northwest. In no other industry did the federal government, through the military, find it necessary to intervene so directly. Yet, while much of the working class of the time was marginally nourished, loggers ate extremely well. Why?"

All loggers burn a lot of calories. *Courtesy of Earl M. Kreuzer*

Conlin answered this question by citing Robert L. Tyler's *Rebels in the Woods: The I.W.W. in the Pacific Northwest* (Eugene: University of Oregon *Books, 1967); Melvyn Dubofsky, We Shall Be All: A History of the Industrial Workers of the World* (New York: Quadrangle Books, 1969); and Harold M. Hyman, *Soldiers and Spruce: Origins of the Loyal Legion of Loggers and Lumbermen* (Los Angeles: University of California, Institute of Industrial Relations, 1963.)

Silas Kimm saw many changes in his 84 years. *The Collected Works of S.C. Kimm, Educator, Historian, Rhymester & Author*, assembled by his grandson Gilbert H.H. Jordan II, is a storehouse of interesting history. *Courtesy of Pat Payne*

Conlin wrote, "Improvements took five forms: (1). the introduction of fresh meats, vegetables, fruits, and even eggs, butter and milk—in abundance and as a matter of course: (2). variety—no more same-thing-every-meal-every-day; (3). baking—often with extraordinary skill; (4). professional, specialized cooks to handle the job; and (5). distinctly separate, sit-down dining—the famous "cookhouses"—with tableware and table service."

While the articles centered on logging camp conditions in another part of the United States, Silas C. Kimm penned a personal memory that adds to the social history of food in an Adirondack logging camp he worked in as a youth. His recollection tells about the workers who lived in the boarding house of a Mrs. William Warner, and the food served in what he described as a "vanished village north of Salisbury…in [a] rough back woods settlement of Herkimer County."

Eating a Simple Task. There was one long table made of rough boards and at each end of the table was a big plate of spuds, a pile of bread and a dish of pork. Occasionally we had a chunk of native beef. Beans and black molasses was a staple article of food. Occasionally we regaled or reveled in dried apple pie, but our pastry for the most part was either molasses cake or "poor man's cake." We worked so far from the camp that we carried our dinner. One of us carried a large pillow slip of big loaves of bread, another took a 6-quart pail of beans and a third was entrusted with several slabs of molasses cake. We were expected to start to work in the morning in the short fall days as early as we could see to stumble along the trail. Two men made a team to saw down and trim the trees and cut them into logs. A third man cut a trail to the logs and a fourth man drew them to the skidway with a horse or yoke of oxen. At the skidway were two men to roll the logs into a large compact pile where they remained until winter to be drawn to the mills on large lumber sleighs. When the sub-boss yelled for dinner, we all met at some central place, preferably by a spring brook so that we might have a drink with our luncheon.

The Boy With Ten Fingers. I recollect on one occasion we had a special treat for dinner. We had succeeded in piloting several pies to the log cutting and at meal time these were spread out on the ground ready to be carved and divided. We sawed off huge slabs of bread and spread these thick with mashed beans and proceeded to satisfy the longings of our stomachs. In our group was a youth nearly six feet tall and with feet to match. He had five well—developed fingers and a thumb on each paw. A big overgrown kind-hearted chap. He had in his hand a

big slice of bread and beans which so occupied his attention that he
walked directly into our pies. The one he stepped on shot dried apples in
all directions. Six pieces of pie all squished, and who would be the six
unlucky chaps to go without that delectable pie? The talk we spilled on
that ten-fingered youth would shock a sailor.

Silas worked in the northern forests from 1875 to 1881, when he was a teenager. During that time, he was encouraged by someone in the lumber camp to further his education, which he did. In 1881 he entered Fairfield Seminary, became certified as a teacher, and was teaching in 1882. Continuing his education, he went on to earn the degree of Doctor of Philosophy in 1899 from Taylor University, Indiana.

Dr. S.C. Kimm served for a quarter of a century as Herkimer County's District School Superintendent, and was one of the nation's pioneers in the development of central school systems.

Dr. Kimm's grandson, Gilbert H. Jordan II, assembled and published his grandfather's vast writings titled *The Collected Works of S.C. Kimm, Educator, Historian, Rhymester & Author* in 2004. Kimm's recollections of an Adirondack past are some of my favorite readings. His poem "The Sounds From the Kitchen" reflects a time in my own past when I listened from an attic bedroom to my grandmother preparing breakfast in our camp kitchen.

How often I dwell on the fond recollection
Of sounds that came from the kitchen below,
While I slumbered in peace in the loft just above it,
Under the roof deep covered with snow.

The smell of the sausage that came up the stairway,
The sizzling of pancakes so steaming and hot;
The clattery dishes and the frying potatoes,
The boiling and gurgling in the old coffee pot.

Heaven itself has no sounds to compare
With the old morning sounds from the kitchen below.

Courtesy of the Lewis County Historical Society, from Larry J. Myers Collection

A staple among the woodsmen was hot dogs, which Joe Conway always referred to as "frankfurters." They were cheap, readily available, and could be cooked in a number of different ways—on a stick over a campfire was the easiest, although boiling them in a pan on an already-hot cook stove was just about as fast. Fried, they could serve as a stand-in for bacon or sausage for breakfast, and as a substitute for "real" meat in stews and casseroles. Here's a quick and delicious recipe Madge Conway used.

Recipe **SAWMILL MUSTARD BROILED HOTDOGS**

Ingredients:

3 tablespoons Dijon-style mustard

1 teaspoon Worcestershire sauce

2 tablespoons chopped parsley

1 pound hotdogs

Directions: Stir together mustard, Worcestershire and parsley. Place hotdogs on broiler pan and spread with half the mustard mixture. Broil 4 inches from heat 4 minutes, turn, spread with remaining mustard mixture and broil 4 minutes longer. Serves 4.

CHAPTER 26

William McCoy's
Logging Camp Accident

William J. O'Hern

Accidents in the lumber woods were frequent, both to the 'jacks and to the draft horses. There were bad cuts and gashes, close calls with death, and odd-ball imaginative first-aid techniques. The following tale grew from John Duffy's accidental slip causing a serious injury to his partner William McCoy, miles from any hospital or doctor. It is as it was reported in *The Malone Farmer*, September 9, 1903, issue on page six:

> *It is said a curious case of surgery performed a year ago in the Adirondacks has just come to light. William McCoy, a woodsman, was the person on whom the operation was performed. While getting out some long poles to repair a log chute on the mountainside at a lumber camp with a fellow workman, the latter let his axe slide out of his hands and it struck McCoy, the keen edge shaving off part of his cheek. A Utica nurse took him in hand, and after partially stopping the flow of blood, he took a fawn that some of the boys had captured a day or two before, shaved the hair for about nine square inches off the animal's side, removed the skin and applied it immediately to McCoy's face, fitting it in place firmly and covering it over with a thick coat of balsam gum, over which he placed tight bandages. The skin adhered, the bandages were removed in about a week and the graft proved to be a success. McCoy's*

later experience is hard to believe but the story goes as follows: "Soon afterward, however, McCoy noticed when he drew his hand across his cheek that hair was growing on the grafted skin. In a few more days the hair had grown so thickly that its color and nature were plainly visible. It was the hair of the fawn growing, and, moreover it was spotted like that of a fawn. He did not dare to shave for fear of breaking the skin and allowed the hair to grow until the fall of the year. Then the spots disappeared and the "blue" coat of a full grown deer took its place. When spring came around he saw that the hair of the cheek was falling out, and fine red hair was growing. At last the blue or winter coat was entirely gone, and the red summer coat took its place. In fact, he and

A teamster takes time out to pose beside his reliable horses. *Courtesy of George Cataldo*

*the other woodsmen, to their merriment, saw that the hair varied and
changed precisely as does the coat of a deer."*
— *The Malone Farmer*, September 9, 1903

I told this tale to Indian Lake resident Ethel Tripp, the day I interviewed
her about her father's life in the Adirondacks, when lumbering was still in
its heyday. She thought the innovator of the surgery must have sedated the
poor fawn with a prodigious amount of whiskey. Then she offered me a glass
of her homemade eggnog. I was familiar only with the store-bought variety
until then. Ethel said back in her younger days it was typical to make your
own. Ethel's father was Mossy Maxium, a well-known Raquette Lake guide.
I had recently found the former site of his Squirrel Top camp. Ethel was
thrilled something still remained of the place. I regaled her with details of
the challenging bushwhack east of Sagamore Lake that day as we drank our
eggnog, which was far superior to any store-bought variety.

Ethel laughed as she remembered liking the holiday drink so well that as
a young girl she would slip into the family's ice house to sip it out of a large
blue-speckled crock. That afternoon she sang to me her Squirrel Top song,
so I named her parents' recipe in honor of her dad's Adirondack camp.

Recipe   **SQUIRREL TOP EGGNOG**

Ingredients:

½ pt. heavy cream

1 quart milk

4 eggs separated

4 rounding tablespoons sugar

1 cup white rum

*Directions: Beat yolks and sugar, add rum slowly, beating in.
Add 1 quart milk, the whipped egg whites and whipped cream.
Chill well.*

CHAPTER 27

Thirty Dozen Doughnuts

William J. O'Hern

"Thirty dozen doughnuts, thirty-five dozen eggs, mountains of pancakes, 30 fruit pies, 150 pounds of meat, 175 pounds of potatoes, a sack of beans, gallons of piping hot coffee…" The provisions went on. This partial list of the amount of food a camp cook prepared each day was just part of the earful I learned at Joe Conway's home about Adirondack logging camp cookery.

Few people today can understand the hunger created by the intense labor of a logger. Food—and lots of it—lifted spirits, calmed tension, filled a lumberjack with a sense of comfort, and provided needed calories.

I was fortunate to know Joe Conway. Joe was a native of the Tug Hill region of New York State. He was born in Highmarket and grew up in Port Leyden, a logging community, surrounded by old-timers and characters who ran the gamut of trades. In Joe's adult years he relocated to Woodgate, a small southwestern Adirondack community. Lumber men—actually anything related to the old days of the logging industry—were his favorite hobby because he related to the forest and the people who used to call it home.

During Joe's retirement years, he turned his hand to writing regional history. His confab sessions with old-time loggers were a sensation. Joe was as colorful as the autumn changes in nature's scheme.

I was invited to attend evening gatherings with former 'jacks, river drivers, road monkeys, men who were part of loading crews, Linn tractor drivers and other hard-working, brave and trustworthy men-of-the-woods who had been involved in the operation of lumber camps and various logging operations. Joe told me he hoped the informal chit-chat would provide me "with a review of life in the Adirondack woods before that which is hailed today as 'progress' had had its effects. And, perhaps it would provide a chuckle or two and much nostalgia."

The cook and his assistant produced dozens of loaves of lumberjack bread and donuts day-after-day. California prune pie was a favorite cookroom recipe served on tin plates.
Courtesy of George Shaughnessy

I can only describe the rowdy crowd as being much like the multi-hued outburst of fall color outside Joe's living room. Autumn was the time we typically gathered. Unfortunately, as I think back, I wish I'd had had the foresight to bring a tape recorder. I could have captured and preserved a way of life that has now vanished from the scene. At least I took notes.

Isaac Bourdage's son Gerald said his father told many stories about the meals in the camps he worked in. "His lifetime taste for salt pork and gravy began the evening he returned to camp very late," Gerald recalled of his father's severe hunger in one 1880s Tupper Lake camp. "All that was left in the kitchen were the dregs from a pork dish, comprised mostly of salt pork and gravy. He proceeded to devour every last bit. From that time on, salt pork in gravy was his favorite meal." He added that Isaac "craved it throughout his life."

I suspect Isaac also enjoyed many a meal of baked glazed ham, sweet potatoes, vegetables, and blueberry muffins in the company of his fellow workers, and that the shared repast gave him a feeling of friendship and togetherness that prevailed in lumber camps.

Doughnuts are often off the breakfast menu for many people today, but period cookbooks suggest they were standard fare for earlier generations. They are also fun to make.

Recipe   **RIVER DRIVER DOUGHNUTS**

Ingredients:

3 tablespoons shortening

¾ cup sugar

3 eggs

3 cups flour

¾ teaspoons salt

¾ teaspoon nutmeg

3 teaspoons baking powder

6 tablespoons milk

Directions: Cream shortening, add sugar, and gradually the beaten eggs. Mix and sift dry ingredients. Add alternately with milk. Fry in hot fat which will brown a 1-inch cube of bread golden brown in 60 seconds.

CHAPTER 28

McCarthy's Logging Boom Days

William H. McCarthy

The story of the logging boom days and woodland lumber camps is told through the memories of the late William H. McCarthy, a man who played an integral part in an earlier logging era. The Gould Paper Company had always contracted out their Tug Hill operations to McCarthy, of Lowville, while Gould did its own lumbering in the Adirondacks. Over time, McCarthy took on the role of wood buyer for Gould.

McCarthy's lumbering experiences stretched from the days when straining teams of heavy bay horses dragged big bulks of logs to the time when logs were moved by trucks to the sawmills.

During McCarthy's retirement, he reflected that from 1898 to 1948 one thing didn't change. Lumbering was still no job for "pantywaists."

"I have seen and experienced a great many changes in the lumbering business," said McCarthy. He was talking about gasoline-driven caterpillar treads having taken the place of horseshoes and the good old days when lumberjacks were for the most part bachelors, and how new logging methods had replaced the need to be up at 2:30 in the morning and work by kerosene torches until it was light. Those old-timers would "never get a chance to eat from breakfast until dinner about 9 or 10 at night," he said. McCarthy's early days were spent with an outfit that required this dedication. It's assumed he might have carried some kind of food in a rucksack. He just didn't elaborate.

By the end of the logging season the 'jacks all looked gaunt and hollow-cheeked, Mary Ruth White reported in a 1950 the *Lumber Camp News* story. "And were the men ugly? You couldn't even say 'Good morning' to your crew; they'd have eaten you alive," declared White.

Bill McCarthy, Camp 7. Found in a 1950 office publication of the Gould Paper Company (*Plant Echoes*) were logging and pulp contracts the company entered into with Bill McCarthy. The paper pointed out that in 1918 a lumberjack was drawing $3.25 per day; in 1950 he received $8.00. In 1950, it cost $2.25 per day to feed a man; in 1918 it was 78 cents. And finally: "The old-time logging camp cost $900 [in 1918]—try to build one today for less than $8,000." *Courtesy of Lawton Williams*

McCarthy's and White's memories were the kind of silage that piqued the interest of Joe Conway, whom I came to know through my logger friend, Leigh Portner. I have always thought of Joe as a true friend, admirer, and historian of the old days of logging. When I listened to Joe talk, he had a way of making me feel as if I was back in the day, with Joe Gordon making a winter trip in his modified Model-T snowmobile from Gould's McKeever headquarters to the camp deep in the Moose River area.

Joe Conway was also an entertaining story-teller. Here's one of his narratives he swears is true. The preacher to which he refers might have been Rev. A.L. Byron-Curtiss.

A logger attended church one Sunday at Camp 7. After the service, he approached the preacher with much enthusiasm. "Reverend, that was a damned good sermon you gave, damned good."

The Reverend replied: "I'm satisfied that you like it, but I wish you wouldn't use those terms in expressing yourself."

The logger replied: "I can't help it, Reverend, I still think it was a damned good sermon, and I was so impressed that I put a fifty-dollar bill in the collection basket."

To that the Reverend exclaimed: "The hell you did!"

Joe was captivated by logging memories of all the old-timers he spoke to like, McCarthy and Mary Ruth White. McCarthy's following description stands as a primer to the lifestyle of the 'jacks who appreciated the meals prepared by the cookhouse bull cooks.

The crisp, clear sound of the horses' sleigh bells travels far through an untouched world of white. *Courtesy of Lawton Williams*

"The equipment used in my youth would be a curiosity today in the lumber woods. Our log sleighs were built solid with 3½-foot length runners, three 3½-foot wide beams and four-foot bunks connected together by a short neap. The loose-jointed sleigh with 8-foot runners and the 10- and 12-foot bunks used today have been developed over the years. About all the logs were moved on sleighs from the woods to the mills or to streams where they could be floated to the mills. In the early days of logging, manpower and horses were the only power used.

"Most timber was cut by choppers or axe-men. There were few crosscut saws and the modern bucksaw and chain saw were not thought of.

McCarthy not only embraced the early Linn logging tractor with 6-cylinder motor and sled steerage for hauling timber he was a proponent of the later-day mechanical and power equipment, such as log loaders, bulldozers, snow plows, large motor graders, power saws and diesel power equipment. *Courtesy of Ernest L. Portner*

"Bark-peeling was the main job in the woods. The hemlock bark was taken to tanneries for the tanning of leather. In those days, tanneries were located in about every hamlet and town. The best hemlock logs were sometimes got out and sawed into lumber for local building. My father delivered hemlock logs to the sawmill for $4.00 per thousand board feet and thought he was getting a very good price.

"Days were long, cold and wet during log hauling and driving season. There were no eight-hour days, and strikes in those days were not thought of. The average day was from 10 to 16 hours, but every man in the crew was a lumberjack and worked at no other trade, so didn't mind the long, tedious hours.

"They were hard workers and hearty eaters. Oh, yes, they occasionally took a drink or went on a 'bender,' but they always returned to camp ready for work. If a buddy or a friend needed a helping hand they were always ready even though it may have meant giving or contributing their last dime. These men were all capable of doing any part of the work or taking over any particular job when necessary and they did it with pride. While they weren't as good as the legendary Paul Bunyan, they were next to him in power.

"In 1898, all pulpwood was rough. When peeling started most of the lumber-jacks objected—today [1948] peeled wood is the rule and is more economical in every way for the producers as well as the consumers. In those days the main cost in the pulpwood was delivering it from the woods to the mils. Today most delivering has been reduced due to truck-hauling over roads built by bull-dozers and dump trucks. Pulpwood and logs are being lumbered in places where fifty years ago it would have been a losing proposition for any lum-berman to get them to market even if given the stumpage free of charge. Chain saws, tractors, bulldozers, log loaders and trucks have changed all lumber-ing methods."

John Carney recalled that he had seen his share of changes in logging camp life. Carney also knew that no matter how rough his earliest days of work were, old-time bushworker George Lanktree's earlier experiences were considerably more harsh. Lanktree had told John how he started cutting with his father when he was in his early teens. When he signed on to his first camp, he bull-cooked for a start, then went on to cutting and driving oxen.

Lanktree remembered: "The salt pork was handed out in huge chunks for breakfast, lunch and dinner, and the day's supply of bread was laid out in a sack in the morning. When you were hungry, it was an A-1 meal…but I guess it wasn't up to the grub today."

During Lanktree's earliest work as a notcher and sawyer he encountered austere conditions.

He admitted the menu was a little monotonous. Salted pork—fried, boiled and pickled—was the main dish, served along with pots of green and black tea, bread and butter, and potatoes. "I've been in old-time camps all winter and never seen a tablespoon of sugar on the table," he swore. There was no coffee, fresh fruit, milk or vegetables to speak of."

George Lanktree's recollections of the old days of lumber camp tales were easily interrupted by memories of more recent meals, at the family table laden with baked glazed ham, sweet potatoes, vegetables, and blueberry muffins. It was clear he enjoyed the feeling of family and togetherness, yet he still defended those former days of tea that often was cold but could "still whet a man's whistle," and the plates of salt pork and beans that "sure kept your belly from rubbing against your backbone." Those rough times were never far from the old man's mind. When he had eaten the main meal and was offered a slice of his granddaughter's tomato soup cake, which she had produced as a special dessert from her pantry, George was on Cloud Nine. He recalled, "When the frosting was cooled, she proceeded to cut that cake into six pieces, placed them on plates and passed them around."

Life could not have been better for an old bushworker.

Recipe   **ADIRONDACK TOMATO SOUP CAKE**

Beat together 1 cup sugar and 2 rounded tablespoons
    softened butter

Add: 1 can tomato soup. Beat thoroughly.

Sift together in separate bowl:

2 cups flour

2 teaspoons baking powder

1 teaspoon baking soda

½ teaspoon salt

½ teaspoon each of nutmeg, cinnamon and cloves

(Whisk together well to mix before adding to wet mixture.)

Add to wet mixture and beat until blended

Add: 1/2 cup chopped nuts, walnuts or pecans.

    (Some people prefer to add raisins.)

Grease well and lightly flour a 9 x 13-inch square pan. Glass is preferred. Bake at 350°F. for about 35–40 minutes, until cake tester comes out clean. (Hint: Cake will bounce back when touched, if done.)

FROSTING

1 cup confectioner's sugar

1 3-ounce package of softened cream cheese

½ cup softened butter

Mix together and beat. Spread on well-cooled cake. Some people like to add chopped nuts on top of the frosting. Eat, enjoy, and tell some family stories.

Courtesy of the Lewis County Historical Society, from Larry J. Myers Collection

CHAPTER 29

Pat O'Brien Remembers His Lumber Camp Days

William J. O'Hern

lthough I had already included other loggers' camp descriptions I incorporated Pat O'Brien's remembrances of his lumber camp days even though some narrative is repeated or is similar to earlier loggers' accounts. I met Pat twice at gatherings of former loggers held at Joe Conway's house. Pat was an engaging story teller who had been around the block. He'd worked in many camps, personally knew Clarence J. Strife and John E. Johnson, two of the biggest logging operators and worked when logs were transported from the logging job to the mill largely with Linn and Holt tractors. Throughout the years, Pat had observed many changes in logging life and methods. I wanted his memories on record. Pat O'Brien began with a summation: "The Adirondack camps were all similar. There was one continuous building that housed the kitchen and dining hall. That portion was separated by a breezeway. On the opposite end was the bunkroom. The camps were of peeled log and tarpaper construction—usually fashioned from spruce, white pine, and hemlock. Hemlock bark was needed in the hide tanning business. Hardwood was also used—all cut on site. The buildings were designed to last only a few years. The kitchen contained a large wood-burning cook stove, and a storage area in one end of the room with a table on which the men could write letters, read or play cards, but there was little of that activity until the weekend."

The camps Pat was familiar with "were built to accommodate teams of horses. There was a barn, and a blacksmith shop for equipment for shoeing horses, filing saws, and doing repair work that needed doing around camp. Another room was the clerk's office and there was a main office where the foreman and clerk slept with extra bunks for others like the superintendent, log scalers and so forth whenever they came into camp. And then there were some small outbuildings."

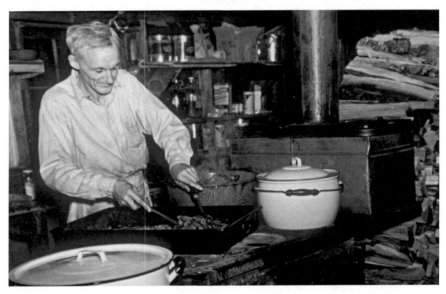

Old "Red" Louie, Camp 7 cook. Sleep was never a problem for cooks. Louie's counterpart, Ed Wheeler, said this of his workday: "All I have to do from 9:30 p.m. to 1:30 a.m. is just sleep." *Courtesy Lawton Williams*

The outhouses were unconventional. "Not your regular variety. No individual seats but instead a peeled pole stretching across a dug trench where 10 to 15 men could sit together...across it. I recall this one camp I worked at had a number of awfully big men and it must have been the biggest man who had constructed the slit trench outhouse because he (Pat stretched as he demonstrated) was about as high as the peeled poles stood off the ground horizontally. I'd have to get a running leap to get up on it and you sure as shooting wanted to keep your balance and not slip off. Since your feet couldn't touch the ground you'd have to concentrate on what you were doing because you sure as well knew where you'd fall if you didn't."

An American engine at a jackworks. Pat O'Brien's logging experience began in the early Gould Paper Company days' headquarters at the wood industry village of McKeever, N.Y. A spur of the railroad went out from the village to the Moose River. At one time above Remsen Falls there was a receiving and sorting boom for upriver log drives, and a steam-operated loader at the jackworks loaded logs from the holding area in the river onto rail cars for transport out from the works. *Post card image courtesy of Ernest L. Portner*

Sometimes 50 to 75 men lived in the larger camps. The covered breezeway that connected the bunkroom and the cook and dining room was where they washed up.

"The smell of the bunkroom…well, nothing was worse. You can't imagine it where some 50 to 75 men lived and slept with never really any chance to bathe thoroughly, launder their socks and clothing, bedding, whatever." Bed bugs and body lice were recurring. It was the job of each 'jack to shake all the straw out of his personal cloth-covered mattress and boil the cover in great black iron kettles also used to boil clothing. The covers were then refilled with new straw. "A deterrent for bed bugs was to spray the bunk bed boards with kerosene," Pat said. A pasty mixture of roofing tar and lard spread over one's skin helped ward off mosquitos and punkies. "Oh, and there was red lice. They come in under the wings of bats."

Pat joked, "I liked to go down to the big horse barns because they smelled so much better than the men's camps."

It was the cook shack, however, that Pat gave his full attention to describing. He explained an improved bill of fare from the old pork and beans and corn bread days. "That's where the donuts, pies, breads, candy, sugar cookies, massive amounts of donuts, lots of coffee…were prepared and served. After you'd worked ten to twelve hours in the cold air, even stale bread would taste good. Cooks made a lot of dried fruit pie—raisin, prune, apples, apricots. Oh, how I well remember the prune pies! Remember, Bub, there were no indoor toilets…."

Pat's recollections were a walk down Memory Lane. "It was a tough life, but a good life," he pointed out. I understood his meaning. The physical labor in the old logging camps was hard work, the wages were low and living was rough. His earliest days were spent first as a laborer in a 1937 logging camp on the Tug Hill "about ten miles from Boonville, operated by the Gould Paper Company. We had to walk about two miles into the woods to reach the camp. It was terribly muddy."

Some of Pat's recurring comments were about the food at the lumber camp, such as, "The food was good; they fed you well," followed by lengthy descriptions, one of which was about Orange Ice-Box Cake—his favorite sugary dessert at camp. "It was Irene Munger's doing. I'm sure any white layer cake today could be used but her scratch recipe was outstanding." His reminiscences continued to wander.

"Oh, I remember the wood stoves and their pipes well. Those pipes were run all over the place." He meant the pipes that rose from large chunk stoves, then ran horizontally, held to ceiling rafters by bailing wire. Heat radiated from the winding pipes until "they went right through the roof. There were no [masonry] chimneys in those days. It's hard to believe with all the tar paper [on the roof] and dry bark [siding] about that there weren't fires." However, he pointed out an accidental fire seldom happened because, "there was never a time when everyone was asleep. Someone was always up"

Pat's stories made the old days come to life. Take the way the lumbermen dressed. "They pulled on wool long johns in fall," he said and never took them off until spring. "They kept them on because the woolen long johns couldn't be boiled [washed]. By February, people were hoping for an early spring."

Over the years Pat worked himself up from a simple laborer cutting firewood to skidding logs, hitching log sleighs to Linn tractors and scaling timber.

He recalled, "It was a dangerous job. I had to get between sleighs and the tractor driver couldn't see or hear me. He'd back up the tractor to the sleigh to make the connection. If you weren't alert, you could get hurt or killed."

Despite the danger present in most logging jobs, O'Brien said accidents were not common because "you knew if you got hurt and lived they [the employers] would fire you."

Frozen ground and good horses were required for winter logging in the Adirondacks.
Courtesy of the Lewis County Historical Society, from Larry J. Myers Collection

Listening to Pat O'Brien was a pleasure. He was well into his seventh decade when we talked, and yet he retained his youthful jokester image. I learned about him from Terry Cataldo, who described Pat in her childhood memories in my book, *Spring Trout & Strawberry Pancakes* (2015). "If the school sleigh happened to arrive at the one-room schoolhouse before the teacher, we were usually entertained by Pat O'Brien and his half-brother, Alton Longway." One of Pat's friskiest clowning antics was to crack a hard-boiled egg in a single blow against his fore-head—a clever trick no other kid could match, no matter how much they tried.

CHAPTER 30

Lumber Camp
Cook House Etiquette

William J. O'Hern

No logger would deny that putting in a winter working in the woods was hard work; most would agree that before and after each of those hard days they looked forward to a meal fit for a king. Food took top billing. Cooks reigned supreme.

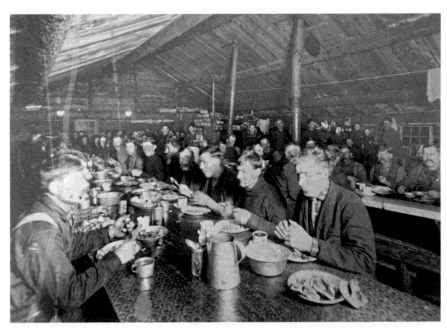

Cooks prided themselves on their ability to gauge quantities to serve huge and tasty meals to the deserving workers. *Courtesy of John Donahue*

Lumberjacks in the Goerge Colvin operations camps had hearty appetites and had chow with a few modern comforts and conveniences. *Courtesy of The Northeastern Logger, August–September, 1952*

Comments of men at Joe Conway's gatherings said newcomers to the lumber camps learned at their first meal that a hierarchy for seating existed at the long tables. Each man had his own place. It was customary for newbies to wait until everyone was seated before the cook directed them to an assigned spot. This hard-and-fast rule helped to maintain order, since taking another man's place at the table would result in at least a verbal and more likely a physical challenge.

Meals were not social gatherings. In the morning it was necessary to fills one's stomach as quickly as possible, then be off to work. If you wanted food passed, you simply pointed to it. The cook and his (or her) bull cook (helper) stood watch and immediately replaced any empty platters and refilled coffee pots.

"Cook House Surprise" is a dessert found in The Reverend's collection of papers. Perhaps the sweet course is a modern variation of an Ed Wheeler recipe.

Recipe | **COOKHOUSE SURPRISE**

Ingredients:
1 graham cracker crust
1 can apple pie filling
1 box lemon pudding
whipped cream topping

Directions: Prepare lemon pudding. Pour apple pie filling into crust. Pour lemon pudding over top. Chill. Serve with a topping of whipped cream.

The author's take on "Cookhouse Surprise" using a traditional pie crust. *Photo by Stephanie Frey*

CHAPTER 31

Flapjacks for Lumberjacks

Rev. A.L. Byron-Curtiss

The following is a tall tale of Rev. Byron-Curtiss's own making. He told it in honor of those skillful logging camp cooks to an audience at Utica's Masonic Club in the early 1950s.

✷ ✷ ✷ ✷

"Trouble was brewing in Camp 5 of the Gould Paper Company, an Adirondack lumbering operation. It came about from an insistent demand for pancakes for breakfast—a morning foodstuff the men indiscriminately called flapjacks, flannel cakes or sometimes chokedogs. But no matter what the label, all needed maple syrup for consumption.

"The cook was bewildered. How was he going to fill two hundred hungry men each morning? Every one of them would need to leave the dining room fueled so as to meet the demanding needs of their half-day of work in pure, crisp mountain air before the bull cook brought their snack in pack baskets. [This was an improvement from early logging days when a 'jack was responsible for carrying into the field his own lunch.] In vain the cook declared the task of hand-mixing batter in either wooden or white-enameled bowls too time-consuming, the wood-burning cook range not big enough and the cast-iron griddles too small. It was impossible to bake sufficient cakes in the morning.

Camp 9's root cellar was partially dug into a dirt bank, lined with logs with a heavy, wired bear-proof door. The cold storage kept perishable foods from freezing in the winter and kept them cool in the summer. The Goulds' "cottage" stands in the background. *Courtesy of Fred Worden*

"Most of the labor force had previously worked for small lumber camp operations throughout Vermont, New Hampshire and Maine, where pancakes were standard morning fare. The I.W.W. [International Workers of the World] had no influence on the Adirondack crew. I.W.W. agitators had not penetrated the Adirondacks to exhort the work force to organize and then demand higher pay; it was purely the gang's stomachs that were demanding more cakes, and some even talked that they were willing to strike over the matter. Mutterings and growls increased each morning as the men filed into the cook house and seated themselves on wooden benches that were lined parallel to the long oilcloth-covered tables. Eating was invariably done in silence, but the vibrations of discontent from two hundred men were ominous.

"At long last the cook brought the beeswax to the straw boss's attention. In turn, the straw boss took the matter up with the head boss, who reviewed the subject and then asked "Billy" Graff, the bookkeeper, to weigh the financial considerations. The bookkeeper then took the problem up with the walking boss, who brought the issue to the superintendent of forest operations

Adirondack Logging

when he made his weekly visit. The superintendent cursed his luck and questioned his judgment for importing so many Down-Easterners from New England camps, whose staples included 'pan-i-cakes' and beans. He should have known they would have warped tastes and strange appetites.

"To pacify the necessary, albeit troublesome, body, for there were twenty-five thousand cords of pulpwood to be skidded out of the woods and into the river by spring, the 'super' declared the company would foot the additional expense so the cook could please the crew. The task of baking four thousand cakes daily seemed impossible—two hundred men would eat twenty average-size cakes apiece.

"The cook, a faithful fellow who took pride in his work and who did not like to own up to defeat, had an idea. He proposed that if the company would provide an elite hotel restaurant-model cooking range, the new equipment would allow him to bake cakes the size of barrel heads. That would reduce the number of cakes to be handled. 'That,' he declared, 'would be the cat's pajamas.' He could then 'turn the trick.'

"The superintendent withdrew to his little log office and sat behind his desk to mull the suggestion over. Then with a nod that signified he had finished thinking, followed by a wink out the window, characteristic of his typical manner of showing he had found a solution, he set the necessary wheels in motion.

"In due time his order was shipped to the Forestport station. From the railroad it was hauled to the foot of North Lake, loaded on a scow and transported to the company's landing from whence a teamster drew it the final miles to camp. The large and heavy carton at once created quite a stir. Mechanics immediately set to assembling the massive cast-iron monstrosity in the cookhouse.

"When the work was completed the new cook stove proved to be quite a looker. The lustrous black porcelain shined; the nickel plating gleamed. Every casting was carefully detailed with elaborate scrollwork and fancy curlicues. There simply was no other lumber camp kitchen in the mountains that had the likes of this. The cook declared it was every bit modern. It had an extra-large window to let him check roasts and pies without opening the door! There was also a fold-down shelf for softening butter, huge warming closets with balanced swing-up doors, a solid copper water reservoir, towel bars and stay-cool hardwood door handles. The cooking surface was as long as a shuffle board! Carpenters rigged up a platform near the stove where they placed a boxcar-sized sprinkling box taken from one of the sleighs used for icing the winter haul roads over which logs are taken to the landing on the river. Connected to the tank was a flexible hose borrowed from a gasoline pump. A concrete mixer was then hoisted on top of the sprinkler. With that final platform the mixing and baking of flapjacks could commence.

"Amid the crowd of onlookers were a number of skeptics who claimed they doubted the apparatus would work. Most, however, had latent faith. On the hope that they would finally find platters stacked high with their favorite breakfast, the men rose from their bunks in the morning before the old horse-shoe rising bell hanging between the bunkhouse and cook house was clanged. Their conversation as they made their way over the short distance was char-acteristically monosyllabic. Hours earlier they had heard the rattle and whir of the concrete mixer. It had now stopped. In spite of the biting cold of the early-winter morning they crowded into the cooking area for a look-see. This is what the favored ones pressed around the front of the door beheld.

"The straw boss, wearing his caulked shoes, had a side of bacon fastened to each foot with hay wire, and was skating up and down the twenty-foot cook top greasing the cooking surface. Close behind the straw boss was the cook who was squirting batter onto the smoking surface from a hose. Behind him tracked the bull cook, boss and bookkeeper, following at a more leisurely pace, each armed with snow shovels. As directed by the cook, the bull cook and boss were to flip the cakes as bubbles in the batter indicated that they were done on the bottom side. The trailing bookkeeper's job was to shovel the cakes as they became ready into dish pans, dripping pans and even wicker baskets. The task of carrying those full containers to the tables fell to the superintend-ent, who had come the day before to assist in the great experiment. He was very red in the face before he got through his job that morning.

"The team of men deployed to produce cakes had scarcely started on the second lap around the stove when a buzz penetrated to their workstation. It was a rumble of pleasure coming from the men who were the first to assem-ble at the tables in the dining room. 'Flapjacks as sure as preaching!' 'Pan-cakes, by jingo!' and, 'Flannels!' or, 'I'll be damned,' and an occasional 'Mon Dieu!' from French-Canadian 'jacks, were heard. All discipline in the lumber camp dining room was broken when the comments culminated in a mighty cheer as the superintendent carried a great pile of the barrel-head size cakes to the last table. Each golden brown disk was the exact size of the extemporized platter, for the cook had by this time learned to calculate and gauge the squirts of batter from the hose to standardization. The experiment proved to be a great success. The lumber camp crew ate their cakes with happy sighs and expressions of satisfaction, the griddle cakes being washed down with gallons of strong coffee, an essential drink apportioned at every meal.

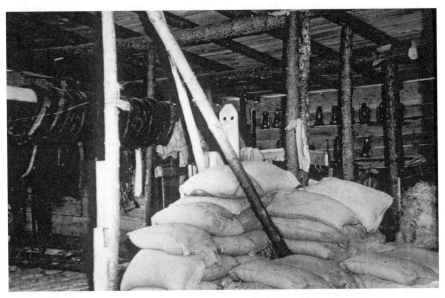

Camp 9's dry storage room for grain, rice, peas, beans, flour, sugar, and other food that needed to be stored for a year or more. However, there were other supplies like lamp oil, chains, blacksmith coal, saws, files, etc. that also needed to be stored, all as rodent- and bear-proof as possible. *Courtesy of Lyons Falls Pulp and Paper Company's archives*

"This outfit for making flapjacks for lumberjacks proved so successful that Gould has since incorporated it into its other Adirondack camps—a string that extends from the North River clear into the Moose River Plains. Minor improvements pertaining to the necessary manpower have since been incorporated into the operation. The essential ingredients—two barrels of flour, two sacks of corn meal, ten pounds of baking powder with other ingredients in proportion—however, have not been altered. If you were wondering, about a face cord of well-seasoned hardwood is also required to stoke the stove

Interior of Camp 9's cold cellar. *Courtesy of Lyons Falls Pulp and Paper Company's archives*

Adirondack Logging

and the great slabs of skating bacon are worn down so quickly to the rind that rail cars are needed to bring in the meat. If you don't believe all this, why, visit a lumber camp in the Adirondacks yourself sometime."

Courtesy of the Lewis County Historical Society, from Larry J. Myers Collection

Recipe   SKY PILOT GRAHAM BREAD (yeast)

This recipe was attributed to a Mrs. Aunsworth [sic].

Perhaps she was a camp cook.

2 cups scalded milk poured on 4 tablespoons molasses.
     When lukewarm add ½ yeast cake dissolved in ¼ cup
     lukewarm water.

1½ teaspoons salt

3½ cups graham flour and enough white flour to knead.

Cover. Let rise. Mold and place in pans. Let rise again. Bake.

There was a time when cooks knew everything they needed to know about yeast baking. Yeast is the oldest and still the newest means of making bread light and palatable. The abundance of today's bakeries has eliminated much of the need to make yeast dough recipes at home, but there is a certain satisfaction in doing so, and nothing can beat the aroma of baking bread or the taste of the first warm, crusty slice.

THIS IS A REAL PHOTOGRAPH OF A WILD DEER
BEING FED FROM THE HAND. ADIRONDACK. MTS.

Courtesy of the Lewis County Historical Society, from Larry J. Myers Collection

Adirondack Logging

CHAPTER 32

The Mincemeat Lady

William J. O'Hern

Long before sunrise, Bertha Gill stood over a large cast-iron wood-fired kitchen cooking range at a remote North Country logging camp, checking the oven's temperature, mixing and kneading, stirring and beating. There were mountains of doughnuts, pans of cakes, pies galore and loaves of bread to be prepared. And, that was only the beginning of the list.

Affectionately called "The Mincemeat Lady" by the loggers, Bertha had an endless job. She had to be up hours earlier than the crew, ready to feed the men before the gangs of choppers, skidders, sawyers and teamsters went to work before sunrise. A family story goes that Bertha had to have a small meat pie for each lumberman to take with him when he left in the morning.

"My grandmother was a dear lady," said Jane D. Lormore as she reminisced. "Grandma Gill turned the kitchen into a magical room."

Jane and her sister, Mary Lou Norte Leene, say their earliest memory of staying with Grandma Bertha and Grandpa Fred was in 1932 on their farm in Shinhopple, N.Y. The girls were four and five. "We went blueberry picking and sat at night visiting by an oil lamp," said Mary Lou, "as Grandma cut doughnut dough. My sister and I begged for the holes. Gram's raw dough was so good."

Jane and Mary Lou had heard the old stories of their grandmother's pre-dawn responsibilities as a younger woman, and how she might often have

Bertha and Fred Gill with daughter Ethel, 1904. *Courtesy of Jane D. Lormore and Mary Lou Norte Leene*

been forced to improvise when there were shortages of supplies. But the girls' strongest memories centered around their young years in Grandma's kitchen.

"By the time we would get up in the morning, the pies, cakes, doughnuts and cookies would be ready for the day!" said both sisters. "Our grandparents owned several little hotels in Copenhagen, N.Y. and had weekly renters who benefited from our grandmother's delicious food."

Later Adirondack lumber camps provided a host of improvements that elevated working conditions for the workers. *Courtesy of the Lewis County Historical Society, from Larry J. Myers Collection*

Mary Lou recalled an image that has never left her mind that happened in 1937: "At the Cottage Inn in Copenhagen, Grandma had chickens which ran free. Before dinner she would snatch one (She was quick!), give it a sharp *FLICK* to break its neck, slap it down on a stump, and with one swift wallop with a hatchet—off came the head. A pail of HOT water was at hand for dipping the bird to remove the feathers. Then into the kitchen to eviscerate the hen, wash it and into the pot to cook for the very best chicken and biscuits. Gram always swore by Rumford baking powder and liberal amounts of butter.

"She churned her own butter too, with an old fashioned butter churn. The butter was put into a wooden bowl where it was 'worked' to release any liquid, and lightly salted. Then she let me make butter pats, which were put on a plate sitting on ice.

"Later when Gram and Grandpa ran the Davenport Hotel—again in Copenhagen—she fed her help breakfast."

Jane and Mary Lou concurred on their memories of the first-rate way Bertha Gill pampered her hotel staff. Jane began, "I don't think the idea of feeding numerous people ever left her. Her staff at the hotel would come to work and sit down to a full breakfast before they started their work at the hotel. They were also recipients of her corn bread, currant pie, bread pudding, pickles, stewed prunes, pancakes and maple syrup and three favorite soups: bean, pea and rice.

"The hotel staff ate on china dishes, but in the cook camp, which had two rooms—a kitchen and a dining room located next to the men's camp—the custom was to use tin dishes, as china would only be broken."

Mary Lou added. "She also fed her staff bowls of soft-boiled eggs family-style, and stacks of the best pancakes that were often sodden in real maple syrup. And there was always a plate of molasses cookies. She could bake pies with her eyes closed and they were out of the oven by mid-morning so meat could go into the oven for later in the day."

Jane offered Bertha's "lumber camp cooking carried over into her own kitchen was very apparent. I think of all the food she prepared before my sister and I arose in the morning when we visited her!"

Jane began to tally up additional examples of how hard their grandmother worked. "Gram made soap using ashes from the wood stove. I remember the soap was strong and used to do all the hotel laundry.

"In the fall a pig was butchered and all the fat was rendered to make the lard, which was used in her pie dough. And if all the cooking and necessary household chores wasn't enough, she always had quilt pieces in a little pantry to be made into squares to make a quilt which was tied. An empty bedroom upstairs had a quilt frame ready. I am in awe of this little lady."

Jane is convinced that in today's world, because Bertha seemed to be able to prepare meals and complete tasks with little or no effort, "Grandma Bertha would be considered a multitasker!

Long after Bertha stopped cooking in the camps, her hotel clientele included men who worked for lumber mills. *Courtesy of the Goff-Nelson Memorial (Tupper Lake) Library P426*

Grandma was indeed a dear, gentle, and assiduous lady. She threw her energy into the work of the day but also had time to help Jane and Mary Lou find the first spring violet and spend contented evenings around the wood stove playing dominoes and Parcheesi, crunching popcorn and munching apples.

The girls thought so much of her recipes that their sister-in-law, Carol Nortz, shared Bertha's mincemeat formula with *Adirondack Life* magazine in June 2014.

"Bertha's mincemeat recipe is delicious," said Jane. "I make it every few years, since it lasts forever in the freezer. It is still a real hit with some of my 80- to 93-year-old friends who remember this flavor from when they were younger."

I was pleased to find Jane included in her correspondence three of Grandma Gill's recipes from her days as a cook in the lumber camp. Jane was surprised to learn that the prevailing method of wiping the men's knives, forks and spoons was to place them in a dry grain bag and thoroughly shake. Then they were poured out upon the table, as clean and dry as the most scrupulous housewife could reasonably desire.

Recipe **BERTHA GILL'S MINCEMEAT**

This is how Grandma recorded her recipes. It's anyone's guess what size bowl she was referring to. —Jane Lormore

4 bowls chopped apples

2 bowls ground venison

1 bowl molasses

1 bowl sugar

1 tablespoon ground cloves

1 tablespoon allspice

2 tablespoons cinnamon

½ pint vinegar

1 pound raisins

1 pound currants

1 teaspoon pepper

1 teaspoon salt

Cook slowly until apples are soft.

Recipe **GRANDMA'S ICE BOX COOKIES**

"Bertha's cookies were as spectacular as her dinners." —Jane Lormore

½ cup shortening

1 cup brown sugar

1 egg

½ cup chopped nuts

2 cups flour with a bit of cinnamon

1 teaspoon soda mixed with flour

Vanilla

Form into long roll—put in waxed paper and store in an ICE BOX overnight! Slice thin and bake at 350°F.

C.J. Strife's crews dinner table at the McKeever Camp in 1952. Strife's logging operations reached a high peak during the Korean War and the 1951–52 season when the Big Blow timber from the November 1950 hurricane created a great emergency and fire hazzard. *Courtesy of the* Northeastern Logger, *November, 1952*

Recipe ⬛ **GRAM'S LUMBER CAMP OATMEAL COOKIES**

Grandma was very good at making up recipes. There were often no directions and limited reference to amounts. —Jane Lormore

1 cup sugar

1 cup lard

Salt

2 eggs

1 tablespoon molasses

6 tablespoons sweet milk

1 cup ground raisins

1 teaspoon soda

2 cups oatmeal, ground

About 2 cups flour 🥾

CHAPTER 33

Former Lumberjacks, Seward Beach and Tony Harper's Favorite Recipes

William J. O'Hern

Kamp Kill Kare employee Seward Beach didn't bat an eye at whatever carpentry or general maintenance task he was asked to do, nor did he ever miss a meal cooked by the Adirondack Great Camp cook Mrs. Clara England and her assistant Evelyn Longway. The women worked as cook and housekeeper for the Men's Camp for many years. Beach had long placed England on his list of favorite persons and grew quite friendly with Clara. There were those among the Summer 1963 maintenance crew who believed that Beach, more than any other seasonal employee, had inspired the remarkable cook to prepare specialty baked goods and meals fit for a king just because of his glowing remarks about her culinary skills, delivered with Beach's ruddy facial expression and chipmunk smile.

Roy E. Wires's family lived year-round for ten years at Kamp Kill Kare. His father was the Adirondack great camp's superintendent. Seward Beach, as Roy recalled, was a man who "never fussed about his food; he knew the good life of '3 Squares.' I can still see Seward following a meal enjoying his hot tea by drinking it out of the saucer.

Roy recalls, "Seward Beach was a hardworking, non-drinking, bent-over, frail little man who lived in an old travel trailer on the North Lake Road in Forestport, N.Y. I think he was originally a carpenter, but as age caught up with him, he resorted to any job that paid a decent wage and gave him a roof over his head and three square meals a day. I knew Seward when he was working at KKK in the Raquette Lake area, in the 1960s. Seward was the ideal employee, as he did exactly what he was told, no questions asked. Case in point: One day Seward was told to mow the lawn in front of the main house. In those days, only rotary push-type power mowers were used. You need to realize that these lawns were mowed and manicured frequently enough that you might only be cutting half an inch of grass each time. This time, however, Seward mowed the entire main lawn without a blade on the lawn mower, as it had been removed for sharpening. He felt kind of stupid afterwards, but he was not one to ask questions, only do as he was told.

Tony Harper at Kamp Kill Kare, 1964. *Courtesy Roy E. Wires*

"I visited Seward one winter day at his North Lake Road home. Seward had installed an old cast iron pot belly stove in the middle of his small trailer for heat. It took him a minute or two to answer the door, but when he appeared, his face was totally black except for his eyes. Not having any electricity, he had been reading a book by opening the stove door, holding the book close, and reading by the light of the flickering flames.

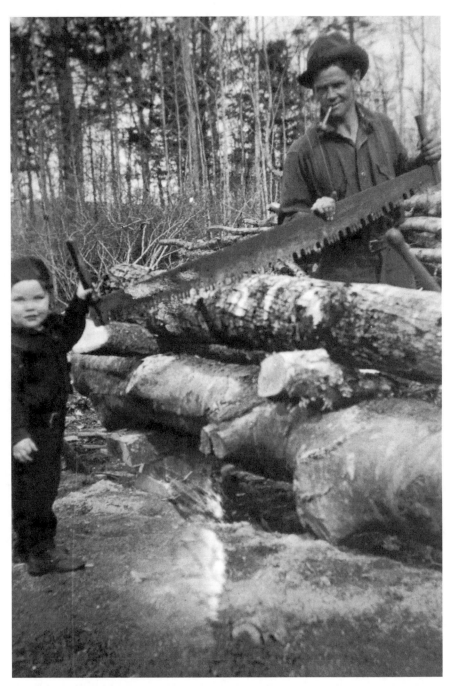

Harper's and Seward's fathers believed it was never too early to teach the younger generation about the use of tools. *Courtesy of George Shaughnessy*

Adirondack Logging

"Unfortunately, Seward had a stroke one year while working, but the Great Camp, which he called home during the summer months, hired him back the next summer, allowing him to do small tasks within his capabilities. Seward died a year or so after that, a small, hard-working man, and a veteran of the north woods."

Seward Beach and Tony Harper were products of the old days in the lumber woods.
Courtesy of the Lewis County Historical Society, from Larry J. Myers Collection

The following recipe was one of Beach's favorites.

| Recipe | MRS. ENGLAND'S DOUGHNUT MUFFINS |

Ingredients:

⅓ cup oil

1 cup sugar

1 egg

1½ cup flour

1½ cup teaspoon baking powder

½ teaspoon salt

½ teaspoon nutmeg

½ cup milk

Butter, melted

Cinnamon

Sugar

Directions: Cream oil and 1 cup of sugar. Add egg and beat well. In a separate bowl, mix flour, baking powder, salt and nutmeg; add alternately with milk to creamed mixture. Fill greased muffin tins full. Bake at 350°F. for 20–25 minutes. Roll tops in melted butter, then dip in cinnamon and sugar.

Tony Harper's Pizza and Clam Shack is today a recognized name in the lineup of Old Forge eating places, but more than half a century ago the retiring logger-woodsman-jack-of-all-trades was known at Kamp Kill Kare for his admiration for the culinary delights of Clara England's meals. Breakfast usually consisted of donuts, flapjacks and hot oatmeal. Her noon meals were something only an ex-logger could imagine, consisting of stews, casseroles, bakery goods and lots of cold fresh milk. Mrs. England's cakes, pies, and biscuits were part of the daily fare that never disappointed anyone who sat at her table.

Roy Wires remembers:

Tony Harper was a legend in the Raquette Lake area. Of French Canadian descent, he spoke with a strong French accent. Tony was recognized as an excellent rustic carpenter. He could take a chisel and wooden mallet and turn out some masterful rustic woodwork. I first met Tony while he was doing some carpentry work at KKK. While I was helping him re-deck a porch one day, he kept telling me in his strong French accent, "gotta get some hair to it." It finally dawned on me what he was trying to say. As it turns out the porch was totally enclosed in stone work and he was telling me that to keep it from rotting again, we had to 'get some AIR to it.'

Gordon Gould by his Model A Ford snowmobile on Moving Day, winter of 1929–30 when Camp 7 closed and Gould moved the main headquarters to Camp 9. Seward Beach would tell Roy Wires about the memorable tracked cars with skis that were converted to travel on snow during his days of working in the lumber woods. *Courtesy of Ernest L. Portner*

Another time we were working on the dirt road leading into the Great Camp and needed to dynamite some boulders in the road that the frost had pushed up during the winter. I was designated as the person to get the explosives permit so we could purchase the necessary dynamite to blast the boulders. Tony used to have such a permit and briefed me on the questions I would be asked when applying for the permit. One of the questions I would be asked was "Where do you plan on storing the dynamite?" Tony told me to reply "under my bed." I quizzed him as to why I would give such an answer. Tony would only say that he knew the Clerk of the Court in Hamilton County and that she would accept

that answer. So, sure enough when asked the question, I told the clerk
"under my bed" and she just laughed and said, "You must know Tony
Harper." I said I did, and walked out with my permit.

Tony lived in a small building on Route 28, just north of Raquette
Lake Village, that wasn't more than about fifteen feet square. He lived
there year-round and in cold weather heated it with a small chunk wood
stove. One winter Tony had a bad ingrown toenail infection in his big
toe. Opposed to seeing a doctor, he simply cut off the toe with his axe."

Working conditions at KKK was more favorable than Harper's early days in the
lumber woods. *Courtesy of the Lewis County Historical Society, from Larry J. Myers Collection*

The owners of the Old Forge eatery purchased Tony's property after he passed.
They built a small commercial building, naming it Tony Harper's Pizza and
Clam Shed. They were convinced Tony's image and name were a respectful
use of the former Adirondack woodsman. Today their new, upscale advertising
touting a picture of Tony has made Tony's name recognizable.

Kamp Kill Kare's staff building offered much more comfort than the lumber camp bunkhouses Beach and Harper had known. *Courtesy of Lyons Falls History Association*

In memory of Tony Harper, one of his top-pick recipes prepared at Kamp Kill Kare follows.

Recipe **TONY'S REUBEN PIZZA**

1½ pounds pizza dough

½ pound deli corned beef

½ pound Swiss cheese

8-ounce bottle Thousand Islands salad dressing

12-ounce can sauerkraut

Directions: Grease sheet pan. Spread dough evenly. Allow time to rise. Pour dressing onto dough, spreading evenly. Spread chopped corned beef over dressing. Spread well-drained sauerkraut over corned beef. Lay Swiss cheese over sauerkraut. Bake in preheated oven at 425°F. for 20–25 minutes. Rotate pan halfway through cooking.

CHAPTER 34

God Save the Queen

William J. O'Hern

"God Save the Queen!" That was the signature cry of "Uncle" Jack Yeoman. Jack was a logger in the 1880s and 90s. In his later years Yeoman lived in a tumble-down shanty. He rambled the vast wooded Adirondack lake country between Woodhull and Sand lakes.

Yeoman was an unusual lumberjack. He enjoyed reading. One subject in particular was the 19th-century Victorian Era of British history. Queen Victoria presided over a period of British industrial progress, artistic successes and political empire-building. Benjamin Disraeli was her prime minister. Yeoman admired Victoria's generosity toward Disraeli. He saw the British Empire owing its glorious position to the prime minister.

Rev. Byron-Curtiss was awestruck by Yeoman's depth of acquired knowledge.[18] When "Uncle" Jack learned of Byron-Curtiss's interest in and research about Nat Foster, he quoted Disraeli: "The best way to become acquainted with a subject is to write a book about it." And that is exactly what the reverend did. In 1897 Byron-Curtiss became the author of *The Life and Adventures of Nat Foster, Trapper and Hunter of the Adirondacks*.[19]

OPPOSITE: Bog River, Tupper Lake area. Jack Yeoman accepted the dangers of the log drive. *Courtesy of Special Collections, Feinberg Library, SUNY College at Plattsburgh*

Byron-Curtiss said of Yeoman, "Disraeli was Britain's 'brightest star,' according to 'Uncle' Jack. He considered the queen was an all right lady. Over time he got in the habit of declaring, 'God Save the Queen' each time he came into possession of illegal deer meat. Over time the saying was picked up by locals.

Byron-Curtiss took a page from Uncle Jack's playbook when it came time to provide meat for his family's table. *Courtesy of Thomas and Doris Kilbourn. (The Rev. A.L. Byron-Curtiss Collection)*

"If you ever hear a North Laker muttering 'God Save the Queen' when the law is breathing down the back of his neck, he is not being profane or facetious. He is just sending a brief supplication to the spirit of Uncle Jack Yeoman."

North Country natives shared a private law that did not look on hunting and fishing as a sport or recreational pastime. In the past, some families relied on those activities to sustain life. "Old-Time Mountain Law" is the term I've heard most often used by southwestern Adirondackers to describe the practice of illegally taking wild game. Norm Griffin mentions it in his Depression-era memories and Rev. Byron-Curtiss explained the accepted practice in "Old-Time Mountain Law" and "Adirondack Capers."[20]

The Reverand attempted to justify the illegal taking of deer. He wrote sometime during the early 1900s, "There was nothing baneful in this form of defiance. Working and living among the locals, I saw graphic examples of their indifference to outside influence [newly enacted game laws] time and time again. Natives were staunch individualists. They distrusted a faceless system that made decisions that affected them. Their response was simple; they continued to follow *their* ways. However, the continuation of old customs did mean they could not leave any clues."

Resistance dictated that deer meat be masqueraded as pork, goat or lamb, and it was common for pounds of trout to change hands for the price of the basket or tin pail the fish were stored in. Two common ingredients found in recipes in lumber camps and on the dinner table of woods folks were described in local jargon: "Adirondack Apples" referred to beans. "Mountain Pork" was a well-known term for venison.

Once when hiking along the South Branch Outlet, Byron-Curtiss went off trail and ran into a 'jerk camp.' He said, "from the telltale meat racks and

Bert Lindsey's hunting party at Camp Ann. Old logging camps have traditionally been converted into hunting camps in the South Branch of the Black River country.
Courtesy of New York State Museum

the method the log-wall lean-to was constructed, I recognized the work to be of Burt Lindsay. Later on I mentioned my discovery to Burt and jokingly suggested that the maintainer of the place should share the spoils with their friends. Burt grinned and said, 'Reverend, I know you are no prosecuting attorney.' I replied I could keep what I know under my hat. The subject was dropped, but Burt did not forget the matter.

Lt. to Rt. Paul Sirtoli and Dan Parkin. Summit Camp, an old logging shanty in the West Canada Creek Country. *Photo by the author*

The following summer I was awakened an hour before sunrise by a gentle tapping on my camp door. I came downstairs and there stood Burt with a pack basket between his feet. His hands rested on the barrel of his rifle. He first eyed me, then asked if I would 'ook after' his pack basket and 'use the contents.' I understood as I motioned for him to bring it in.

I reflected seriously on the situation and its moral implications. I hated to see good meat go to waste. Finally the science of the conscience, 'casuistry' we theologians call it, came as the solution. We hold it a sin to waste good food, either fodder for cattle or flesh for man. The law of God is above the law of man, I decided. So I rapped on the stovepipe to awaken my daughters, stoked up the kitchen range, and proceeded to get breakfast. Instead of bacon I prepared venison chops. The girls squealed with delight when they found what was on, and took charge of the rest of the meat in the basket. Besides the spare ribs there was a saddle and a lot of meat for stew. They started the stew simmering after breakfast and prepared the saddle for roasting. The windfall provided us with fresh meat for nearly a week, stored in the ice-cold spring box out back."

Recipe ED WHEELER'S POPULAR LUMBER CAMP BEAN SOUP

Wheeler's recipe is reproduced as it was provided less a listing of ingredients.
Ingredients:

1 pound dry navy beans

2 quarts cold water

1 meaty ham bone

6 whole peppercorns

1 bay leaf,

1 medium onion

Directions: Wash 1 pound of dry navy beans. Add 2 quarts cold water;
soak overnight. (Or, bring to a boil, simmer 2 minutes; remove from heat;

Rice Veneer, Inc.,[21] Camp 6, Moose River, 1952. A cut of 4,000,000 feet was made
on lands of the Gould Paper Company on the South Branch of the Moose River
near Indian and Squaw Lake. The logs were transported over the new truck road
to Limekiln Lake and on to McKeever. *Courtesy The Northeastern Logger, July, 1952*

Chow Time at the Rice Veneer Company's Camp 4 in the Moose River Plains where food was plentiful. The men shown are responding to the sound of the supper bell at the close of a hard day's work during the summer of 1952. *Courtesy The Northeastern Logger, December, 1952*

cover and let stand 1 hour.) Don't drain. Add one meaty ham bone, ½ teaspoon salt, 6 whole peppercorns, and 1 bay leaf. Cover; simmer 3 to 3½ hours, adding 1 medium onion, sliced, the last half hour. Remove ham bone. Mash beans slightly, using potato masher. Cut ham off bone; add ham to soup. Season to taste. Makes 6 servings.

Editor's note: An alternative to this very good recipe is to sauté some onions and a very finely chopped carrot in olive oil for a few minutes, then pour in the beans and water and ham bone—or, if no ham bone is available just use ham cubes. And, here is a little trick if the soup isn't thick enough—add some instant mashed potato flakes, a couple heaping spoonfuls at a time, stirring in after each addition until the soup is the thickness you like. —Mary L. Thomas, recipe tester and editor.

Collection 6
Pork, Molasses, Beans and Gingerbread

L ove it or hate it, create it or repeat it, logging camp cooks once served a lot of pork, molasses and beans. Here is an interesting look at a sampling of the old bull cooks' recipes and their modern counterparts' dishes— a behind-the-scenes glimpse if you will at the growing variety of meals cooks prepared.

The cooks controlled what the camp crews ate. Refinements depended on what provisions were available. With a wider selection of meat, vegetables and fruit came more flavorful, savory food. The tedious and by no means holy trinity of meat, vegetable protein (beans and peas), and carbohydrates that fueled the American lumberjack in the early days changed, as did the equipment the cooks used. The huge Blodgett bake oven and the cookhouse range known as an "iron elephant," with its eight-griddle stovetop, couldn't have measured less than half an acre during the years when cookees hand-peeled bushels of potatoes a day. Camp kitchens eventually evolved, as modern, dependable Delco oil burners, Frigidaire refrigerators, ranges and water heaters and new hand-cranked potato peelers worked their way into logging camp kitchens.

Collection VI features recipes that are as good today as when they appeared on camp tables, but there is more. You'll also learn how a monthly recipe column in a popular logging magazine spurred culinary invention and competition among cooks and added zest to once-routine cooking. Here is the infamous formula for "Jagasee," the surprising meat substitute that was a camp standard in lean times, and here too is the implausible "Hop Toad" recipe that probably would not be on anyone's breakfast table today.

Jagasee and Hop Toad recipes would have appeared in pre- and post-Civil War lumbering camps such as that of early entrepreneur David Swancott,[22] who moved into the southeast side of the Tug Hill area in 1867. He built a dam situated along Fish Creek and established a water-powered sawmill, around which a sizeable settlement known as Swancott's Mills quickly grew up. *Courtesy of Earl M. Kreuzer*

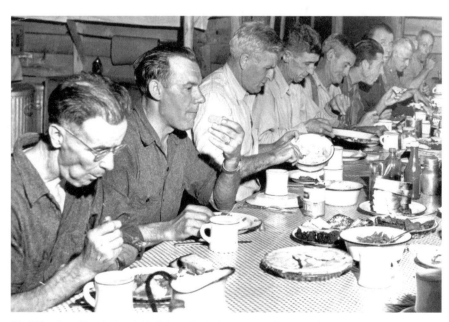

Sky Pilot Rev. Frank Reed (3rd from Lt.) always complimented Pierre. The cook would then exclaim with joy, "Ba gosh! He always eat her all up!" *Courtesy of Lyons Falls History Association*

The Camp Cook Says—Jagasee and Hop Toad. Two old-time recipes.
Jagasee was a not-too-soupy mixture prepared in a big pot made with lima
beans, rice, salt pork, tomatoes, onions, green peppers, celery and sugar.

Hop Toad was merely cooked oatmeal pressed in a pan to cool and
then sliced fairly thin, rolled in flour, and fried in butter or fat until
crisp and brown then sweetened with a primitive syrup made by boiling
equal parts of white and brown sugar and water.

As Adirondack and Tug Hill lumbering enterprises grew, the areas were introduced
to a breed of lumberjack from other regions, especially French-Canadians from lower
Ontario and Quebec. With these new woodsmen "also came the skill, the daring, the
devil-may-care spirit that enabled them to survive countless dangers and hardships,
and this also was quickly emulated by the natives....they encountered and overcame
conditions that would have killed lesser men: living for days on end in clothing that
was never dry, wading through deep snow along stream banks, working endless hours
each day and sleeping a few hours at night in sodden blankets inside hastily-constructed
brush shelters, often in freezing weather. Rough but wholesome food was furnished
by a cook…" —Harold E. Samson, from *Tug Hill Country, Tales from the Big Woods.*
Courtesy of Earl M. Kreuzer

"Pork, Molasses, Beans, and Gingerbread" is a short journey from the humble
beginnings of the old logging days when the only food loggers demanded
was something hot and belly-filling to the pride bull cooks felt when their
favorite recipe appeared in print in a well-read magazine.

Camp cooks were not the highest paid personnel in camp, but they were
important employees.

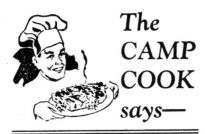

The CAMP COOK says—

MACARONI AND CHEESEBURGERS

Ingredients:

1 7-oz. pkg. elbow macaroni
1 lb. ground beef
½ tsp. salt
1 tsp. Worcestershire sauce
1 tbsp. fat
3 tbsp. enriched flour
1 tsp. salt
1¼ cups milk
1 cup shredded American cheese

Procedure:

Cook macaroni. While macaroni is cooking combine ground beef, ½ tsp. salt and Worcestershire sauce. Shape into 12 small patties and brown in fat in heavy iron skillet. Remove meat, drain all but 2 tbsps. fat from skillet. Stir in flour and 1 tsp. salt. Add milk gradually and cook until thickened, stirring constantly. Add ¾ cup cheese and stir until melted. Fold in macaroni. Pour into greased casserole. Put meat patties on top and sprinkle with remaining cheese. Cover and bake in moderate oven (350° F.) until thoroughly heated, about 15 minutes. Serves 4 to 6. Could be increased in quantity easily to serve 25 and more. *The Northeastern Logger, Nov., 1952*

Rt. to Lt. Mrs. Helen Jones, cookee, and Mrs. Lewis Holland, head cook, at C.J. Strife Lumber Company camp in 1952. Mrs. Holland's favorite macaroni cheesburger patty recipe that "easily served 25 and more," can easily be reduced in quantity to serve 4–6.
Courtesy of The Northeastern Logger, November, 1952

CHAPTER 35

The Camp Cook

William J. O'Hern

There are true stories and tall tales galore that regale readers with the exploits of whitewater men and lumbermen, but equal in legend were the cooks and their assistants, the cookees,[23] who fed the men in camp.

Good cooks' reputations spread quickly among camps. Workers were known to weigh the quality of the cook and their food equally with the pay offered when they decided where to work. Woodsmen knew they could not work unless they were fed, and fed well.

Not only were cooks held in high regard, but their power was respected. Cooks in the Gould Paper Company lumber camps demanded silence at meals. The rule was intended to speed the eating process and allow the cook and cookees to clean and wash dishes and have time to begin preparations for the next meal in an efficient manner.

Cooks were also known to "cold food" when they believed the men had eaten amply. If a boss demanded something they deemed unreasonable, they threatened to walk off the job. And a boss knew a camp without a cook, or one with a bad cook, would not survive.

This did not mean all the power rested with the cook. If the loggers were unhappy with the food served, they broke the silence rule and talked during meals, and carried out other disturbances to compel the boss to fire the cook.

★ ★ ★ ★

"The Camp Cook Says—" was a section developed in the *Lumber Camp News* in the later years of the newspaper's program.

The publication's rapid circulation expansion was made possible by the interest of sawmill operators, forest industries, and manufacturers of logging equipment and cooking appliances and utensils, who were hospitable and cooperative in providing advertising and furnishing information for the columns.

"The Camp Cook Says—" encouraged cooks to submit favorite recipes representative of choices that were being offered from their kitchens. Each month in the *Lumber Camp News* tempting new recipes appeared in the "The

Outside the lumber camp cook shed at Stillwater reservoir. The camp cook and her help proudly display some of their labor.

Lumber camp cooks Harriet and Carl Sweeney said the meals they prepared were wholesome, basic foods cooked in large quantities. When Harriet was asked about being thrown together with 25 to 40 'jacks for months at a time, she replied, "I guess I never thought much about it. We were very busy. We had our own quarters and I was never aware of any problem. We never had a single complaint. The men were always very polite. They would compliment us on a particular meal or dish. They especially liked it when we served beef and biscuits." —"Lumber Camp Cooks," by Louis Mihalyi *Adirondack Life* May–June 1988. *Courtesy of Pat Payne*

Camp Cook Says—" submitted by one of the cooks from the many active logging camps in the eastern United States.

The *Lumber Camp News* recipe competition offered cooks the opportunity to showcase their favorite recipes or a formula they found popular among the men they served. The monthly recipe also found its way into many families' cookbooks. Wives of retired lumbermen enjoyed preparing dishes that reminded their husbands of times past. The judging and evaluation was left to the editors. Short-listed candidates had the opportunity to present their personal project to the editorial board in a monthly taste test before they could be declared the winner. The recipe challenge also offered the opportunity to showcase a company's kitchen fare. There was no prize money for the winning candidate—the honor came in just being recognized.

The sample tasty-sounding foods are only a few of the wide variety of choices in the diets of loggers throughout the late 1940s operations. It's an interesting contrast to the "good old days" of logging, when pork and beans, molasses, gingerbread, tea boiled in a pot, salted or canned fish, and—depending on the location—beef were served along with breads, pastries, and pies, at which cooks often excelled.

By the time these choices of foods were being prepared in camp kitchens, the logging camps of former years had begun to disintegrate, and the woodsmen of former years, who had lived and labored there, had retired—some even laid to rest under the spruce and pines.

The one thing the old loggers had in common with the more modern 'jack was that the dining room still remained the absolute domain of the cook.

And, those tales about cooks stirring beans with cant hooks (like a peavey but without a spike on the end), using soap to make biscuits rise, and flipping plate-size flapjacks from an enormous iron griddle into the air to turn them over all add to the folklore of the lumber camp cook.

The following recipes are from "The Camp Cook Says—"

Recipe   APPLE PUDDING

> 1½ pounds apples, diced
> 1½ pounds sugar
> 7 pounds bread
> ½ ounce cinnamon

Procedure: Stew the apples in 2 quarts of water; slice and toast the bread. Spread a layer of the apples over the toast and sprinkle with sugar and cinnamon; continue to alternate layers of toast and apples until all are used. Bake in a 400° F. oven about 20 minutes and serve with a plain or caramel sauce. Nearly any kind of fresh or dried fruit may be used and pudding named accordingly.

The tables were constructed of rough boards and ran the length of the room. Plates and bowls were turned bottom side up to avoid collecting dirt that filtered down between the cracks in the ceiling boards from the second floor. *Courtesy of the Maitland C. DeSormo Collection*

Recipe   CARROTS A LA CHAMPAGNARDE

Just when you might be thinking The Camp Cook recipes sounded all too "lumber campy," a favorite sous-chef-sounding recipe is shared.

Ingredients:

10 pounds carrots

1 cup butter

2 pounds onions

2 cups sugar

1 quart milk

Salt and pepper

Procedure: Cut the carrots in rings, and whiten for about five minutes, drain and put in a casserole with the butter, sugar and milk. Cook until tender. Season and serve.

"We got pretty good meals in the old days, not as fancy—no coffee, fresh fruit, milk or vegetables to speak of—but a man could go for it. I liked it because I wasn't much for pastry and lighter stuff." —George Lanktree. *Courtesy of George Cataldo*

| Recipe | **CHEESED POTATOES** |

Ingredients:

10 pounds potatoes

½ pound cheese

3 pints beef stock

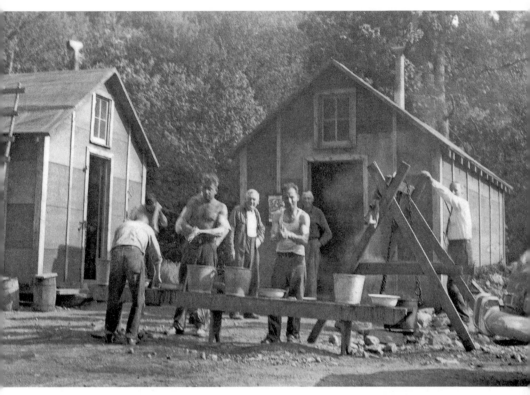

The menu was a little monotonous. Salted pork—fried, boiled and pickled—was the main dish, served along with pots of green and black tea, bread and butter, and potatoes. "I've been in old-time camps all winter and never seen a tablespoon of sugar on the table," swore George Lanktree of his days in the camps. *Courtesy of Lyons Falls History Association*

Procedure: Use any left-over cooked whole potatoes; cut into pieces about the size of a lima bean. Season to taste with salt and pepper and mix with beef stock; then add the grated cheese. Spread 2 or 3 inches deep in the bottom of a well-greased pan and bake in a medium hot oven for about 30 minutes. Feeds 25 men.

Recipe ## CHILI CON CARNE

Ingredients:

8 pounds meat scraps, fresh or cooked, trimmed of fat

1 can tomatoes

about 1 ounce of red pepper

1¼ pounds kidney or chili beans

2 quarts beef stock

Procedure: Soak the beans in cold water 8 hours or overnight, then simmer about 4 hours until soft. Brown the meat if it is raw, add to the stock, simmer until meat is tender. Run about of the cooked beans through a food grinder, and add to the meat and stock. Add remainder of whole beans and tomatoes. Season to taste with red pepper and salt and mix well.

Recipe   **SCALLOPED SWEET POTATOES AND APPLE**

"The Camp Cook Says" Scalloped Sweet Potatoes and Apple
   is a nice change. This will serve fifty.

Ingredients and procedure:

15 pounds sweet potatoes.

   Cook potatoes in skin—peel and slice.

1 pound apples—peeled and sliced

Place alternate layers of sweet potatoes and apples
   in baking pan.

Pour over all syrup, made by cooking:

   1 pound sugar, brown

   8 ounces sugar, white

   1½ ounces salt

   8 ounces butter

   2 quarts water

Bake in moderate oven until apples are done.

Note: During the last 5 minutes of baking, place 1 pound
   of marshmallows on top.

✫ ✫ ✫ ✫

These recipes were a starting point for a whole new adventure in meal-making. "The Camp Cook Says—" was still a young feature throughout 1947–49, with plenty of room to grow.

Nothing meant so much to loggers as having good food to eat. The same can be said for the modern-day logger. Today, the biggest difference is how meals are prepared. We have all types of electrical devices, running water, stainless steel pots and pans, refrigeration, microwaves, dishwashers and so many other kitchen-related equipment to cook good food—things mostly taken for granted.

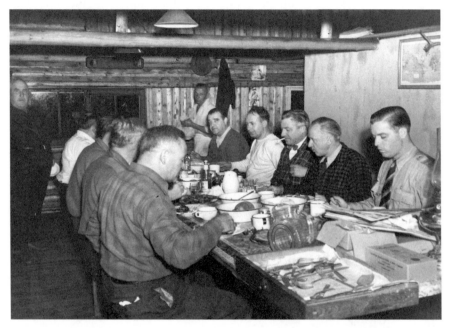

Silence was observed at the table even when "big wig" guests dressed in white shirts and ties appeared. *Courtesy of the Goff-Nelson Memorial (Tupper Lake) Library*

Spanish rice was a typical dish prepared and served in 1950s logging camps. I've seen many variations of the recipe. Liberties were taken with the conventional recipe when there were shortages or an ingredient was not at hand. For instance, if celery was called for but none was to be had, the cook might increase the amounts of tomatoes and onion, or even add some chopped carrots.

Al "Bunyan" Reber's Pork Chop Spanish Rice is a modern-day casserole I've named in honor of a logger with whom I have spent countless hours in the woods. Al is an independent logger who presided over the cutting of my woodlots. His self-reliance gives him a contempt for those seeking something for nothing or trying to ride on others men's efforts—yet no one has more genuine interest in their fellow men or is more ready with help in need, for his greatest interest in life is people.

I've spent many a sub-zero morning talking with Al, waiting for his big green skidder to warm up as he checked tire chains or busied himself at some other preparatory task. Al has a story about everything. His keen wit and ready humor make him an entertaining character. I imagine him to be a boon companion in a hunting camp or on a fishing trip. That same wit and humor might also have helped him through the last weary hour of his long work day.

Al's "green monster" skidder dwarfs the Tug Hill logger. *Photo by the author*

Food was always a favorite topic. One winter morning I promised to meet him before first light. I planned to surprise him with a big square of fresh-baked Johnny cake. We'd eat it around a fire and wash it down with cups of coffee. The corn bread never made it to the woodlot. It was bitter cold that morning; snow swirled in my headlights. I was tense as I drove over unplowed roads. Unconsciously, I broke off bits and ate the warm bread as I drove along.

Eventually I realized what I had done. Knowing there would not be enough for Al, I finished the rest. That morning our talk revolved around how we liked beans, split pea soup, and other favorite dishes.

Recipe	**AL REBER'S PORK CHOP SPANISH RICE**

Ingredients:

5 pork chops, ½ inch thick

2 tablespoons shortening

1 teaspoon salt (optional)

½ teaspoon chili powder

Dash of pepper

¾ cup uncooked long-grain rice

½ cup chopped onion

½ to 1 cup celery, diced

¼ cup chopped green pepper

1 1-pound 12-ounce can of (3½ cups) tomatoes

5 green pepper rings

½ cup shredded sharp process American cheese

(Optional additions are 1 tablespoon Worcestershire sauce, a teaspoon sugar and a half-pound of browned ground beef.)

Directions: Trim excess fat from chops. Slowly brown chops in melted shortening about 15 to 20 minutes; drain off excess fat. Combine salt, chili powder, and pepper; sprinkle over meat. Add rice, onion and chopped green pepper. Pour tomatoes over. Cover and cook over low heat 35 minutes, stirring occasionally. Add green pepper rings and cook 5 minutes longer, or until rice and meat are tender. Sprinkle with cheese. Serves 5 or one hungry Al and his wife!

There were recipes in "The Camp Cook Says" column with interesting names, like "Canadian Grandfather's Recipe"—basically dough balls cooked in and served with sugar syrup—and "Dark Dough," an odd name for basic molasses cookies. The cooking column must have been particularly helpful to other cooks because it gave so many large-quantity recipes. "Corn Cakes" fed 25 men, and from-scratch Chocolate Cake that called for six cups of sugar and nine eggs served 50.

It must be noted that "The Camp Cook Says" was printed long before it became common to include nutrition information with recipes. These days, the health-conscious would probably reject some of the recipes. "Mincemeat Pie" and "Christmas Plum Pudding" were made with copious quantities of suet and sugar. While that might sound like a "heart attack on a plate" to modern readers, the 'jacks worked so hard in such extreme cold that the fat and sugar were the perfect fuel for them. And when they returned from the woods at the end of the day, there was always hope for something extra-special for supper—"Partridge With Cabbage" and "Scalloped Oysters" were two of the gourmet treats enjoyed by tired and hungry men at the end of a long day.

HARRIET AND CARL SWEENEYS' LUMBERJACK BREAD. George Watson, who worked in several lumber camps where the husband and wife team of Harriet and Carl Sweeney cooked said, "We always got real good food. There was always more than we wanted." Bread was a standard offering at every meal.

When the Sweeneys retired from the camps, they opened a bakery in Greig, N.Y. Their bread "achieved a measure of local fame," reported neighbor and writer Louis Mihalyi in his "Lumber Camp Cooks" story that appeared in *Adirondack Life's* May–June 1988 issue. Mihalyi asked the couple if they would share their bread's ingredients. Carl's answer was a bit more than Mihalyi expected, he reported. "I spoke to Carl; he had to search his memory for the recipe, since it had never been written down. 'You need 40 cups of all-purpose flour, more or less. If the day is humid you will need more, if dry, less. Add about a handful of salt. Proof eight envelopes of yeast in two cups of warm water with a little sugar. When it bubbles add two cups of melted lard, four cups of blackstrap molasses, and four quarts of warm water (less the two cups used for proofing).

"'Mix well and add enough flour to make a batter. Add the balance of flour until a dough is formed that will not stick when punched with your finger. Allow it to raise, punch it down and allow it to raise a second time. Place in tins and allow to raise a third time, then bake.'"

Not to be deterred from attempting to "work out a more manageable recipe," Mihalyi said he found a friend to help him work out a formula without "going overboard and baking 20 loaves at a time."

If a buddy or friend needed a helping hand, 'jacks were always ready to help, even though it may have meant contributing their last dime. *Courtesy of George Cataldo*

The following is his successful conclusion.

Recipe — SWEENEYS' LUMBERJACK BREAD

Ingredients:

4 cups of flour.

1 tsp. salt.

¼ cup melted shortening.

6½ Tbs. blackstrap molasses.

1 envelope yeast.

1½ cups warm water.

Directions: Fast-acting instant yeasts may be mixed with a cup of flour and the salt. Then add the warm water, molasses and melted shortening, mixed, to the dry ingredients in a large mixing bowl. Beat thoroughly. Add the flour to make a dough, then knead until smooth, elastic and no longer sticky. (If instant yeast is being used, a fairly good result will be obtained by shaping the loaves at this point.) Allow to rise to double volume in a greased bowl. Grease the top to prevent drying. Shape, allow to rise again to double in size, and bake in a 350°F oven for 30 to 40 minutes. Makes two medium-sized loaves.

PART THREE

The River Driver

The days of the log drive were long and cold. Tons of softwood logs rushing down-stream, striking rocks with a madding rumble, pitching high into the air and falling with a great crash and splash were a match for the whitewater men of old. Florence Western relives those days of glory—and of death to some—in the following poem "The Passing of the Log Drive." *Courtesy of the Town of Webb Historical Association*

Collection 7
Logging's Glory Days

Gone are the Gould Paper Company lumber camps and the picturesque hell-roaring, fist-fighting, hard-drinking and hard-working lumberjacks of a hundred years ago who cut the North Woods forests. No longer do the river corridors hear mouthfuls of sulfurous blue-smoke curses and profanity from lumberjack's voices, see the white-water log drives or the river-hog who was stirred with excitement as he cat-footed over huge, plunging sticks—thrilled at the many narrow escapes and excited that he survived to face the perils of white-water log-driving the following season.

The roar of the track-crawling Linn tractors is silenced. A few surviving models are rebuilt, positioned in museum exhibits. Others are kept as working models in private collector's yards—antique reminders of the age of lumbering when machinery replaced horses. We can only look at the black and white photos of lumber camp life, visual reminders of the past. These, words put to paper, that tell the first-hand accounts that lived on in old folks' memories, and the songs and legends, are all that remain.

THE PASSING OF THE LOG DRIVE
(Dedicated To Those Who Were Part of It)

How we miss the springtime log drive
Down the royal old Moose River,
For we'll never find the old thrill
In a piled-up truck or flivver.

'Twas a time-honored tradition,
And it lives in memory's halls:
Otter Lake, McKeever, Lyonsdale,
Gouldtown and Lyons Falls.

River drivers with pike poles. *Courtesy of Lyons Falls History Association*

Though 'twere cold and wet and dreary,
There were those who'd never fail;
They always could rely on
Webster, Todd, McBeth, McHale.

And the river claimed its bounty;
Some rest in an early grave.
They're remembered now as heroes
Numbered with the many brave.

We who've trailed it down Moose River
With full many a jam and rive
Have both staunch and fond recallings
For the old Moose River drive.

Now we leave the drive behind us,
Though we felt 'twould always last—
One more legend doomed to progress,
Now a milestone of the past.
  —By Florence E. Western, *North Country Life*, Spring 1961

  *Adirondack Logging*

Lumberjacks were strong, rugged individualists who did not fear an occasional test of their athletic ability. *Courtesy of Lyons Falls History Association*

"Leo Graves and an unidentified Indian straightening logs." —Fred Worden.
Courtesy of Fred Worden

CHAPTER 36

The Once Annual Icy-cold, Flood-swollen Moose River Drive

William J. O'Hern

For untold millennia, the waters of the Black and Moose Rivers had coursed freely from their source in west-central New York through the less mountainous but rugged and remote central Adirondacks, where they ultimately emptied into Lake Ontario. By the mid-1800s the rivers of the Adirondacks had been legislatively declared "public highways" for the transmission of logs from remote cuttings to sawmills and later to pulp mills more favorably located downstream. *Courtesy of the Town of Webb Historical Association*

Opposite: Spring, to all not connected with logging, promises the return of budding pussy willows, the joyful song of birds, vernal greenery and warmer temperatures. To the lumberjack of old, spring meant only one thing—the annual log drive.
Courtesy of the Town of Webb Historical Association

Each spring the Black River and its tributaries had been filled with softwood logs from bank to bank until the early 1900s. Regarding the spring log drives on the Moose River, Hazel Drew penned in her *Tales From Little Lewis* that, "For the first time in 50 years—in 1948—the turbulent Moose River made its way down to its confluence with Black River without its burden of thousands of spruce logs." This would place the first annual log drive on the spring-flooded Moose-Tekahuniando (Native American for "Clearing an Opening") at about 1898. Possibly that figure could be stretched to include 1896, the year that Gould's Mill at Lyons Falls became operational—and perhaps even earlier.
Courtesy of Lawton Williams

January thaw on the South Branch of the Moose River Landing. Thaws caused enforced idleness. There was little for the men to do on those days. Few of them could read and little reading matter was available anyway. The 'jacks typically played cards, and much tobacco was purchased from the company van on days when there was no work.
Courtesy of Fred Worden

  *Adirondack Logging*

Local author and interested historian Matthew J. Conway, in his book *Port Leyden: The Iron City, a Passing Glance*, mentions seeing a picture of six of Port Leydon's white water men "in front of a [river] driving tent with their boss, John McBeth, Sr." The caption mentioned the crew was to use the boats on the North Branch of the Moose River. Since it's known McBeth got out two million feet of timber the spring of 1881, Conway speculates the logs had been "destined for G.H.P's first sawmill up the river from Lyons Falls at what was later called Gouldtown." He feels the Moose River was used for the transport of logs for closer to seventy years, all ending after the last drive on the Moose in the spring of 1947. In this year, Conway wrote that Gould's successor, Continental Can's wood operation, "had been mechanized to the degree that all future pulp wood would be trucked to the mill's jack works. The days of the 'corked croghans,' the 'stagged woolen britches,' the 'peavey,' the 'pike pole,' and the 'pig yoke' were over for the white water men on the Moose-Tekahunlando River, as the Native Americans so aptly named it...Clearing an Opening and its tributaries, Limekiln Creek, Indian River, Red River, et al." *Courtesy of Lyons Falls History Association*

For history's sake, it is also important to mention that rising waters in late May from a heavy rain storm were responsible for washing out the dam at McKeever, N.Y. on June 3rd, 1947. The June, 1947 edition of *The Lumber Camps News* reported the full story that attracted an unprecedented number of spectators. Here is a portion of the story that appeared in Rev. Reed's newspaper following the 6:30 P.M. break in the log and gravel dam. *Courtesy of John Todd (The John B. & Scudder Todd Collection)*

"Moose River Landing. Almost a full house." —Fred Worden. *Courtesy of Fred Worden*

  *Adirondack Logging*

At the mercy of the raging Moose River, a 15-foot head of storage water along with 1,500 cords of pulpwood that was being held in the log boom sent logs crashing below the McKeever dam into "two old iron bridges. There the water level rose until the dam timbers and the logs could no longer pass, and jams were formed. Soon the pile of logs rose until the bridge floors became covered, halting traffic. "As the dam waters reached the high bank stretching below the bridges, the river rose an additional seven feet, but soon began to spread out and fill the low places, bringing the water level down gradually so that when the crest reached Lyons Falls at about ten o'clock it was not too noticeable." *Courtesy of John Todd (The John B. & Scudder Todd Collection)*

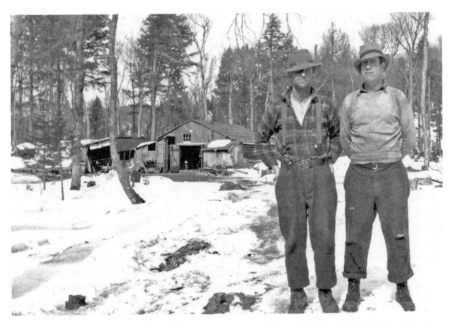

"The lumberjacks and the [river] drivers are two different things," Hugh Dowling is quoted as telling *Daily Sentinel* writer Conse R. Delutis in 1939 when the Rome, N.Y. columnist visited Gould's Moose River logging operations, "and there aren't too many of either left." *Courtesy of Lyons Falls History Association*

Bog River, 1915. Stories and songs abound of the fearless whitewater men, but the truth of the matter is there were heroes and heroes' widows left with children and bleak futures. Conway wrote, "There were no entitlements whatsoever! No compensation. No Social Security." A bleak remembrance of the men who engaged in a yearly sixty-day superhuman effort for a couple of bucks a day was a high risk game with the daring 'jacks gambling their families' future and inviting watery graves for themselves. For some there must have been a strange and compelling attraction to those yearly hazardous trips down the icy, flood-swollen streams." *Courtesy of Special Collections, Feinberg Library, SUNY College at Plattsburgh B-2-13*

Adirondack Logging

A cook camp followed the spring log drive. *Courtesy of Lyons Falls History Association*

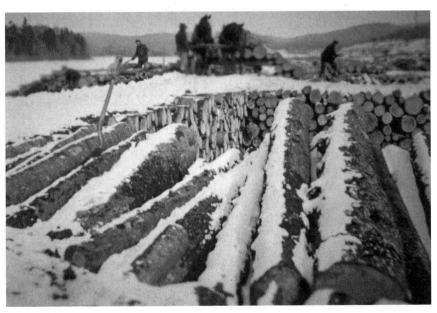

Cold decking of logs on the Moose River for the spring drive. Beyond forester Joe McDermott's and Superintendent Gardiner Poore's preparation at camps 10 and 9 for spring 1928's "Break-up time" at The Landing, there had been 14,000 more cords of timber stacked further down the Moose River near McKeever. Long after those winter weeks of work, when the valleys filled up with water from the melting snow in April and the smaller streams flooded rivers, the log piles would begin to groan. It was then that the white water wonders would be on their way with the pig yokers following in the rear. *Courtesy of Pat Payne*

There were generally 75 to 80 river men involved in Gould's spring drive down the Moose. Ice jams were anticipated. In 1938 one of the largest jams ever witnessed occurred at McKeever, at the site of the dam and mill once owned by former Governor Dix. Working feverishly in twelve-hour shifts to save both dam and bridge, cases of dynamite were resorted to, blasting open a channel for thousands of tons of ice and 10,000 cords of wood to flow into the river below. *Courtesy of Ed Kornmeyer*

"Flat Feet" were men who followed the drive along the bank. Their job was to dislodge logs that had become caught in rocks or beached, and to move the sticks back into the river. *Courtesy of Ed Kornmeyer*

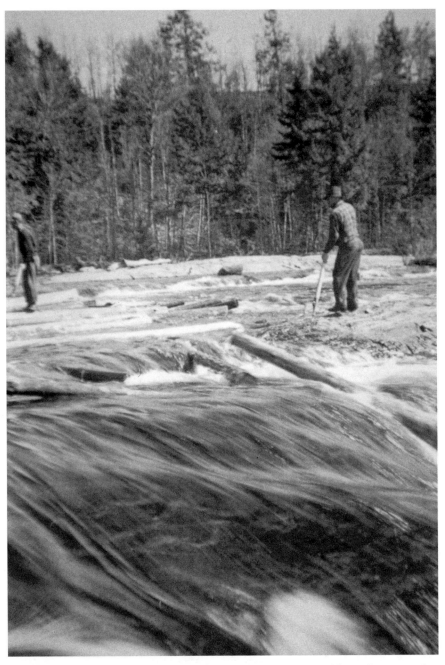

The log driver needs to be able to ride logs, handle a peavey and know how to work himself out of a jam as well as ride a bucking log out when a jam gives way in order to save his life. *Courtesy of Lawton L. Williams*

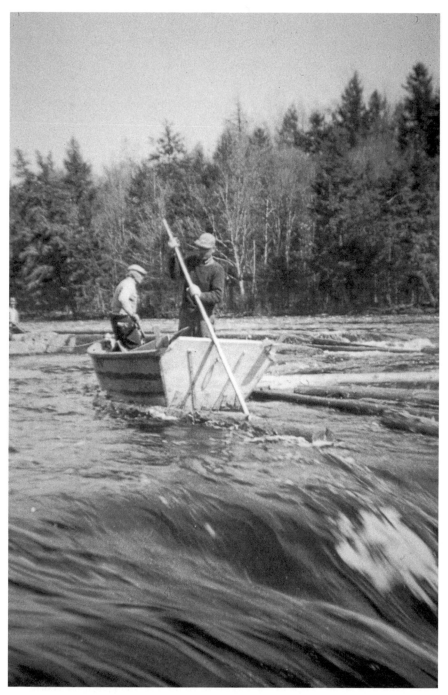

Possible death or injury surely hovered in the back of river men's minds.
Courtesy of Lawton L. Williams

  *Adirondack Logging*

There was a lack of talk among log drivers when working. Very few orders
were given and those that were, were given in a quick matter-of-fact tone.
Courtesy of Lyons Falls History Association

The bumping of logs, the rush of the water, rattles of peaveys, and the click of calked
shoes on stone is about all that could be heard. *Courtesy of the Town of Webb Historical Association*

Boom! Dynamiting a log jam. *Fynmore Studio photograph. Courtesy of Lyons Falls History Association*

Stout, flat-bottomed Moose River boats shown at Camp 9 accommodated three men: a bow man with a pike poke, the man at the oars and a man in the stern with a peavey. The job of these teams was to untangle resistant logs that had piled up like jackstraws to start the whole mass moving downstream again. *Courtesy of Fred Worden*

"The River would drown you as quick as a wink if your caulks didn't hold in a log. No man would save you if you fell in, it was you, or the devil or God."
—Patrick O'Brien, *Memories of Lewis County, New York*

Gone are the days when, in a good year, the Gould Paper Company worked 20,000 cords of wood from the forest to the South Branch of the Moose River Landing using a combination of horse teams, tractors and trucks. Trucks have since hauled timber directly to the mills. *Courtesy of Lyons Falls History Association*

The last logs to ever be decked on the Moose River Landing, 1947. *Courtesy of Fred Worden*

PART FOUR

Life and Times in Adirondack and Tug Hill Lumber Camps

For more than a century and a half since logging began in earnest in the Adirondacks and Tug Hill Country, academics and folklorists have been making hay with the proposition that lumberjacks embodied a distant voice from America's guileless, rural past.

Men came into the lumber woods from various regions. Some were the hard-bitten-old-sinner types, those with a professional air and a swinging gait. The 'jacks wore distinctive shirts, sturdy pants, high, laced boots and flaming mackinaws with pride.

Then one year there came into the woods a man the likes of whom no one had ever known. His origins were a mystery. He gave his name as Bunyan—Paul Bunyan.

Courtesy of Clifford H. Gill from The Memoirs of Clifford H. Gill

Collection 8
The Memories

Lumberjack traditions continue annually each August with the N.Y.S. Woodsmen's Field Days held in Boonville, N.Y. This three-day, wholesome, family-oriented occasion features a wide variety of events, exhibitions and displays for men, women and children as well as adult and junior Lumber Jack and Lumber Jill contestants who compete in a wide-variety of woods-related competition. *Photographers George Capron and Betty Haig. Photos courtesy of the Boonville Herald*

An idle logging camp moment with woods workers and their husband-wife camp cooks. *Courtesy of the Lewis County Historical Society, from Larry J. Myers Collection*

CHAPTER 37

Old George S. Worked During Logging's Glory Days

William J. O'Hern

Every former 'jack I spoke with had a memorable experience to share. All graciously invited me into their homes to sit and listen, to ask questions, to videotape and tape record their personal experiences. All spoke of a demanding but fulfilling woods life. Due to injury, age, family obligations, or the need for a less rigorous job, they all had long ago left behind their logging lives for good. They now relax in retirement with memories of their long-ago times in the woods. They tend their gardens and look at vintage snapshots taken when they earned their livelihoods cutting trees deep in the forests.

Old George Shaughnessy is one example I sought in my daytrips throughout the the Adirondack region to interview old-time loggers. I talked with "Old George," as he called himself, on subzero February 2, 1991 in Minerva, N.Y. The logger-woodsman proved anything but routine, as I found out from the moment he replied to my knock on his door.

"Door's open. Come on in," he called in a voice that seemed time-worn.

"George. George Shaughnessy. It's Leigh," my comrade who had arranged the meeting answered back as he opened the door.

"Hello, young fellers." George's greeting was warm, earthy and inviting, typical of the many men and women I had met over the years. (George immediately endeared himself to me. Well over 90 himself, he assumed anyone younger than himself should be labeled a "young feller.")

A brief rush of sub-zero air entered the kitchen with us. George was typical of North Woods natives: he was born and raised in the mountains and lived off the land, mostly from a large garden and fish and venison. He worked hard with his hands to earn a living for his family.

George S. Shaughnessy (the short one in the first row) began his career as a young boy working in his father's 1890s logging camp. *Courtesy of George Shaughnessy*

"Glad to meet you," he told me as we shook hands. "I'm Old George S. Your buddy told me about your interest in my albums and stuff."

As he spoke, I spotted a huge kettle of navy beans that were beginning to boil on the stove top. Reading my expression—I must have looked to Old George as if my eye balls would leave their sockets—he seized the moment. "That's one big pot of beans, ain't she?" George commented. "By golly, when I was in the lumber camps we never had a problem getting the likes of them eaten down. They're still a favorite food of mine."

My observation had opened a door for Old George. I was about to become a mark. George sized up people quickly. George, being a salty veteran of experience, did it right off and with warmth and humor. George did me in, in first-class fashion.

"Yep, them beans always produced results too. A timepiece could be set for the beginning of the grand fan-alley. You ever consider the stench of those old lumber camp bunkrooms?" (I knew he was referring to gas, the volatile substance of beans.)

He continued. "I can list them in order of their headache value. First, bunkroom odor. Wet, sweaty clothing. Lines of rank woolen socks drying overhead. Second, bedbugs. You know, lice and cooties. The straw mattresses were lousy with 'em. And third, GAS. Natural human internal combustion gas!"

I nodded knowingly. "That's why we're here, George. Word in the community is that you are a masterful storyteller of those days." And he was. One of a dying breed.

"I've lived through both good and hard times. It's never been easy to make a living in the mountains. But, I love it here. Wouldn't trade a single day outside 'em." With a glance back to the kettle on the stove, he refocused my attention. "You know, I prick every single one of them beans. Eliminates the gas," he volunteered.

"That so," I countered. "My grandmother used to throw in a pig's head when she boiled up a pot. It addressed the same issue, only took less work."

He smiled, then delivered his grand "fan-ally" to the banter. "The camp bosses used to have a saying: 'A fartin' horse never tires and a fartin' man is a man to hire.'"

"Indeed," I replied, "and that holds true to this day."

Old George S. was a picturesque character—savvy, sage. He loved to talk about his past life as a timber harvester and driving logs on the Hudson River. George's life has bypassed historical records. His experiences are one example of the untapped history I see disappearing.

I like listening to people talk—the dialects and rural heritage. All those years-ago stories come to life through memories.

Adirondack Logging

CHAPTER 38

Norm R. Griffin's Official Lumberjack Status and Notions of Hula Girls

William J. O'Hern

Norman R. Griffin was seventy years old and living in Homer, Alaska, when I interviewed him in 1986. Norm worked for the Gould Paper Company in 1936. The passage of time had not dimmed his memory.

Norm assured me, "Those are the kind of reminiscences that I'll never forget." He said it was during some "hard times in America. I was nineteen years old. My brother, Red, was eighteen. I had worked on a farm from the time I was eleven years old until I was nineteen, then I joined the Civilian Conservation Corps, staying until I was twenty-one. The CCC is one thing that shaped my life along with the brief time I was with the loggers." He supposed it was the camaraderie of shared accomplishment and a feeling that he was a part of a big family in the CCC and with Gould. He felt it "was unmistakable in that era."

The Civilian Conservation Corps was formed by President Franklin D. Roosevelt in March 1933 to relieve unemployment during the Great Depression.

As a 19-year-old from the Adirondacks, Griffin joined the CCC, and got the World War I-issue khaki outfit, "the big, old black clodhopper leather boots from the war," and denim work outfit. Best of all was the $30 monthly, $5 of which went to Griffin and the other $25 home to his family—the standard arrangement for the millions of young men on the CCC payroll. "Back home, without the 3-Cs, the boys often had nothing to eat and couldn't find a job to help their families make ends meet," Griffin said.

"The experience added to my discipline and confidence," Griffin pointed out. He had been raised in a rural area, and knew hard work—probably never had known otherwise. He was proud knowing he had once served his country in a CCC camp. As for his lumber camp experience, he found that was "a real treat."

Norm warned, "All this was more than fifty years ago so I might be a little foggy in some areas," but I felt his recall was sharp as a tack. I enjoyed listening to so many of Norm's memories.

"That fall [1936] my brother and I decided to try for a job in the woods. We were broke and needed socks and mittens. Howard James owned a general store in Buffalo Head [outside Forestport] and he gave us what we needed on credit.

"Howard James was a good man. He was always ready to help if he was needed. No one went hungry... James trusted everyone. Like me, he'd grown up in Forestport. Sometime in the 1920s he opened a store in the Buffalo Head area. It wasn't the usual grocery store. It was a country store. You could buy just about anything from boots to penny candy or gasoline. Travelers, summer residents, natives, and the lumberjacks traded there.

"Folks have said 'Howard James[24] was Heaven-sent for he saved so many people from lots of Hell.'"

While at the general store, the Griffin brothers learned that Gould had purchased the timber job on the Adirondack League Club property but it was a considerable distance by foot. Gould's headquarters was at Camp 9. This was approximately one half mile south of the log landing on the South Branch of the Moose River, and approximately 20 miles east of McKeever.

"That evening, my brother and I packed a little poke of personal belongings and travel food. The next day we walked from the Buffalo Head to a North Lake [logging] camp called Johnson's. We arrived just before noon. The cook was finishing up a hog he had butchered on a large pile of horse manure. He took us to the boss and said they didn't need any more help but said maybe Gould was hiring at McKeever. He let us stay for lunch. We were pretty hungry and the lunch hit the spot. The mess hall and kitchen were in a room with heavy tables like picnic tables. I forget just what lunch was but it certainly included beans. We called beans 'Adirondack strawberries.' There was plenty and we took advantage of it.

Norm and his brother began their nineteen mile hike in to Camp 9 from the Fulton Chain Road at McKeever's dam and mill. Circa late 1930s or early 1940s. *Post card image courtesy of Ernest L. Portner*

"With our stomachs filled with plenty of good grub we walked back to Buffalo Head, arriving at a friend's house just in time for supper. We covered a lot of miles that day. We would run a while and walk a while. It was something we did to break the monotony whenever we had a long ways to travel. The next day we caught a ride to McKeever. We found the company store. I remember a long counter and a clerk who asked what we wanted. We told him we were looking for work. I was not uninformed about a logger's life. Lumberjacks of my day were not like the old-timers—you know, the swaggering, hell-roaring, fierce fighting, hard-drinking 'jack of years past.

"The desk clerk told us we had to see the walking boss, Hugh Dowling at Camp 9. We asked directions. He pointed out the window as he told us to follow the telephone lines, 'They'd take you fellas right to the camp.'

"We took off on a pretty good dirt track but it soon turned bad. All the swampy areas were corduroyed with logs laid down side by side. There was no snow to fill the gaps between the poles. That would have smoothed out the uneven surface, but we had to step carefully from log to log much of the day. It wasn't a comfortable way to walk. Deer were a common sight as we traveled along."

The cookhouse was one of the first buildings the Griffin boys would have seen as they crossed a small bridge and walked over the final section of corduroy that led to Camp 9. "Many stretches of this road were muddy and corduroyed with few scenic diversions." —Norm Griffin. *Courtesy of John Todd (The John B. & Scudder Todd Collection)*

Most people are not familiar with walking on corduroy roads and could miss the point of Griffin's short description. Corduroyed byways got their name from the way logs of varying sizes were laid side-by-side, with gaps between them. Mud or snow normally filled the gaps. The rounded surfaces of the logs could be slippery when either icy or wet, and it was not pleasant to step into the mud-filled holes either. It's easy to see the difficulty of such

Adirondack Logging

walking conditions. The brothers would have constantly needed to adjust their stride, and risked straining their back and leg muscles as well as falling.

Norm's narrative continues: "We walked and walked until we came to a road that crossed our trail. We figured we'd walked for three or four hours by then but had no watch to know for sure. We were positive we had taken the wrong way though, because the clerk had said nothing about a road to cross. But because the road was decidedly better maintained, we made the decision to follow it and see where it took us. After a mile or so on the road we met a man driving a truck loaded with potatoes. He said he had come from Old Forge. He stopped and asked what the hell we were doing out there. I told him we might have gotten off on the wrong trail. The McKeever clerk told us it was 6 to 9 miles to the camp and we had certainly gone that far on the trail. The truck driver laughed and said, 'The clerk more than likely told you six or nine hours!' He gave us each a large raw potato and took us back to our original trail and told us to continue on it. He figured we still had about nine miles to go.

"The shadowy twilight of the coming evening sky began to creep in but we kept on. As it grew darker our thoughts went to wolves and bears. Nothing bothered us though, and suddenly we found ourselves on a bridge. From the plank decking we could see a small building on the left and down on the flat we could make out several small buildings. Not a light could be seen. We approached one building on the left and could hear and smell horses. That told us that someone must be in the area. As we approached we saw another long log building and could just see a crack of light coming from underneath the door. Carefully pushing the door open, we peeked in. It was a bunkhouse—all bunks empty but one. Way on the far end we spotted a big fat guy sitting on a bunk. He looked up and motioned us to come over. He said he was a teamster; his name was Frank. Then he said, 'Hey Uncle Billy, see what we have here.' The door from the kitchen opened and the cook came out. He had two clubbed feet. We told him we were looking for Hugh Dowling to ask for a job. He informed us that Dowling, the walking boss, was at Camp 8, eight miles farther up the trail. He brought us in the kitchen and fired up the big stove. He heated beans, fried potatoes and ham, and we topped it off with apple pie and big mugs of tea. It sure tasted good after having nothing but a raw potato earlier in the day.

"It was after nine by that time; we were pooped. We crawled into a couple of bunks and slept until the cook roused us at six the next morning. The bottoms of our feet were so swollen that we could hardly get our boots on. And then it hurt to walk. We ate breakfast and then followed the trail on toward Camp 8. Our sore feet gradually improved; there didn't seem to be as much corduroy on this trail as there was on the road to Camp 9.

"We came to a small river—the Indian River. Some lumberjacks were repairing a log bridge. The boss was a cantankerous old boy they called Jack McVay, if I remember right. He didn't like the way one of the 'jacks was using his ax. He yanked it away from the guy and leaned over to chop as he said 'I'll show you how it's done.' When he over-reached and fell into the cold river, the crew pulled him out and he ran to the camp to get dry clothes. The air was blue with his cursing. The men said he was a seventy-five-year-old S.O.B.

"We got to the camp just before lunch. Dowling, the 'Bull of the Woods' was there. He was a pleasant man. From him we learned he'd been working for Gould for 20 years. To our disappointment, he said he didn't need any more help until the snow came, when it was possible to skid logs. Timber harvesting began in mid-May when the balsam, hemlock and spruce are 'ripe'— that is when the timber crop is cut, trimmed and peeled or spudded (when the bark is removed) from pulp trees while the sap is still in the pulp.

"We'd seen plenty of log piles located beside the corduroy road we traveled along. They set there waiting for the last operation before the spring river drive. During the winter the logs are taken by sled loads pulled by 'cats.' That was loggers' lingo for Linn tractors that took them to the landing on the river.

"With no prospect for work, Dowling invited us to have chow with the eight or ten lumberjacks that were around, but as we left his office, he called us back and asked us what we were going to do now. I told him we were thinking about trying to join the Army. 'I've got two boys and I'd hate to see them try to go in the Army,' he said. 'You fellas know how to cut firewood?' 'You bet,' we answered, 'we've cut plenty of wood.' 'Okay then,'" Dowling said. 'I'll pay you a dollar a cord for fourteen-inch wood and $1.50 for eighteen inch wood.'

"Following chow, Dowling walked with us back to Camp 9. On the way he pointed out where we were to cut and how he wanted it stacked. 'Split it in slabs and pile it tight,' he directed. 'Don't leave any holes for the rabbits to jump through.'

Opposite: Norm and Red Griffin at Camp 9. Norm's experiences had "lasting effects" upon him in later life. Norm claimed he gained more knowledge about the world in the CCCs and lumber camp than all his formal schooling. The experience taught him discipline and sacrifice and that hard work would keep him going. *Author's collection*

When we reached Camp 9, Mr. Dowling gave us a tour. The lumber camp was extensive. It consisted of Dowling's office, a mess house with bunkhouse attached, blacksmith shop, repair shop, 10-stall garage, root and ice houses and a cottage for the 'inkslinger'—the timekeeper and camp clerk. The cottage also had beds reserved for officials when they came into camp.

"Dowling showed us where to sleep—which we were ready for—and issued us a crosscut saw, two double bitted axes, two wedges and a handful of files. We were officially lumberjacks, we thought.

"We worked day after day felling hardwood trees, bucking and splitting and piling. We tried to cut and pile four cords a day. That would give us two dollars each per day, out of which we each paid a dollar a day for board. The food was good and plentiful, but otherwise things were pretty crummy. The bunks were full of bedbugs, our drinking water was in a galvanized bucket with a dipper, and there were two big log-burning stoves in the bunkhouse. Double decker bunks on each side, no sheets or pillowcases, dirty straw bags for mattresses, blankets that felt like some kind of paper. Long wires were stretched down the length of the shack on each side to hang wet socks and mittens on. I won't try to describe the stink, but we got used to it. For light we had one kerosene lamp in the bunkhouse and 'Uncle Billy' had two lanterns and a lamp in the kitchen. A Russian man called John wanted to write something and went to the kitchen and said, 'Uncle Billy, you've got too many lanterns,' and he reached for one. Old Billy roared, 'Get out of here you Russian S.O.B.,' and as John ran out the door Billy threw a stove poker that almost broke the door. Poor John didn't get the lantern.

"By this time the snow had arrived and the camp was full of men. After the first week I got up enough nerve to ask the cook how we took a bath. 'Bath!' he bellowed. 'Go down to the creek and chop a hole if you want a bath.'

"Before the lumberjacks came in there was only Uncle Billy, Frank, the teamster, my brother and myself. Uncle Billy called me in the kitchen one Sunday morning and showed me a Winchester 32-40 he kept under his mattress. 'Do you think you could get a deer with this rifle?' he asked. 'Sure would like to try,' I answered. This was very mischievous, because we were on Adirondack League Club property. Hunting by non-members on the private preserve was forbidden. And, the ALC had a caretaker with a reputation that had everybody scared to death. But the thought of fresh venison dulled my fear.

I took the rifle and Uncle Billy's last three cartridges, and told my brother to listen for shots and come and help if he heard any.

"After a while I spotted a nice fat doe. I shot and missed. She ran a bit and stopped. I sneaked forward, keeping bushes between us as much as I could. When I got as close as I dared I got down on my stomach and squeezed one off. Down she went. By the time my brother located me, I had the deer all gutted and I had a brush pile over the remains. We carried her into camp. Frank told us to hang her in a water sprinkler box so we would have fresh meat for a while.

"In the middle of December I noticed my brother acting funny. His face was all red and he didn't have any pep. I knew he was sick so we went back to camp. Uncle Billy made him some hot tea and gave him some molasses cookies. Hugh Dowling had just come into the camp; I told him Red was sick and we had to go out. He went with me to measure the wood we had cut, and then we returned to his office. He gave me a slip to give to the clerk at McKeever for our pay. He said he was sorry that there was no way he could get us a ride out, but he did say that as long as he had anything to say we would always get a job in his camps.

"We left Camp 9 about 11:30 in the morning. There were several inches of snow on the ground—enough to make it hard walking. We did pretty well until we were about halfway. At the road that crossed the trail, there was an old abandoned car. My brother wanted to stop and camp in it for the night. He was pretty sick by then. I knew we couldn't stay there because he would be too cold and besides, with no way to keep warm, we might both be dead by the morning. I talked him into staying the course. He did for another mile or so and then he began flopping down into the snow and refusing to get up. I'd get him up and on we would go for a while until down he would go again. I tried carrying him, but it was too much for me. He got down once and refused to get up. I swore at him and got him mad enough at me so that he would get up and chase me. Finally he settled down and kept on walking. It was dark at this time and I figured we had 4 or 5 miles to go. The trail seemed endless.

"Suddenly I heard a dog bark a long way off. I knew it was McKeever, so we kept on and finally got there. The store was closed but the lumberjack hotel was open. We got in there about nine at night. The room clerk asked if we were lousy. I told him 'no' so he gave us a warm room. The next day we got paid and hitched ourselves a ride to Forestport. Red had pneumonia and had to go to the hospital. We had earned eight dollars each. The reason we had so little was because they had a little company store, a 'van,' that sold smokes, chewing tobacco, snuff— known to loggers as 'Scandinavian Dynamite'—candy, socks, mittens, clothing and so forth at inflated prices.

"So as my brother was taken care of, I went right back to McKeever. This time I was lucky and got a ride back to Camp 9 on a flatbed sleigh pulled by a Linn tractor. There were four or five men besides me. It sure beat walking. When we got cold, we'd drop off the end of the sleigh and run for a while. The Cat only went about 10 mph or less. One fella wouldn't do that, said he'd 'ride like a man' rather than 'run behind like a dog.' When we arrived that guy had to be lifted off the sleigh and carried in to thaw him out.

"Mr. Dowling put me on the payroll again and sent me on to Camp 8 as a road monkey for two and a half bucks a day with a dollar a day off for board. My task was to work on the roads which were not much better than trails in tiptop condition. Holes caused by heavy sleighs and tractor treads needed to be filled with snow and then sprinkled with water so the snow would freeze and form a solid and safe foundation. Soft roads, holes and bumps could cause breakdowns or worse—disasters.

"We were roused at 5 AM for breakfast. One guy used to say how good they were to us. Wake us up in the middle of the night to feed us. After breakfast we went out to inspect the roads under our charge and shoveled snow into the road from the sides. It was hard work but most of us were pretty tough and didn't complain. It was dark so early in the morning, so we worked by the light of kerosene lanterns mounted on long poles stuck in the snow. Some called it 'daylight on a stick;' others called it 'moonlight in the swamp.' We chewed plug tobacco because if we stopped to light a cigarette the boss would growl at us. At that time I was the youngest one in the camp, but everyone treated me very well. I heard many wonderful stories, true and otherwise. I also learned some verses of traditional logging songs. One song is about a fight that went on for forty minutes involving a Christian logger named Jack Driscoll, during which he lost two teeth and his opponent, Bob, who lost an ear. Here's a bit of it:

Jack he got Bob under
And he slugged him once or twice;
And Bob confessed almighty quick
The divinity of Christ.
So fierce discussion ended
And they rose up from the ground;
Someone brought a bottle out
And kindly passed it around.
And they drank to Jack's religion
In a quiet sort of way.
And the spread of infidelity
Was checked in camp that day.

"My favorite stories were told by the old-timers called 'bunkhouse historians.' There were tales of how cold it could get in the woods and one about a 'jack who trained a woodchuck to dig postholes and how the logger retired from the woods and made a killing by taking on fencing jobs for farmers.

"When we filled the road with snow, a Linn [tractor] would come along pulling a big wooden rectangular water tank with two drain holes that let water run into the runner tracks. That would freeze and make a good road for hauling—like a railroad in reverse, grooves instead of rails.

"I never worked on the hills. That job was for the 'Sand Hill Men.' Generally, they were 'jacks with years of experience but they'd grown too old for the more strenuous jobs. While on duty, they stayed in 'huts,' or 'caves' cut right into the sides of hills. They kept a fire going inside. Those log fires were never allowed to die out during the hauling season. Evergreen boughs and branches were arranged as protection against freezing temperatures and biting wind. When they heard the approach of a tractor hauling a train of logs, they would come out and either spread pails of sand or sometimes spread hay on the hill so that the loads would slow down on the hill and not jack-knife. They called them sandhillers.

"Sleigh loads of logs were hauled to the loading yard with horses. Twelve loads made a train and the Linn tractor hauled them all to the landing at Camp 9. As each sleigh weighed between four and five tons, a string of 12 sleigh loads could weigh as much as 60 tons. Only the largest tractors and most experienced drivers were used for these extremely heavy loads. Cat drivers got four dollars a day but they had to haul two trips a day to earn it. If something happened to slow them up they lost money for that day. The driver's helper, the "whistlepunk," got $2.50 per day.

Lt. to Rt. Unidentified Gould supervisor and Louie the road monkey at his station on the sand-hill that led down to the Moose River Landing. *Courtesy Lawton L. Williams*

"I remember Scottie the blacksmith. He shod horses, made wedges and did all kinds of repair work. He was kept very busy. Everybody liked Scottie. He was a good man.

"I also remember a timekeeper, Arthur Barnes. We labeled him a young man from a more tender environment. We figured he must have been related to somebody important. He was all right but very gullible and very inexperienced. His pocket watch stopped one day. One of the older lumberjacks told him that Scottie fixed watches. So the young innocent took his watch to the shop and asked Scottie to fix it. Scottie thought he was being kidded, so he took the watch, laid it on the anvil and hit it sharply with a heavy hammer. 'That watch won't give you any more trouble, Sonny,' he said.

"One of the road monkeys was an ex-soldier who had been to Hawaii. He told wonderful stories of the hula girls and the beaches, the hula girls, warm climate, hula girls and all the wonderful pineapples and bananas and of course the hula girls. This sounded good to me, I thought, as I stood up to my knees shoveling snow into the road.

"One day I developed a toothache. I told the boss I'd have to quit and go on out to have it pulled. 'Scott will pull your tooth, boy,' he said. But, I didn't want Scottie pulling my tooth after what he had done to Barnes's watch. When I got home my brother was out of the hospital and we went to Utica and joined the field artillery and I went to Hawaii. Facing hula girls sure beat snow."

The original Rt. 28 curved through McKeever then crossed the Moose River.
Courtesy of the Lewis County Historical Society, from Larry J. Myers Collection

CHAPTER 39

Visiting Grandfather's
J.B. Todd's Lumber Camps

William J. O'Hern

Dorothy Payton and John Todd were two of John B. Todd's grandchildren. Todd, Superintendent of Woodlands, had been employed by the Gould Paper Company since the days when the company was founded by G.H.P. Gould.

Dorothy and John's remembrances are based on their childhood years of vacationing in the Adirondack logging town of McKeever, and at Gould's Camp 7 at the eastern base of Ice Cave Mountain in the North Lake country.

"Grandfather was known by all as 'JB,'" said ninety-three-year-old John Todd. "My father was Scudder."

Barbara Kephart Bird,[25] wife of Royal G. Bird, is the author of *Calked Shoes, Life in Adirondack Lumber Camps*. Her husband was a forester for the Gould Paper Company. JB Todd was Royal's immediate boss.

Bird emphasized the risks of logging. "Lumberjacks characteristically led a life of danger. A typical example is an accident that happened near Camp 7 when two men were felling a spruce and had not noticed that a loose limb, seven inches in diameter and fifteen feet long, was lodged in a fork of a nearby beech tree with the upper end of the limb leaning on the spruce. When the spruce fell, the loose limb crashed down on one of the men and knocked him to the ground, crushing the eyes out of his head. Such a limb is known, in logging camp vernacular, as a 'widow-maker.'"

John touched on another spruce tree his grandmother Hazel Todd wrote a story about that became a Camp 7 legend.

Hazel's story is of an extraordinary spruce and of the events that lived up to the prophecy. John said, "It was said that a curse would follow anyone who cut it. And so, it grew to an enormous size until my father, Scudder, who was the foreman of the Gould Paper Company camp ordered it cut, and from the time it was cut to floating it to the mill several men died—proving the curse."

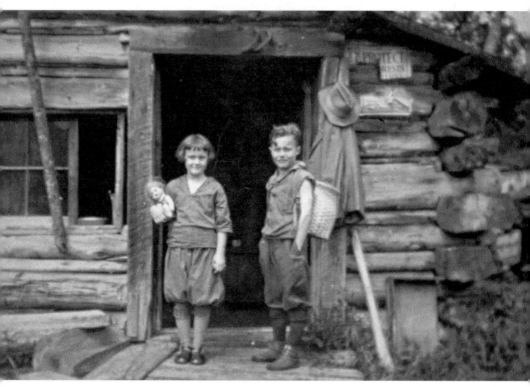

Dorothy Amsden Payton and John Amsden at the entrance of Camp 7's cookhouse, 1928. *Courtesy of Dorothy Payton*

John and Dorothy's earliest images of a family vacation at McKeever, the gateway village to the central Adirondacks date back to 1928. Recalled Dorothy, "McKeever was always one of the places we went in summer and once in a while in winter. I stayed there for a few weeks because Grandma and Grandpa Todd were there. Grandpa had an office outside of Forestport—the Buffalo Head, it was called. There used to be a hotel there. He had his office in it. I stayed at that headquarters too."

Lt. to Rt. John Todd and John Amsden fishing Cobblestone Creek. Circa 1924.
Courtesy of John Todd (The John B. & Scudder Todd Collection)

Their memories are a fabulous addition to Adirondack logging lore—because they show the viewpoints of two children who were personally connected to the era, and Dorothy's female viewpoint gives the account added charm. The transcript of their memories is conversational. In plain words they intertwine, adding detail to each other's statements, wandering between Dix Camp, Forestport Station—The Buffalo Head, Camp 7, and the Moose River. As we talked, something one said often brought up or gave rise to something the other had forgotten.

"Both my Uncle Scudder and Grandpa, John B. Todd, worked for the Gould Paper Company in Lyons Falls, Dorothy continued as she handed me snapshot after snapshot of family excursions and of the Gould Paper Company's logging operation in the woods above McKeever, and some thrilling images of a spring log drive—for many years a familiar scene on the Moose River.

"My fondest Adirondack reminiscences are the vacations with my grandparents at ex-Governor Dix's camp in McKeever and staying at Camp 7. Gould bought virtually the whole town of McKeever, including the governor's old camp.

"McKeever was comprised of a railroad station, a hotel, a general store, post office, clubhouse and company homes lined around a curved road. A schoolhouse was located a short distance down the Moose River road. Camp Dix was opposite the hotel and mill. Nearby were a railroad station, a general store, post office, and a clubhouse. The rest of the buildings where the road curved were company homes and a schoolhouse, I think. The cottages were attractive and nicely furnished. This was all before the state built the new road [Route 28]."

Front row. Dorothy (with doll), John, Grandfather J.B. Todd, Mrs. and Mr. Amsden, at Camp 7. "My brother and I are standing in the doorway of a shack down by Ice Cave Creek where the Linn tractor drivers used to warm up. This was during the time when women first began wearing culottes, or divided skirts. My grandfather frowned on that style but he was tolerant of other things." —Dorothy Payton. *Courtesy of Dorothy Payton*

The Dix camp Dorothy referred to was built by John Alden Dix, governor of New York in 1911–1912 and the person for whom Dix Mountain in the High

Camp Dix complex overlooked the Moose River, McKeever, N.Y.
Courtesy of the Lewis County Historical Society

Peaks is named. An article under the heading "No Debt To Pay To Any One—Dix" in The *New York Times*, November 13, 1910, credits the existence of the Adirondack foothills village to Dix. "At this little village the outward manifestations of the Dix energy and the Dix aptitude for business and for industry are to be seen on every hand. McKeever is virtually the creation of Mr. Dix. Until his advent in 1903, when he harnessed the water of the Moose River, the wilderness held undisputed sway here. Now the low rumble of a Dix pulp mill blends with the muffled roar of the Moose River, and a new row of workingmen's cottages flanks a railroad station and a Post Office as evidence that nature has been made to yield her toll to industry."

Dorothy continued, "One day I'll never forget, the evening my cousin Lucille and I slept in one of the cottages (Grandfather and Uncle Scudder owned three of them). Apparently a lumberjack had recently come in needing a place to stay for the evening. Grandpa permitted him to sleep in the cottage bed we used. We did not know it was infested with bedbugs. You can imagine our surprise and discomfort that night! Grandmother was livid. I can still see her mopping the sheets in the yard with boiling water, kerosene and, Pesky Red Devils Quietus next morning and castigating Grandfather the entire time."

"I enjoyed watching the spring log drive on the Moose River. Grandpa would call me early in the morning saying, 'Dorothy, up and at 'em.' The log drive will be starting soon.'

My bedroom's back window overlooked the Moose River."

Dorothy and John agreed nothing equaled the thrill of the log drive—the sight of big logs rushing down the roaring stream—the booming of them as they pounded over falls. The destination of the Gould Paper Company's logs was the mill at the junction of the Moose and Black Rivers in Lyons Falls. Once

The central fireplace with the ornate hood was a favorite gathering place in Camp Dix. *Courtesy of John Todd (The John B. & Scudder Todd Collection).* Inset: Camp Dix. *Courtesy of Dorothy Payton*

there, the 13-foot logs were cut into 32-inch lengths, then stored in huge piles until needed at the mill in the making of groundwood specialty papers.

Far left: Hazel and J.B. Todd stand next to their early RV "traveling house" parked outside Camp Dix, McKeever, N.Y. *Courtesy of Dorothy Payton*

"Grandpa and Grandmother owned a home in Utica," Dorothy said. "Grandpa would come down weekends; Grandma Hazel stayed there during the winter months.

"Grandpa Todd was a big heavy-boned man. Barbara Bird described him as 'fine-looking with broad shoulders, distinctive features and heavy gray hair. He gave an impression of rugged strength of sinew and mind.'

Opposite: August, 1931. Dorothy Payton and her mother rest on Ice Cave Bridge on their way to Camp 7. Dorothy recalled, "I could never decide if I should walk on each one of those logs or on every other one. It was difficult. Boy, it was rough! I pulled a seedling on my way out to replant as a souvenir." *Courtesy of Dorothy Payton*

Adirondack Logging

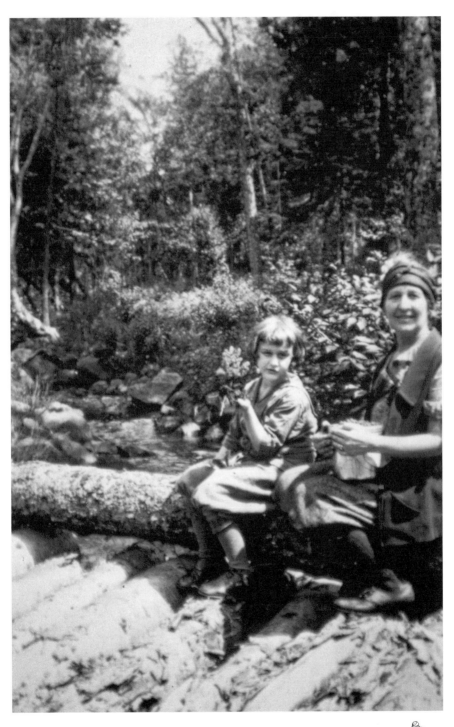

"Grandpa was well adapted to woods work. He related to the lumberjacks. They would come out of the woods at the end of the pay period, you know. I can remember them coming along and talking with Grandpa. There was some kind of a hotel or bar in Otter Lake and the 'jacks would go there and next morning they were destitute. I remember them coming along. Grandpa would listen to them and the first thing they would want was a small loan that could carry them over.

"Gould acquired Camp Dix soon after the governor left. It was in mint condition. The complex had a central camp, one big room with the kitchen off the main room and a storeroom. At one end was the fireplace and at the other end was a kitchen with a big eating table. We ate at a round felt-covered table that we also used for card games. There was always a running card game going on. One of the cottages the Gould family kept for themselves.

As John slipped an almost hundred-year-old 8x10 inch photograph that has been staring out from its frame, he said, "I've heard so many stories about these strong hard-wearing machines. This is one of my favorite pictures of Grandpa [J.B.] Todd. He is standing [far left] by the first Linn tractor, at Camp 7, purchased from the Linn Manufacturing Company in Morris, N.Y." —John Todd. *Courtesy of John Todd (The John B. & Scudder Todd Collection)*

Adirondack Logging

It was self-contained with a kitchen, various rooms—even a room just for dressing. Can you imagine that—a room just to get dressed in! Of course there was a bathroom and sleeping quarters. Next to that was another cottage with two large bedrooms. Uncle Scudder had the cottage. The hotel or lodge or whatever it was called was opposite the mill. Our lights would dim about 10 o'clock at night because the company would turn down the power for the evening. All the cottages had sleeping porches.

"My grandparents had one of the first RVs but they didn't use it much." Dorothy pointed to the early camping vehicle parked by the Dix camp. "Can you imagine that truck on those roads?"

"In 1929, Gordon Gould told Grandfather he had a million dollars' worth of logs in the river and no market for them. He told Grandfather, 'I might go broke." I didn't understand anything that was going on in the country at that time, but I remember hearing the word 'Depression.'

"Dad usually took his vacation in August after the bug season, but not always. One summer when I went up to McKeever it was when women were just beginning to wear culottes. My grandfather frowned on that sort of dress. He was tolerant of other things, but a divided skirt was not one of them.

"Besides going to Camp Dix, we also vacationed in a lumber camp that I used to think looked just like a jumble of logs. Now, as I think back, I know it was rustic. The first time I saw it I didn't know what to expect, so I had no expectations." The rustic camp Dorothy refers to was Gould's Camp 7, in the valley between Ice Cave and Canachagala mountains at the head of Ice Cave Creek.

She recalled, "Grandfather told many stories to my brother and me." John Todd added, "Grandpa and the lumberjacks in camp were terrific story tellers."

Dorothy said, "Most loggers had heard, and a few actually claimed to have seen, the Lopsided Ridgerunner and the Side Hill Gouger emerge from the deep crevasse on Ice Cave Mountain."

John thought Grandfather Todd probably told the boys more logging stories than he told the girls.

Bears in camp were also a rich source for stories, John recalled. One in particular stayed in the back of his mind before going to sleep. "It had to do with the black bears that were always trying to break into the meat storage locker." His grandpa told him he should pay no mind to those bears—that they were not able to climb into a first-floor window—but somehow could manage, once in a while, to climb up and enter the window in the kitchen. "I was reminded that if I happened ever to be woken up by a lot of rattling, that it was only a bear rummaging through the kitchen and that when he got his belly full he would go away. I should just go back to sleep. And that's exactly what I would have tried to do."

"I was only 10 years old in 1928," Dorothy recalled as she looked back on her lumber camp days. "Grandpa said one time Gordon Gould traveled to Morris, New York, to pick up some parts for the Linn tractors. He was flying his plane back to deliver the parts to Camp 9. Fred Worden, the head mechanic, mentioned to Gould to drop the parts from the air in the clearing beyond the tractor barns. Gordon miscalculated when to drop them at the target, and they landed in the Moose River. Fred and some other men had to go and fish the parts out. It was common for Grandpa to fly down to Morris to negotiate for tractors and parts."

John added, "Gould died in a plane crash near Morris Airfield in July 1937." "He liked fast cars and planes—well that's what I've heard," added Dorothy.

"By 1929–30 Gould established Camp 9. Deeper in the woods, it became the headquarters for Gould's Moose River logging operations. Following the relocation, Camp 7 was slowly phased out, but my family still enjoyed visiting the lumber woods around North Lake. We usually only stayed a week.

"Our first stop was Forestport Station and Grandfather Todd's office in the Forest House hotel. The Buffalo Head Hotel was nearby.

"We always traveled to Camp 7 over the North Lake road from Forestport Station. Oh, how that dirt road was rough. Mostly we traveled by horse and wagon; I don't remember going in by car all that much but when we did we'd park at the State House, the reservoir keeper's home at North Lake. From there we would either meet a company truck or take a barge or boat to the dock at the head of the lake, transfer our baggage onto a truck or horse and wagon, or walk the final miles.

"The Ice Cave Mountain camp was rustic, comfortable and pretty in the evening. I liked seeing the deer graze in the clearing. I remember there was all kinds of machinery to play on," John added. "Dad and grandfather held Linn tractors and trucks were ideal 'all-'round' machinery for logging, township and county work. A Linn kept busy.

"The Cottage was the name of the cabin we slept in. It was a two-story-high log home in the woods. It was on a hill overlooking the main tractor shed across Ice Cave Creek.

Outside the cook shack at Camp 7. Lt. to Rt. Eldridge Kelly, Katie Kelly, Hazel Todd, Hazel Amsden, Dorothy Amsden [Payton], John Amsden, J.B. Todd. The last three people are not identified. *Courtesy of John Todd (The John B. & Scudder Todd Collection)*

"A big water tower was at the foot of the hill from The Cottage. There was a pump house to fill the big tanks with creek water. In winter, it was sprayed from sprinkler boxes to ice and harden the main haul roads following their being rolled and packed.

"Grandpa took us berry-picking and fishing at the various streams around the logging camp. We were never bored. It was like camping."

The children viewed staying in the lumber camp as a fun-filled vacation, but Grandpa Todd might have secretly entertained another reason to have

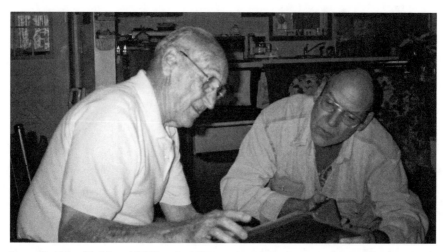

Lt. to Rt. John Todd and William J. O'Hern. "Dorothy and I never realized, at the time, what an experience it was to live in a lumber camp. Without pictures to look at, it would be difficult for anyone to imagine Camp 7 ever existed." —John Todd.
Courtesy of Scott Todd

his grandkids in camp. John mentioned that JB "always had an interest in education." He had served on the school board in Lyons Falls and was instrumental in building the high school. John learned from his grandfather's obituary when Forestport Central District was formed, one of the first in Northern New York State, he was elected to the Board of Education and was still serving at the time of his death in 1942. John and Dorothy have never forgotten the double-crusted pie filled with finely minced pork and the delicious 'panicakes' Pierre, the cook, served to them piping hot from the camp kitchen. Whether it was camp food, camp stories, or the experience of living in an Adirondack logging camp, Dorothy and John unknowingly absorbed an education they've never forgotten.

John recalled, "There were not many lumberjacks in camp during the summer. I ate in the cookhouse with everyone else.

"The camp wasn't being used that much between '29 and '30. Everything was being phased out and moved over to Camp 9. Gould still used the haul road but the area was pretty cleared of timber by then. Once we took a Linn tractor ride along the main haul road from Camp 7 to Camp 9."

Vacation life in camp was bliss. The children scoped out the machinery sheds, poked around the tractor driver's shack where they used to warm up by the creek, and followed Ice Cave Creek toward North Lake, but they never hiked to the summit to see the ice cave.

John remembered eating in the cookhouse. "There was a cook that stayed in camp and prepared our meals. The lumberjacks were not there when we came to stay. They were out at that time of the year. Because no one was in there I suppose that was why my grandfather felt it was a good time for us to come.

"We would play games and do various other things." They both agreed, "At the time we never realized what an experience it was."

John said he still likes to take a yearly drive with his son Scott from Forestport Station to North Lake. "Several miles out of the village there's a stretch of open country known to the lumberjacks as 'Louse Hill.' It hasn't changed much from the days when I was young." Louse Hill is a colorful name that came from the loggers who worked the forest surround Ice Cave Mountain-lore had it that not even a louse could find a living in the sand.

Dorothy concluded her picturesque memory as she handed me the final snapshots and pointed out a picture of her with her creel. "I used to follow my brother John around everywhere and there's me and my little tree. I could never decide if I should walk on each one of those corduroy logs or on every other one. Either way, it was difficult."

PUBLIC SQUARE
BEFORE-THE-FIRE.
MᶜKEEVER N.Y.

Courtesy of the Lewis County Historical Society, from Larry J. Myers Collection

CHAPTER 40

An Adirondack Logger

Casber C. Thompson, *North Country Life*, Spring 1950

The following remembrances are wood industry-related stories. They were written by contributors to long out-of-print North Country Life (*later called* York State Tradition) *from 1946 to 1974. George Glyndon Cole was the editor-publisher of the magazine. Cole enjoyed a life-long interest in the regional history and lore of America. The authors of these four accounts took an interest in preserving memories of early logging and lumbering. Each is different in its focus and in the way it adds to logging's rich history.*

I was told by my grandfather, Jacob Hillier, who was a Northern veteran of the Civil War as a bounty man (an alien selling his military service to a United States resident as a replacement for his son), that New York State was a land of golden opportunity. As an experienced young bushman, I crossed to the Adirondacks in company with a fellow named Boyd. We were offered a job on the Watertown police force if we'd apply for citizenship, but we preferred to search the tall spruce timbers of the Adirondacks for employment.

We found employment in a lumber camp at McKeever. Boyd and I were engaged in log cutting and trimming 200 pieces each day or we were given the ultimatum by the employer: "Bring in your tools and look for another job."

It was the duty of the foreman or camp owner to patrol the bush each day where his men were operating. A man caught wasting time would be sternly reprimanded once. The second offense brought forth the old saying: "Take the hay road home."

One day Boyd remarked that he knew some new wrestling holds. He expressed a desire to put me on the mat (dead leaves) with this new tackle. I accepted the challenge. We had struggled for about three minutes when we heard the sound of feet and felt the presence of someone. Behold! There stood our boss. With his arms folded and a sly grin on his face he said, "Good stuff, boys, but that's not cutting logs for the Goulds."

"The lumberjack was a happy, clean-living individual in camp," said J.C. Ryan, who claimed he had worked in "more than 70 camps. Most camps had a small building where men could wash their clothes and 'boil-up' to get rid of lice. The men themselves did a good job of policing. If a man came to camp that they thought might bring lice, they insisted that he 'boil-up' before sleeping in the bunkhouse. There was always plenty of soap and hot water available." *Courtesy of the Town of Webb Historical Association P2253*

CHAPTER 41

Life in the South Woods Lumber Camps

Mary Rita Gadway, *North Country Life*, Fall 1958

I n the 1880s the Adirondacks were sprinkled generously with lumber camps. A large proportion were located around St. Regis Falls, Tupper Lake, Long Lake and Saranac Lake. My grandfather, along with many other men, mostly of French Canadian descent, went south to work these lumber woods.

Grandfather worked for a company which operated a string of camps. In one camp were 120 men who paired up and cut logs by the month. In the woods, physical prowess was indispensable because the men were paid, not

These lumberjacks and their families of days-gone-by were not so pressed for work that they couldn't take time out of their day to pose for a traveling photographer.
Courtesy of the Town of Webb Historical Association P5941

Adirondack Logging

in proportion to the time spent, but rather for the specific number of logs cut. For example, $20 a month would be paid to two men who could consistently cut 100 logs a day, $18 for 90 logs, or $15 for 80 logs.

The logs were drawn to the St. Regis and Raquette Rivers to be driven down to the mills in the spring. Grandfather often used to talk of the excitement of the drives, of the men who skillfully rode the logs, and of others stationed along the banks to aid the drive by pushing the logs out of coves and eddies into the swifter waters with pike poles.

The camp cooks used Dutch ovens, or large iron pots with covers, which could be fastened securely, in which to prepare the daily meals. If a man didn't care for pork and beans with bread and molasses for dessert, he must have been "powerful" hungry by spring, because this was the menu for every meal every day. The cooks would dig a pit, fill it with coals, and bury pots of pork and beans and others of bread dough under the coals. At mealtime the pots were dragged out from the pits with long iron hooks. To the morning meal every man wore a grub sack around his neck into which he scraped bread, beans and pork to be eaten at noon in the woods.

THE "DOG ROOM." The camp sleeping quarters, consisting of a long room with shelf-like bunks along the walls, was called the "dog room." After a long, wet day in the woods, there was neither room nor time to dry the clothes of 120 men before a single stove in the center of the "dog room." Therefore it was customary to dry one's wet clothes during the night by sleeping either in or on top of them. Kerosene, always available to the men in order that they might keep their saws free from pine pitch, was just as often put to a far different use. It was sprinkled on the men's clothes to ward off the curse, or "bête noir," of the lumberjack—the irritating, sleep-stealing lice, which infested the camps.

The "dog room" and cook camp were under one roof, with an open space, comparable to a breezeway, between. Here on a large bench were kept the barrels of molasses, each with a wooden plug in the bunghole. Outside were numerous pigs and a stack of straw for them to sleep in.

According to one of Grandfather's stories, one morning the men, still groggy from sleep and on their way to breakfast, were astonished to see a number of little straw piles walking around the yard. During the night the pigs had worked the bung out of the barrel of molasses, wallowed in it, rolled in the straw, and made repeated trips between molasses and straw until they had become animated straw stacks.

THE STORY TELLER. Though the lumberjack of Grandfather's day was an early riser and a hard worker, he was seldom too tired to participate in the evening fun. An indispensable figure in every camp was a story-teller, or "conteur," and though he was not paid specifically for his art, the "conteur's" camp job was always an easy one. Every wise woods boss appreciated the worth of one possessing an uncanny ability to keep 120 sinewy giants of the woods contented by merely acting out his simple tales with gusto. Most of the "conteur's" stories revolved around Petit Jean, a brave little fellow who was constantly imposed upon by two older brothers. I'm sure that Grandfather would have made an excellent "conteur," for he knew scores of Petit Jean tales and never tired of dramatizing them for us.

PETIT JEAN. I was introduced to one of my favorite characters through Petit Jean's adventure with "the ship that sailed by land or sea." In this story, Petit Jean acquires three helpers—a man who can see two weeks ahead or behind the present; another who hears people's thoughts; and finally, my hero, the fastest runner in the world. At his first encounter with the runner, Petit Jean is surprised that the man has mill stones tied to his feet. When asked for an explanation, the character in question patiently explains that he is hunting rabbits, and without wearing mill stones, he finds it impossible to run slow enough to catch them.

In another of Petit Jean's adventures he acquires a fiddle, which makes everyone dance for seven miles around. The wicked old king is afflicted with rheumatism, and oh, how Petit Jean makes him suffer when he plays on his persuasive fiddle.

Petit Jean once found an ant, a lion, and an eagle fighting over the carcass of a deer. As a reward for dividing the carcass suitably, he received an ant leg, a hair from the lion's tail, and an eagle feather, enabling him to transform himself instantly into the smallest ant, the biggest lion, or the fastest eagle in the world. The unique power proved very helpful in rescuing numerous damsels in distress and foiling the evil schemes of countless wicked kings.

Adirondack Logging

As children, we re-hashed these stories and many more, and often came near to blows in defending before Doubting Thomases the veracity of the hero's deeds.

After a good meal, logging ballads were one form of popular entertainment for guests at Kenwell's Sportsmen's Hostelry. Besides published songs, there were many verses made up to fit the location. One song originated from the death of an unfortunate logger named Fred Hynes, who died of hypothermia. His grave was within eyesight of these camp guests at the South Branch of the Moose River. *Courtesy of Margaret Wilcox*

THE CAMP FIDDLER AND FOLK SONGS. Even while the "conteur" held the interest of one group of men, in another part of camp the fiddle, harmonica, and Jew's-harp would be claiming attention, and some of the men would kick up their restless heels to do the Buck and Wing or Soft Shoe to the catchy beat of favorite lumberjack tunes such as "Money Much" or "Moccasin on the Rack."

A wealth of songs originated in the lumber woods, and almost as many, sad to say, never left their birthplace, yet these are North American folk songs. The lumberjack "Alphabet Song" was a very popular one in our region. Here is a fragment of it:

> *A is for axes you very well know;*
> *And B for boys that can use them also;*
> *C is for chipping that we did begin;*
> *And D is for danger we're all the time in.*

Another song, and my favorite, is "Flat River Girl." It has a snappy tune and forty or more verses, one of which is this:

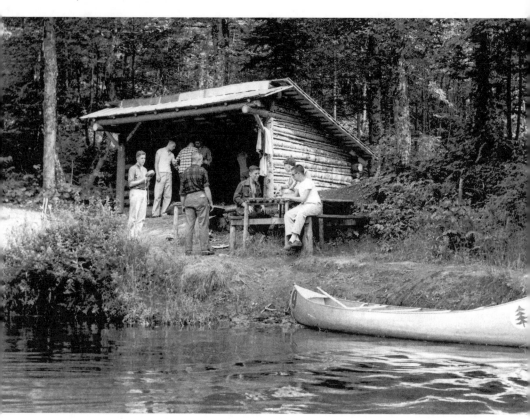

Here, where logs used to flow down the Moose River a century and more ago to a distant mill, today the water course is a popular canoe route. *Courtesy of the Town of Webb Historical Association P5733*

Adirondack Logging

Ghost and stories of the supernatural go hand in hand with the Adirondacks. The spirit of Fred Hynes is reported to still be active around Ice House Pond in the Moose River Plains where this wooden marker once stood before it was destroyed in a volley of gunfire in the late 1890s. *Taken from the front page of "The Governors" last complimentary club supper menu given in honor of guides Dick Burch and Tom Savage held at The Pafraets Dael in Troy, New York, December 31, 1894.*

Come all you shanty boys
With stout hearts and true,
Don't depend on a woman,
You're beat if you do,
And if you ever meet one
With a bright chestnut curl,
Remember Jack Haggerty
And the Flat River girl.

The Adirondack region is no longer the dominion of the rough-and-tumble lumberjack. Far superior equipment, wages, and living conditions have been introduced into the life of today's woodsman. No one could wish otherwise. Yet there is no need to abandon completely the gay world of Petit Jean. Just as the beautiful Northern New York landscape is ours, Petit Jean and his friends belong to us, too. They are a part of our heritage.

CHAPTER 42

Branding and Driving
in the Adirondacks

Dr. Harry F. Jackson, *North Country Life*, Spring 1960

The branding of cattle on the Great Plains and the driving of great herds along the trails to the railroads is a story well told in books, movies, songs, and television. The romance of the exciting and dangerous life has become a part of our heritage. I too have enjoyed the romance of cattle and cowboys, but I believe I enjoy even more the romance of log driving down the Adirondack rivers.

In the West, cattle had to be branded because they became mixed on the great free range. In the Adirondacks, the logs had to be branded because they became mixed in the free rivers or lakes. The practice of burning brands on the hides of cattle was common on the frontier long before settlers reached the Great Plains. The marks on the logs were called brands also, even though these marks were not burned.

The driving of the great herds up the Abilene or Dodge City trails was similar to the driving of the logs down the Upper Hudson or Raquette Rivers. The destination of both was the railroad, which would take the product to market. The logs were nearly always sawed at the mills before marketing. The cattle were sent live to Eastern markets until better meat packing was developed. Both log and cattle driving required careful organization and strenuous, dangerous effort by strenuous, dangerous men.

Logging for cabin building took place at the edges of the Adirondacks before 1800, and some sawmills were established by that date. However, the markets were the local population, and log driving was developed only when more distant markets were available. Norman and Alanson Fox were the first (1813) to organize such a system, their operation being on the Upper Hudson and at their mill at Glens Falls. Their woods crews cut the trees during the winter on the upper parts of the river, stacked the logs on the banks and rolled them into the water at the first major spring thaw and rise of the river. Booms were built near the mill to catch the logs and hold them for sawing.

Ordinarily the boom was a line of logs, probably double, chained together end to end in flexible, floating log catchers. Some booms were stretched directly across the stream from bank to bank, but these were suitable only for small catches. Other booms were attached at one side and anchored in the middle of the streams—the upper end, or fin, being swung from one side to the other to open or close the boom. In this manner the debris of the rising water would float past the closed boom. It would be opened for logs and then closed when it was filled to capacity. These booms were suitable for small operations and were used by the first lumber companies. When additional companies had become established, more complicated arrangements had to be made.

The branding of the logs became a necessity, and every company had its peculiar mark. The marks were imprinted in the ends of the logs with a branding hammer with the brand mark properly raised on the head of the hammer. Each sharp tap of the hammer left the mark, and of course several were made so that one was bound to show above water when the log was afloat. Sometimes a patch of bark was skinned off the side of the log for a brand to discourage log pirates, who would saw off the branded ends and sell the logs to a nearby mill, in some cases to the rightful owner.

When several mills were established in the Glens Falls neighborhood, a more substantial boom had to be built. In 1849 the Hudson River Boom Association constructed the Big Boom at Glens Falls. This was composed of cribs or pens of logs with rocks inside to form a solid pier. The cabin of logs stretched from crib to crib and was meant to withstand all the floods and the battering of logs and ice. The remains of such cribs can still be seen at various spots in the North Country. The Big Boom first constructed was not equal to the expansion of the cutting, however, and in 1859 broke under a load of some half a million logs and a heavy flood. Most of the logs were recovered ultimately, some getting as far as Troy, forty miles downstream. The loss was expensive and the boom was rebuilt strong enough to hold this time.

When booms were ready on the lower parts of the rivers, the companies sent their crews into their tracts of woods to do the winter cutting. On the smaller, subsidiary streams splash dams were built to augment the main log drive. These dams, made of cribs and earth, provided a pond in which to roll logs; but, more important, they provided a crest of water that was released through gates and carried the logs down the small stream several miles to the next pond.

When the first big spring thaw came, the drivers began to send the logs down to the main streams and to release the logs in the stacks along the banks. Now the drive of a half million logs began. With pikes and cant hooks, the drivers started down the sides of the stream, rolling stranded logs back into the current, watching the curves and narrows to prevent a log jam, keeping the whole mass moving as steadily as the rise in the water allowed. The less experienced drivers did the shore work. The more agile, experienced and daring men went into, or rather onto, the water. No cattle herder had to be more poised or daring on his pony than a driver riding a log in the swift river. The log driver had to change mounts like a circus rider, only without planning. And a false step or a sudden shift of his mount meant probable injury or death—at least a soaking in icy water with the attendant chills before dry clothes were available. And if a log mount struck a boulder in the stream, a driver was bucked of as effectively as any bronco could do it.

Where the stream entered a lake, a common occurrence in the Adirondacks, the danger in the drive was lessened, but not the work. To get the logs across the lake to the outlet generally required night driving when the wind was down. The logs were rafted loosely by encircling a mass of them with a chain of logs. On the forward part of the raft a windlass was set up with capstans. A long cable was anchored ahead and then the drivers trudged round and round, winding up the cable and "kedging" their way across the lake. The logs were then released into the current to continue the drive.

As the stampede became the dread of the cattle drives, so did the logjam become the dread of the loggers. In the stampede the need was to stop the action; in the jam, to start action.

Adirondack Logging

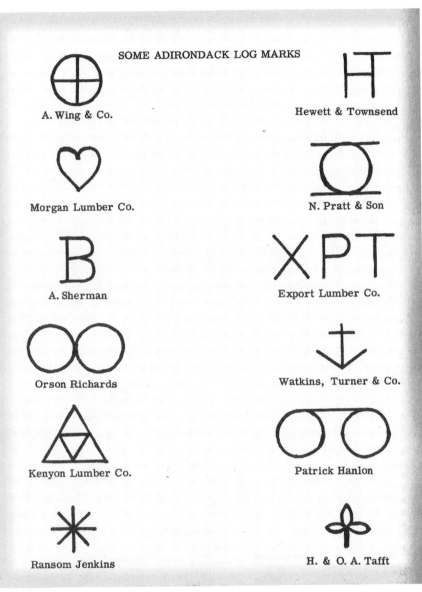

SOME ADIRONDACK LOG MARKS

A. Wing & Co.

Hewett & Townsend

Morgan Lumber Co.

N. Pratt & Son

A. Sherman

Export Lumber Co.

Orson Richards

Watkins, Turner & Co.

Kenyon Lumber Co.

Patrick Hanlon

Ransom Jenkins

H. & O. A. Tafft

Log marks are from the *1900 Report of the Forest, Fish and Game Commission.*

In every jam there was a key or king log that held the piled-up logs, a pile that became greater and greater with each passing moment. Only the most daring and skillful drivers would volunteer to go to the head of the jam and pry out the king. If the judgment of the brave man was correct, the mass of logs would begin to move when the king was free. Just a few seconds were available for the man to reach shore before the whole mass came tumbling and seething around him. Perhaps he rode the king log to shore ahead of the mass. Perhaps he jumped nimbly from log to log in the few seconds when they were gathering momentum. Those on shore were ready to receive him with shouts of acclaim if he made no false step. If he missed, they could only honor his daring and give his battered, broken body a belated burial when he was found. Hardly a driving season passed without a death or serious injury. Almost all the woodsmen carried scars or stiff joints as evidence of the peril.

Log marks were as important to early loggers as brands were to western cattlemen.
Courtesy of Earl M. Kreuzer

Adirondack Logging

But all was not hardship and danger. Even though the drive itself had to be conducted from start to finish with as much continuity of action as possible, there were times when the logs gave little trouble, and then banter and jokes gave pleasure and relief. Whiskey too reinforced the spirits of the drivers or helped them stand the chill weather or the accidental fall into the icy river. Drunkenness was reserved for the off-season or for weekends in camp during the chopping season. Many a logger knew the jails of the Adirondack region because of his drinking and his uninhibited enjoyment of the town life. The wild cowboys who shot up the western towns were only a little more expressive. Frequently the drinking among the loggers led to fighting, sometimes with cutting or shooting. But the fun and good spirit must have exceeded by far the quarreling and violence.

The meals around camp or at the cook wagon were tremendous. The food was plain but nutritious and plentiful. The basic foods were coffee, baked beans, and bread. If the cook wagon could get to a good location, additional foods were prepared. At one meal it is reported a crew of forty loggers ate a bushel of boiled eggs (at least 400), three hams, and uncounted loaves of bread.

When the logs were successfully herded into the booms, the drive was over. The sorting and rafting for distribution was generally safe and unexciting. If a jam remained unbroken and left the river full of thousands of piled-up logs, then months of hard work ensued in tearing it apart, log by log, to salvage for the next season.

Railroads made such log driving unnecessary and unprofitable in the same way that railroads eliminated the great cattle drives. The literature of the cowboy is unlimited, but those who know the Adirondacks know that the log driving was unexcelled for romance and excitement.

CHAPTER 43

Tug Hill Lumbering—
from 1867 to 1953

Mary Ruth White, *North Country Life*, Winter 1953

The logs they haul through the streets of Camden these days on big bulks of motor trucks look exactly like the ones straining teams of heavy bays used to drag to the sawmills forty years ago.

Except for the fact that they still cut down trees and haul them to market, that's about the only similarity between then and now.

Camden, as a furniture center, has seen lumberers come and go for quite a few years. It is on the southern fringe of the Tug Hill section, lumber center of New York State, and many residents of this area know how to ride a crosscut saw without dragging their feet.

The old grey mare ain't what she used to be in the field of lumbering, though; gasoline and caterpillar treads have taken her place in the hearts of big-time operators. Motor oil has kicked elbow grease out of top place in the lubrication field.

Lumbering is still no job for pantywaists. It takes a muscleman to carry a chain saw, oil, gasoline, lunch, axes and wedges through deep snow.

The area north of Camden was originally lumbered for the bark, not the wood. Hemlocks were left lying in the woods while the bark was shipped to tanneries for processing leather. The Costello tannery was located in Camden…and there was a good-sized tannery in Altmar, besides those in Florence, Osceola, Redfield and other places.

In the early days, softwood, mainly spruce, hemlock and pine, was lumbered for building purposes. Lumbering probably started around Camden in the first half of the 19th century.

Seventeen-ton load of "chemical" wood being hauled by a 1919 Linn tractor driving through Morris, N.Y. At one time it was common to see large loads of logs being drawn down a town's main street. *Courtesy of Ernest L. Portner*

David Swancott established Swancott's Mills in 1867, twenty miles north of Rome....

He sent crews into the wood in July to fell the trees and cut them. When cold weather froze the ground, loggers and teams came in to get them out. The logs were drawn to the pond and floated there until the sawmill was ready for them.

Waterpower was used to run the sawmill. There was a broom handle and paddle factory at Swancott's Mills. The mill supplied handles to the Amsterdam broom works, and Mr. Swancott had brought in paddle finishers from Tennessee, Ohio and Georgia, as it was a new industry in this section.

The mill also shipped out railroad ties, lathing and raw lumber. Forty to fifty men were employed and as many as 75 teams were used to skid the logs and draw them to the railroad at Rome. Single horses were used to skid the logs to the skidways.

This saw mill is typical of the mills once found in the Adirondacks and Tug Hill country.
Courtesy of Earl M. Kreuzer

The camp was a complete village with a school, general store, boarding house, company houses for the married lumbermen and a dance hall. They even had a baseball team. The tract was sold in 1920 to the Gould Paper Co., … and nothing now remains to show what a complete community once occupied the site.

The first mechanical method of drawing logs was used at Smartville. It was a steam engine mounted on a wagon, called the "Smart team wagon."

A lumberman named Stuper, between Camden and Osceola, used to hook up two or three wagons behind a steam tractor.

John Kirch began lumbering sixty years ago, at Stillwater, between Altmar and Redfield. The logs, spruce, hemlock and pine, were cut about seven or eight miles above Redfield and floated to Stillwater, then drawn to Altmar by team to be put on the train. Mr. Kirch also cut long timbers for use in the Oswego dock at the Stillwater mill. The sawmill, run by water, was about a mile above the Salmon River falls at Stillwater, on a site now flooded by the big dam there.

Lumber was taken from Osceola for use at the Conant chair factory and the Harden furniture works. Dean Williams, Redfield, operated a mill there for many years.

To see how modern logging methods differ from the above, we visited the McDermott & Hogan concern, which last year cut two and a half million board feet from land on Tug Hill northeast of Osceola.

Before the coming of mechanization, loggers had to skid by horse and oxen.
Courtesy of the Goff-Nelson Memorial (Tupper Lake Library) P396

Only nine lumberjacks stay at the lumber camp in the woods; the rest live with their families in Osceola or at a nearby boarding house. This is one change the years have brought to lumbering. In the old days lumberjacks were for the most part bachelors; now the greater share are family men.

Including truck drivers, about 45 men work for this outfit. The trees are felled and cut up by gasoline chainsaw by two-man teams. The skidding arch, a tractor-drawn piece of equipment with caterpillar treads and high arched axle, is brought to the logs and they are strung behind it on cables, several abreast.

The cable goes from a winch over a sheave on the high arch to the logs, so the pull on the logs is upward instead of parallel to the ground, to avoid their digging in so much.

Howard Wieman removes logs from a cold stack. *Courtesy of Howard Wieman*

Adirondack Logging

The logs are dragged to the logging roads and piled there while the arch goes back for more. Tractors collect the logs and take them to central loading zones; where a swing crane is used to sling them on trucks. Three men handle this operation, one top loader on the truck pushing the logs into position with his peavey, one man setting the loading tongs into the log, and the third operating the crane.

Logs are not left in huge piles for shipment all at once, as they used to be, but truckloads are constantly going out so it is often a matter of only several days from standing tree to the sawmill.

The term for the old method is "cold decking," where the logs were heaped in huge piles and shipped out of the woods later all at once. The system by which they continually go to the mill from the woods is called "hot logging."

The crane replaces skid arrangements, which formerly were used to roll the logs on sleds and doubleheaders, platforms from which the logs were rolled on trucks from a bank near the road. Bulldozers are used to nose roads through the woods, casually pushing aside rocks and trees. One team is still used at the McDermott and Hogan camp for very short skidding and for bunching logs for the tractor.

Loads carried by the skidding arches average seven tons, or 1,000 board feet. This arch is the descendant of earlier high-wheeled carts, which had axles about six feet above the ground but were horse-drawn. The axle served the same purpose: to apply the pull from above the level of the logs. One of the first to use the mechanical skidding arch in this section was Oliver Judson, now of Speculator, who has lumbered the Tug Hill section for many years.

Mr. Judson said, comparing the old and new logging methods, "Remember how we used to work? We'd be up at 2:30 in the morning and work by kerosene torches until it was light. We'd never get a chance to eat from breakfast at 8 until dinner about 9 or 10 at night. By the end of the season we all looked gaunt and hollow-cheeked. And were the men ugly? You couldn't even say 'Good morning' to your crew; they'd have eaten you alive."

CHAPTER 44

In the Adirondack Country

Arthur S. Draper

In December 1946, editor Frank A. Reed, of the Lumber Camp News, *published the following letter. The writer's point of view is that humans cannot happily survive without a sense of purpose and self-worth. The lumbering industry and the rich agricultural land made up a large part of the North Country's employment. But Draper saw something more in many of his neighbors who took joy in the hard work and responsibility that gave their lives meaning.*

Mrs. William Hill must have been born a train dispatcher because her husband's truck begins snorting at exactly 6 a.m. every day of the year. He is a lumberman and my nearest neighbor up here in the heart of the Adirondacks. Pretty soon thereafter, the buss and hum of a mill starts up, less than a mile away, and so another day of lumbering is in full swing. The North Country is turning out board feet of lumber in a way it has never done before. Modern machinery is the answer.

Kenneth Murphy has the last word in modern lumber mills in this section, built for both winter and summer use. Bill Hill has another, which he moves from place to place. Both started from scratch and they have developed their plants beyond belief. They have ready markets for everything they can produce, and they are taking a long view of their future. The experts say that 64 billion board feet of lumber will be needed in the next five years [1947–1951] to carry out the housing problems in this country. That is no small job, but it will be done. During the war and since, lumbermen have had priorities at all times, and rightly so. Thanks to them, all sorts of buildings

Logger with an early-era chain saw felling old growth red spruce.
Courtesy of Eric Johnson, Executive Editor at The Northeastern Logger

SONG FOR THE SAW (poem)
by Helen Hays, Johnstown, N.Y.

My man and I still cut our wood
But never take down a tree that is good.

Pulling together just has to be
When two on a crosscut make logs from a tree.

Not cash in the bank, Book learning nor law
Can bring rhythm to living like work with the saw.

for the armed forces were erected, and now in the post-war period, they have been supplying lumber for the building of hospitals, barracks and various other places for veterans.

Modern lumbering is an expansive business. It covers many fields: the felling of trees, their exit from the woods, the loading of logs, the sawing and planning, and the business of putting the boards on trailers for long hauls.

For every man engaged in this industry as long as 50 years ago, 10 are working at it at the present moment. Skill, strength and experience are needed, and most experienced oldsters can still find jobs without difficulty. Wages are high. The lowest average wage runs to $40 a week; experts earn more than twice that amount. This is one of the reasons why this section of the Adirondacks has never been so flourishing.

All this is only a preface to farming conditions here. Some few years back, we had a young fellow who raised chickens for us, did a bit of farming and was paid $16.50 a week. He was happy until the early summer of 1941. Then we sold some 1,500 chickens at $1.00 each, closed up the place, and I went into the war service. My man went into a place where they raised rats for experimental use in Europe. He earned three times as much as I had paid him. Some years ago I received $10.00 a ton for hay on the place; the past summer I could not get it cut unless I paid $10.00 a day for the cutting. No farm worker around these parts works for less than $6.00 a day and it takes a bit of urging to get him on the farm. Even painters, cooks and bartenders have taken a shot at lumbering.

If this might seem a bit despondent, we want to say that there never was a happier lot than the poultrymen and farmers in this section at the moment. For instance, Jimmy Moriarilty had the sense to buy a large flock of cockerels and to sell them as broilers to the summer camps before July 15. Len Fraser bought 500 poults, raised them for a couple of months in an improved pen, and sold the turkeys at a good profit. Len lost only one poult and that creature had its neck caught in a door. Many lumbermen here have successful small gardens, from which cellar shelves are well stocked with canned vegetables in variety for their families.

Now we come to George Ellsworth, lean, lanky, driving a wheezy car summer and winter and always delivering his milk every morning, Of all the self-sustaining persons I have ever known, he is tops. He has almost lost track of the number of farms and grandchildren he has in Warren County, N.Y. Comes a meat shortage, but not with George; comes a butter shortage, but not with George; comes an egg shortage, but not with George. If the family wants a loin of pork, George has it. Grain prices go high. We call him Old Man Diogenes, always going around with a lantern to find the answer to life; he does. George is up at 5:00 a.m., winter and summer; his good lady is out of bed at the same time: Neither needs to do it, but they love the work, making butter, canning vegetables, meat and doing a thousand and one things. He has been on the town board for years, he is keen on school and all local affairs, he knows a sick bird or animal, and he knows a weakling in the human race. Among his places is one with some lumber on; there he has established his own sawmill, and it's going right now. Some of the boys who deserted his farm because of the higher wages paid for lumbering are again working for him. He smiles as he tells the story, but it is the smile of the cat who has gulped down the canary.

Long since we learned that just making money was not the answer to life. We discovered that it was making ends meet and getting happiness.

> "Lord, I am glad for the great gift of living,
> Glad for the days of sun and rain;
> Grateful for joy with an endless Thanksgiving,
> Grateful for laughter and grateful for pain."
> —A 1951 prayer by Rev. Frank A. Reed

Courtesy of the Lewis County Historical Society, from Larry J. Myers Collection

CHAPTER 45

Life in a Lumber Camp—1899

Helen Escha Tyler

Mortimer Moss was a well-known name in Lewis, AuSable Forks, and Westport, New York. This story is about Moss's efforts to support his family. As Adirondack Mountain folks would say, he "turned his hand to just about anything." Moss was a man of many talents who cared for his family's welfare—you might say he had "their future in his veins." Stories and memories from his daughter, Helen Escha Tyler, in her out-of-print series, Folk Tales of the Adirondacks, *add a personal touch to Adirondack history. Helen's daughter, Dr. Martha Tyler John, was invaluable in sharing the use of this unique perspective of her mother's family in 1899.*

Helen Escha Tyler was born in 1893 in the village of Lewis, New York. She lived her entire life in the Adirondacks.

In 1917, Helen married Albert Tyler of Vermontville, N.Y. Shortly after the couple's marriage they bought a farm a half mile from Albert's birthplace.

In 1931, Mrs. Tyler began a writing career for the Adirondack Daily Enterprise, *which was and still is published in Saranac Lake, N.Y. In 1953 she developed a weekly column titled "This 'n' That."*

Her writings were personal, referencing local people, places, and events for her youthful readers—real happenings, and, as she said, tales sprinkled throughout because "the Adirondacks have always had their 'tall stories,' which were so much loved by our forefathers."

In 1969, enthusiastic readers of Tyler's column asked Helen to assemble a collection of her weekly columns in book-form.

Helen's readers' requests were a real incentive. Fine newswoman that she was, the challenge could not be turned down. Between 1968 and 1983 she published...in them

Helen Escha Tyler's (inset) family's life in an Adirondack lumber camp made an indelible memory. *Courtesy of Dr. Martha Tyler John. Inset courtesy of Lyons Falls History Association*

thar hills, Log Cabin Days, Mountain Memories, and This 'n' That. *The books in her series are sought after by collectors of folk tales of the Adirondacks.*

"Life in a Lumber Camp—1899" is one of Helen's stories from This 'n' That. *The story doesn't stop at just what she knew of lumber camp life, but reports the common*

childhood experiences of four curious children who never forgot their short logging camp experience. It was a time when both father and mother earned an honest day's wage for an honest day's work for a lumber company jobber, when relations between the 'jacks and camp manager were important to their mutual success.

A primitive Adirondack lumber camp. *Courtesy of the Town of Webb Historical Association P3879*

This remembrance is Helen's cherished "grass roots" celebration of a phase of Adirondack life that sheds light on logging's social history. It won't be found in formal logging histories. Helen's story adds to the autobiographical history about the Adirondacks' early natives. I also feel it defines success in her own words, for success is when you look back at your life and the memories make you smile.

Much local history of this type has unfortunately probably been lost because the cost of publishing the material in book form is usually prohibitive. This remembrance has been preserved through its inclusion here, along with many other excellent remembrances. The result brings to life interesting first-person historical information about people, places and events associated with logging in the Adirondack region.

Each time I have climbed to Giant Mountain's summit and gazed off into the far distance, I have thought of a little lumber shanty, where Helen stayed, nestled deep

in the dense woodland and how challenging life during her era was compared to mine,
even while laboring up the rough, rock-strewn trail on a pleasurable outing.

One day, during the latter part of August 1899, my father came home and told my mother that he, or rather they, had the chance for a few weeks of work if she thought she could do her share of it.

I don't know what my father had been doing that summer, but he was spoken of as a "day laborer," meaning that he had no steady job, but worked a day or two—or sometimes a half-day in a place. Sometimes two half-day jobs might be completely across the village from each other. For several years—away back there—he went to Vermont and worked on some of the big farms throughout the haying season. Back at home when he could find nothing to do around Westport, he usually went to Keene and worked in the lumber woods, cutting logs. We hadn't lived in Westport very long—perhaps a year or so—but after people got to know my father they were always glad to hire him, if possible, because he knew how to do most anything in the line of work and they could depend on him to do a good job.

I remember the loneliness of having Papa gone so much, for cars hadn't yet come to our town. We had no horse and not even a bicycle then. Of course there was a stage line between the two places, Westport and Keene. But most always Papa felt that he must walk and so save the price of the stage-fare, which I presume likely to have been around 50 cents or possibly 75. Anyhow, by walking and saving money, he had that much more instead of less. I think the distance between the lumber camp and home must have been right around 25 miles, far enough for a good afternoon's walk. Consequently, he only made the trip once every four to six weeks. Just often enough to keep Mamma supplied with the money to buy provisions.

When he worked in the woods at Keene, it was usually for the late Jim Hall, who almost always had a lumbering job going. He liked my father because he was a good worker, handy at anything, and didn't have spells of drinking and then laying around to sober up. I don't know whether Papa had come from work in Keene that day, or whether Mr. Hall had come over to see him. But he was looking for a camp cook. Something had happened to hinder the couple he had engaged from coming then, and they would not be able to come for several weeks, and he had expected to open the lumber job in just a day or two. So he had to have a cook.

The horse and wagon team that delivered the Escha family were working camp horses. *Courtesy of the Goff-Nelson Memorial (Tupper Lake Library) P397*

Of course we girls were to go along. There were four of us: Fleda, just past nine; I came next and was seven and three-quarters; then Ida, just past five and Vera, not quite four. I don't know the wages they would get, but we would all have our board, and the wages offered to Papa and Mamma were good, for the times. Of course it meant keeping three of us out of school for a few weeks, but our parents decided we should have to get along, as they needed the money so badly. And besides that, they wanted to accommodate Mr. Hall, who needed a cook and helper immediately. So after talking the whole thing over, they decided to take the job and started immediately to get ready to go.

It must have been some problem for my mother to choose the clothing to take for us, for that time of year we would still have some real warm weather and could also expect some real cold times. The bulk of the clothing would have been too great as we hadn't many changes. However, we were always kept reasonably clean, though sometimes it wasn't easy. (Many a time we had only one school-dress each and, to have them clean for school, they were washed by hand after school, dried through the night, ironed in the morning and put on fresh and clean for school again.) The problem was to take as little as possible, but still have all we would need.

Papa and Mamma were wanted in camp at once, so we were soon on our way to Keene Valley, by stage I suppose though I can't seem to remember. From there we were taken to camp by team and wagon, and a good supply of groceries, food for the horses, tobacco of all kinds for the men; work gloves, mittens, etc. were taken along too. The last several miles were through heavy forest, over a rough woods road. We finally arrived late Saturday afternoon to find a good-sized one-story, two-roomed log building, located in a cleared space in the forest.

I don't know how my mother felt, but to us girls it was all a new and interesting adventure, although Fleda was pretty much disgusted at being taken away from school, for she loved it and didn't want to miss any. I liked school too, but I was younger and don't remember that I minded being away.

My mother used to say that she was a coward, but I've always felt it took plenty of courage to undertake that job that fall. We were on a slope, the southwest slope I think, of Giant Mountain, back in the forest a few miles from Keene Valley. We seemed very far away from everything and everybody.

Papa had lived in that camp before and so felt at home. He was warmly greeted by the one lumberman who had gotten on the job ahead of us. He was known to Papa, and consequently to us, as "Big Henry," and Big Henry he remained to all as he was a tall, broad-shouldered man. The men kept coming on the job for the next few days and we soon had a "Little Henry," who was really a little man, and still another who was just plain "Henry."

We girls only had time to look around a bit that first afternoon, and keep out of the way of the unloading and storing of supplies. Mamma soon had supper ready, and then it was time to make up our beds. We had never seen the like of those beds before. Instead of beds, they were "bunks." The lower one was about a foot and a half from the floor. Instead of springs, it was just boards, about six and a half feet one way, and possibly four and a half feet the other. Each bunk had its own straw tick, of a size in length and width to fit the bunk. (Each tick was made with a two or three-foot long opening lengthwise down the middle of the top of the tick. Good clean yellow oat straw was preferred for filling, unless one had well-dried corn husks left after gathering and husking the field corn. The tick was filled through the opening, which was usually fitted with buttons and button-holes to close it when filled, though sometimes fairly good-sized safety-pins were used too, if the filling happened to have been so uneven that there would be a hump, or a hollow, that made the bed uncomfortable for the sleeper. All he, or she, had to do was to turn the bedding back to the tick, open it and reach in and smooth the hump, or push more filling into the hollow.) We four girls slept in the lower bunk with our feet toward the wall and our heads toward the kitchen. The head-board was a wide board nailed up edgewise.

Papa's and Mamma's bunk was two-and-a-half to three feet above ours and narrower, so that our heads weren't under it. There was a short ladder for them to climb to their bed, and we girls later came to think it a great treat to be allowed to climb into their bunk to doze, or play quietly while the men had their early breakfasts. The making of the bunks was an unhandy process, but they were finally ready and we were all glad to get into them for our first night's sleep in camp.

On that first Sunday, there wasn't much to do. "Big Henry" had been there for a few days and had done some scouting around, and knew where there was a patch of raspberries. Although it was late in the season for them, they were so shaded back in the woods that they were just well ripened. So for the sake of something to do, we all went raspberrying, with the result that Mamma made a delicious pie for supper.

As mentioned before, the camp house had two large rooms. One was the kitchen-dining area and living quarters for our family. Our bunks were in one corner of one end of the room, and the rest of that end of the room was used as a storage place for supplies. The many bags of food for the horses were stacked in a portion of it. Sacks of flour, corn meal, beans and such groceries were stacked there, as well as cereals and what few canned goods we had. The potatoes, carrots, turnips, cabbages and such were put into the cellar, which was just a large hole under the center of the kitchen floor. There was a small trapdoor in the floor as an opening to the cellar, and no stairs, and not even a ladder, to go down or up. So when my mother needed potatoes or other things, papa would open the door, and lower Vera, who was the smallest and lightest of us, into the cellar. She would pick up the vegetables into a pail which Papa raised up by a rope; then she would reach up her hands and he would raise her up out. The tobacco, gloves, mittens, etc. for the men were kept on a wide shelf up over the back corner of the foot of Papa's and Mamma's bunk. The men, of course, had to buy these things as they needed them, and there was also a small box up there in which the cash from such sales was kept. That shelf could not be reached without climbing the ladder to the upper bunk and crawling across the bunk to the shelf.

Our big kitchen room also served as a dining room for the men, and there were two long tables made of rough boards with an oil cloth on top, and long benches at each side for seats. The men came in to eat, but were never allowed to sit around in there after the meal was finished. The second room was theirs. Bunks were built, three deep, along three sides of that room, and there was an old-fashioned, wood-burning heater in the center, and a few chairs. After work got under way there were most always mittens and socks, and sometimes jackets or heavy trousers, laying around on the floor near the stove, hung on chairs, on the edges of bunks, or on strings stretched up here and there, to dry. Usually a strong odor of wet and steaming not-too-clean woolens hung heavy in the air of that room. Soon after daylight on that first Monday morning, things began to hum. Papa went to making up bunks, and assigned them as the men arrived by ones, and twos, and threes. They kept coming for several days until there were between twenty-five and thirty of them. Mamma got busy at the cooking, and soon had pies and doughnuts made, then a big batch of bread going. It seemed as though from then on that she always had a batch of bread in the making. I can't remember now how much flour she used each week, but it was an almost unbelievable amount. Everything had to be cooked. There were no stores at which one could buy a loaf of bread, a pie, cake or cookies. And let me tell you, it takes a lot of food to satisfy twenty-five or more men, who work hard from daylight to dark six days a week. And, of course there were the six in our family to feed also.

Always we girls had had little chores to do, and Fleda and I had helped with dishes from the time we had had to have the dish pans put in chairs for us, unless we stood on the chairs, or stools, to reach the pans on the table. (Perhaps that may sound to some of you as though we were abused. But we weren't. We didn't think we were then, and I still don't think we were. I truly think that the younger a child is when taught that there are certain duties that are expected of him, or her, the better it is for the child. He, or she, comes up expecting to help, and to share in the responsibility of daily living, and is therefore better fitted for adult life. You know it was wise Solomon who said: "Train up a child in the way he should go: and when he is old he will not depart from it…*Prov. 22:6.*" And that is true of work as well as of other things.) And so we helped with the dishes at the lumber camp, and what stacks there seemed to be of them. We also helped with the peeling of potatoes, and the cleaning of other vegetables, and we made our own bunk and sometimes swept the floor of our big room.

Papa wouldn't allow us in the men's room much, and never without him, or if the men were in camp. We would go with him sometimes, when he made up the bunks, and swept and cleaned the floor, but he wouldn't let us touch the bedding, for he was always worrying for fear we would get lousy. Back in those days when such a large group of men worked on a lumber job, there was almost sure to be one or two that weren't very clean. I think we must have had an exceptional group that fall, for I don't remember that even Papa got lousy, and surely he would if there had been any lice in camp.

Papa knew many of the men who came, and seemed proud to have them meet his family. Surely he could be proud to have them sample my mother's cooking, for she was always an excellent and economical cook. It may have been a bit strange for them to see a group of four girls, from three to nine years of age, in such a camp, but I think they rather enjoyed it than otherwise. And even the roughest of them were always careful of their speech and actions around camp because of us.

One chore which we rather disliked at home was picking up [wood] chips. Now, I suppose if you told many of our children today to "go out and pick up a pan-full of chips" they would have no idea what you wanted. But we knew then. We knew that the fire must be low, and that Mamma wanted to hurry it up, and make it burn harder by having the small pieces of wood

"And let me tell you, it takes a lot of food to satisfy twenty-five or more men."
—Helen E. Tyler. *Author's Collection*

(chips) that were left from chopping and splitting the firewood to add to the fire. These chips were to be found on the "chip-yard," so designated because it was the area in the backyard where the wood was piled and cut up for the stove. After many visits to the "chip-yard," the chips that one would find were liable to be pretty small and it took a lot of them to fill a pan. But we hadn't been at camp long before Mamma discovered that there were chips to be had there. And such chips! We girls had never seen anything like them. I don't know how it was in other lumber camps then, but axes seemed to be the main tool used for cutting down the trees, and it seemed, the larger the tree, the larger the chips. Many of them were six or eight inches in length, and nearly as wide, and an inch or so thick. It didn't take long to fill a pan with them. It was rather exciting picking them up. And how they did burn!

At camp we found our outdoor play had to be entirely different from anything we had known. But four lively girls can usually find something to do, and we did. A mountain brook flowed through a rather deep gully, just a bit behind the camp house. The mountain rose rather abruptly beyond the brook, and logs were being cut there. One huge tree had been fallen across the gully, and left there as a walk-bridge for the men, as it made a much shorter distance for them to walk to and from their work. Of course, the men with the horses had to go around. It wasn't long before we girls found the walk-log and used it sometimes to walk on, but more often to ride horse-back on. Our parents didn't let us enjoy that play much, for we were too near the log job, and, too, we could have been badly hurt had we fallen off.

At one place just to one side of the open rather flat space that made up the door yard was an abrupt precipitous rise of ground, like a small hill. A portion of the side of it, toward the camp, had a spot that was a little hard to climb up to, that was just almost pure white sand. The bank was so steep that the fine sand would almost flow down it like water down a waterfall. We liked to play in that sand, but Mamma couldn't see us when we were there. And we couldn't see the camp, so it seemed too lonely to play there and we very rarely did. But we did take pans of sand from there to the big flat rock that we discovered the day they had kept us away from the cabin while they cut the big trees. We also took dishes full of sand to places near the brook where we combined it with water for our play. If only the things that we made had been eatable, our mother wouldn't have had to work quite so hard.

One day the men had Papa take us girls and our mother up onto a small knoll beyond the further end of the cabin, and to be sure that we stayed there while they cut down two or three big trees that were across the gully from the camp. They just about HAD to drop them that way, but there is always a chance that the tree does not drop just where the chopper plans that it will: a broken branch, or a twist of the wind, can send the tree way off as it falls. And those trees were so tall and so large that the men feared for damage to the cabin, or to us, if any such thing happened. So we were sent where we would be safe. As it happened the ends of the branches of one of those trees did land on the end of the cabin, but they weren't heavy enough to do any damage.

We used to like to play around the spring that bubbled up out of the ground to one side of the dooryard. It was among a clump of trees that kept it in continual shade. The reservoir was just a hole in the ground which was about the size of a good-sized wash tub. Because the water bubbled up there day and night the year 'round, the ground, for quite a space around, was wet and sort of swampy—just the sort of place that frogs enjoy. But we weren't allowed to bother the frogs very much, for our mother didn't want us to do anything that would soil or spoil the water, because that was where we got the water for cooking and drinking. But she did often send us with small pails to get water from the spring to replenish the house supply.

I can't remember just what happened but one day I slipped into the spring with both feet, and feet first. I was almost completely covered with water, except for my head. I can't remember why I thought I was deserving of punishment, for we never were punished for accidents—just disobedience. Maybe I was at the spring when I thought I shouldn't have been. Or perhaps it was because I had on a nearly brand new pair of shoes—and I thought I had ruined them. Anyhow, I had a feeling that I was to be punished; but Mamma only had me change into dry clothes, and then put on those soaking wet shoes. It was quite a struggle but I got them on and kept them on until they were completely dry. Had they dried off my feet they would have shrunk so much I would never have been able to get them on again. And they were probably the only shoes I had.

I suppose we played at many other things, but the one we seemed to enjoy the most was rolling downhill in a barrel. The brook which flowed through the gully behind the camp turned and flowed around one side, and it was probably three, or four, or possibly five rods away from the house, down a medium steep hill to the brook. The road out of camp led down that grade, across a rough but serviceable bridge, and on out several miles to civilization. The top was out of our barrel, but the bottom in. We would roll it to the top of the hill, and would each take our turn getting into it for the trip down. When the rider, or should I say "roller," was as comfortably settled as possible, the others gave the barrel a push, and we were off. Of course, there was no way for us to guide the barrel, so we didn't always stay in the road, but unless we happened to turn too far to one side and so hit a tree, or stump, or stone, we always rolled clear to the brook, which was only a narrow, shallow stream at that time of year. Then we rolled the barrel back up the hill, and someone else took her turn. You may be sure we were always careful to keep arms, and legs, and head safely inside the barrel. Even then we got many bumps, for the barrel picked up plenty of speed on its way down the hill. I can't see now why we found it such fun, but it was our favorite outdoor play. When tired of rolling, we would rest ourselves by playing in the brook awhile. But the brook water came from springs back in the mountain and when we first went there at the end of summer, it was too cold to wade in comfortably, so we did very little of that. However it gave a very handy and endless water supply for our pie and cake baking.

I don't suppose we would have thought so at the time, but it was really a blessing in disguise that Mamma could find the few chores for us to do. Play, ANY play, gets tiresome after a while if that is all you have to do. When the weather was good, we managed pretty well but as the cold and stormy days of fall came along, we found the weather too rough for us to enjoy the things we had been doing. Such days seemed long and dark and dreary, and we tired of our game of Authors and other table games. Each day seemed very long. I remember one day the "lumberman's missionary" came to the camp for an hour or so, and we surely did enjoy the many magazines, and the few picture books that he left for us.

The lumbermen seemed to enjoy having us girls in camp. I expect it made the days seem a bit less lonely to them, for many of them had children at home. From the first, "Big Henry," who was there the day we arrived, was our favorite. One reason for that, I suppose, was that he seemed to like us so well. He seemed especially fond of Vera, who was quite small and very blond. He would carry her around in his arms, or on his back, and he tried very hard to teach her a few French words. It delighted him very much to bid her "good-night" in French, to have her reply, "Go and swear." She was very proud of the little gun he whittled out of a thin board, and gave to her on her fourth birthday, and it was among her toys for several years.

Fleda and I liked to get away from Ida and Vera sometimes and play by ourselves. I suppose we thought we were much older than they. I don't know how we discovered it, but we found that by climbing up onto the bags of horse-feed in the storeroom part of the kitchen, that there was an empty space way back in the corner, that went way down to the floor. So, after that,

"It wasn't long before those weeks in camp seemed almost like a pleasant dream."
—Helen E. Tyler. *Courtesy of Pat Payne*

for many evenings, while the men were at supper, Fleda and I would wait until Ida and Vera were busy at something else, and then we would climb up, and over, and down into that corner. We were so squeezed in that we could hardly move, but there we would stay all during the supper hour, and tell stories to each other. The stories were always originals, and usually had to do with ourselves as grown up and very rich, and of how mean some of the boys we knew were to us. We thought we were having lots of fun without the "children" to bother us. Mamma and Papa kept our secret for us, but we laughed too hard at our own tales one night, and that was the end of that bit of fun, for we never could go there again without Ida and Vera knowing it, and there just wasn't room in that corner for four of us.

One day one of the men cut his knee, and when some of the others brought him into camp, my mother was called from the kitchen to care for the wound.

I don't remember how large a cut it was, but it bled a lot, and Mamma couldn't seem to get it stopped. Today a first-aid kit would have been among the necessities on such a job, but not then. I don't know what she used for bandages and pads unless she tore up a sheet. I know she had no absorbent cotton, and finally opened a heavy bed-quilt and took out some of the batting which she bound into the cut, and that stopped the blood for the time being. However, the man had to sit or lie absolutely still, for just the least movement would start it bleeding all over again. His knee still hadn't healed when another of the men received a back injury in some way. My father and mother knew he was badly hurt and would have to be gotten out to a doctor as soon as possible. A litter had to be made to carry him on, for they knew he should not be subjected to the jolting of the wagon over the rough woods road. Another litter was made for the man with the cut knee, for it was decided to take him out also. It was planned for them to leave early the next morning, and late in the afternoon, the man and woman who were to keep the camp during the winter arrived unexpectedly, and so our job was done. A bit more of planning, and my parents did some hurried packing, and we left camp the next morning when they took the sick men out.

There wasn't much work done in the woods that day, for most of the men went out with us, for it took four men to carry each litter, and the carriers had to be changed often. Progress out of the woods was very slow, for the road was so very rough, and each of the men had to be carried very carefully. We girls, and also Papa and Mamma found the jolting of the wagon more tiresome than walking, and so we walked long distance that day. As I have said before, I don't know how many miles we were back in the woods, but it was quite a distance, and we were a long time getting out to a decent road. Even then we were several miles from Keene Valley. I've forgotten if we ever heard if the two men recovered from their injuries.

Although we had enjoyed our life in the lumber camp, we were all glad to be back home. It was good to get back to school, and to be with our playmates again, and it wasn't long before those weeks in camp seemed almost like a pleasant dream.

CHAPTER 46

Earl M. Kreuzer's
Lumberjack Scene

William J. O'Hern

"Just look at them wooded hills, fella," Earl Kreuzer began on a hot, humid day early in mid-July in 1988 when I visited the 93-year-old long-retired logger at his cabin in Hoffmeister, New York. Earl was seated on a makeshift bench facing his vegetable garden. A .20 gauge shotgun lay across his lap. He lived alone along a long winding dirt road that dipped to West Canada Creek.

Earl owned a large assortment of old-time logging photos. His collection was wonderful, but even more interesting were the stories he told. I think he looked forward to people coming by to talk. I gathered his days were mainly waiting in silence to pop off chipmunks, squirrels, and rabbits that scampered from the surrounding woodland on raiding parties to his large vegetable garden. "I'm ready for them critters," he said as he patted the shotgun. "Ya don't live off the fat off of the land around here. It takes work to get by."

Politics, fishing, hunting, logging, gardening, his ancestors and Earl's long life in the Adirondacks were the conversational topics covered as he lit one cigarette after another during the entire time I was there. I believe Earl experienced a good deal of contentment—as well as good luck—to have lived well into his ninth decade. He was seemingly without a single disability or apparent health problem. He had smoked, according to his memory, "since I was a kid." Earl was as honest as the day is long. I liked him.

Generally speaking, the hills Earl was referring to were low mountains covered with second-, maybe even third-growth timber. We moved inside his cabin because the black flies were thick outside. The cabin was an escape from the bugs, but I found there was no escape and no rest for my eyes and lungs. The inside cabin air was thick with the odor of tobacco. As Earl smoked, I choked on both the cloud of smoke he exhaled and the residue of the thousands of cigarettes he must have smoked in the past. Earl himself seemed unaffected by either.

"There was a time before machines came to the logging woods," Earl began, "when this river was the only road in and out, a time remembered now by a handful of woods workers like myself."

Earl was talking about the time when woodsmen cut trees in the Adirondack forest by hand and river drivers moved them downstream. No one had a bit of safety equipment. Earl spent a good portion of his life "growing up" with the logging industry. This is his story in his own words—memories of long logs, sluice gates and lumber camps, heavy suspenders to hold up the heavy wool clothing, of team-work and pride in what lumberjacks accomplished in another era.

"There was a fascination to it. For common flies and black flies, mosquitoes, we'd mix green tar and lard and then smear it all over our faces. You never shaved and never washed except for just around your mouth so you wouldn't get that tar taste when you ate. Why, it was a hell of a place to work, but you couldn't help but like it.

"Anyone today who thinks the working and living conditions of the old 'jacks was terrible is all washed up. I'm here to tell you nobody was exploited. We were fed good, had decent housing, and were paid well. This is the truth. Why I know for a fact older men were kept on the payroll as bull cooks— [that's jargon for "the bottom of the barrel"]—long after they weren't able to produce a hundred percent of when they were in their prime. Those men might have sustained an injury or been disabled, but they were kept on the payroll as long as they were able to make it to the table to eat.

"Oh, it wasn't bad; you got used to it. There were lots of stars still in the sky in the morning when you left camp to work. We didn't know it was cold—

didn't even have a thermometer in camp. We expected the weather to be cold, so we'd dressed to cope for it—dressed in wool from top to bottom with eight-inch-top rubber [bottom] boots."

"Back in those times you worked in the woods or did river driving," he continued. "The men that loaded logs were the best paid. That was an art. [Sleigh] loaders were considered the aristocrats of all the crews. Some men worked for a dollar aday. Choppers earned $2.25 aday. They didn't chop an entire tree down with an axe but first notched them with an axe and then sawed them with a crosscut saw."

Earl's life began during the old-style horse logging days. *Courtesy of John Donahue*

Earl was referring to the two-man saw-gangs with a third man known as a notcher. He notched the trees for falling and the sawyers felled the trees.

"Nobody saw a steam hauler or skidder, bulldozer, and so forth. The only power equipment was horses, and those big old horses were something of the kind." Logging camp horses toted supplies, skidded logs, hauled water, furnished power for hoisting the logs onto the sleighs [with a sidejammer], plowed and hauled logs over iced roads, and performed many different jobs such as transporting hot lunches to the 'jacks in the woods.

"Well before I ever went into the woods, I had learned to use an axe. My father trained me, not only explained, but showed me. He schooled: 'Keep your tools in good shape. Don't pound your axe into the ground or anything like that.' And the saw, when filed right, was three times as fast as you could cut with an axe.

Linn tractors were the "aristocrats" in the new era of mechanization of logging. Earl said he never saw any piece of machinery get "tied up because of weather or ground conditions. They operated through mud and snow and over rocks, stumps and all."
Courtesy of Lyons Falls History Association

"The peavey was used in woods operations—it was about the only tool for rolling and turning a log. With the first snowfall woodsmen followed ox teams and horses upstream to remote camps back in the woods. That was years ago. I went into the woods when I was fifteen. The first year I didn't know too much about the logging woods but I soon learned.

"Each crew member had a specific job. A swamper worked ahead of the skidders clearing trails where logs would be skidded. Filers sharpened the tools—kept them in good shape. Teamsters cared for the horses. Cooks and cookees had to peel potatoes, and they had to get the wood for the cooking and sleeping shack too. Had to also keep the towels all washed out and the camp floor clean, if they could, and they had to lug warm lunches to a central

Adirondack Logging

spot where the teams were working [in the woods], wash dishes, and while they were washing dishes at night the rest of the men in the crew were sitting around, resting, telling stories, singing songs, playing cards, doing them kinds of things. I saw all that [kind of work] and knew I didn't want none of that. I wanted to work with the crew in the woods.

"After you swung an axe or pulled a crosscut [saw] ten to twelve hours all day, about eight o'clock at night you were ready to hit the bunk. I was tired even though I was only in my late twenties. And if you weren't used to the work, going to bed would take some getting used to before you'd get to sleep. You could hear all kinds of notes on a scale—grunting, blowing, talking out loud, talking in their sleep, snoring. I'd try not to pay any attention to any of that and concentrate on a sound night's rest." Other loggers have described the same bunkhouse conditions by referring to their sleeping quarters as "the growl house."

Earl continued: "Six days a week 16-foot-long logs were twitched to central loading areas; teams of horses pulled sleds [sleigh bunks] of logs to the river. This could only take place in winter when frozen earth and packed snow made a packed surface.

"At the banks the logs were unloaded and piled, readied for the spring river drive. Each crew could prepare tens of thousands of logs during a winter's work. To ensure a continuing supply of timber year after year, the companies used forest conservation practices such as selective cutting.

"The forester would come in and cruise the timberland with his compass, maps, notebooks and so forth. The trees were plucked like you would a garden crop. Coming into an area, they might take a third to a half of the existing volume. A typical operation today with mechanical equipment might take nearly everything." In Earl's day, loggers would not have known the word "ecology," but according to J.C. Ryan, another old-time logger, the simple principles of that word…were very much in the minds of all early loggers because nothing meant so much to them as having good water to drink and good food to eat. Today, with our modern conveyances and all types of electrical devices, radio, television, telephone, running water and refrigeration, we take for granted the things that meant so much to the early logger.

While probably more could be credited to their lack of pollution than their prevention of pollution, the early loggers did carry out many preventive measures. And they used only biodegradable materials and rigidly policed their environment.

Earl waxed over his time in the timber woods that spanned the era that began with old-style horse logging and ended with the age of mechanization. "The river has been replaced by company roads and all sorts of mechanical equipment," he went on.

As I read the transcript of the interview, I realize I never asked him how many different crews he worked with. Earl was one of the originals, one of a dying breed, even though that's an overused term. There was no question in my mind when I interviewed him twenty-five years ago that he was one of those self-reliant, hard, solitary men—perhaps a bit competitive, and fiercely proud of his skills. He had to be to still be living on his own, going forward; he was an old-timer for sure but just the same, hell-bent-for-leather.

"When the ice broke [on the river in spring] in my day the most dangerous and exciting part of the operation began. The river drive depended on a system of dams that held back the spring run-off. The water was used to transport the winter cut up to seventy miles downriver to the mill.

"There had to be an experienced watchman on every dam along the river that knew how much water to run through [the sluices] to turn them logs to keep a driving head below where the river drivers were using that water power. Too much flood of water ran the risk of washing someone [over] to take a dive in the icy cold drink and running [the reservoir basins] dry before the logs reached the mill. Too little water slowed the logs' advancement down and they got caught behind boulders and snags. If not cleared, one log would trap others and quickly you'd get a jam. I've seen my share of dragging, rolling, and tossing those wayward logs back into the river. You give me six to eight men with peaveys and they can move an astonishingly heavy log.

"Experienced crews could identify the key log which, when removed, sent the river traffic on its way again. Jams would take hours, days, even weeks to clear. They could block a river from bank to bank and extend down to the bottom. Then too, sometimes long fuses needed to be lit by the dynamite man. His job couldn't tolerate any slip-ups. When a charge went off, it'd blow logs sky-high. The jams roared down in a grand spectacle.

"Just as important to the men as the axes, crosscut saws, cant hooks, and peaveys were a [river] driver's boots—the specially studded boots. Calked

Adirondack Logging

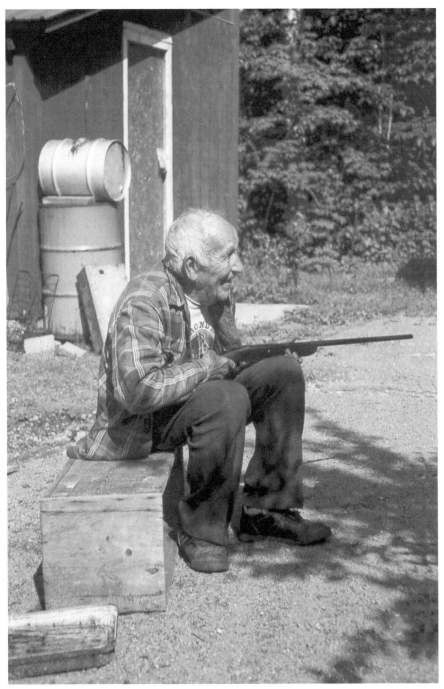

Earl M. Kreuzer, protecting his vegetable garden from unwanted critters, June 1992.
Photo by the author

boots they were called. I never learned to swim. I knew I could keep my balance [on a floating log] and it didn't worry me.

"I often was wet from the start and many times I slept with my [river] driving boots on because if you took them off they would freeze and you couldn't put them on in the morning.

"As the drive moved down river, there were teamsters that used to transport men and supplies to work, camp and eating places. Cooks prepared four meals a day to fuel ten or more hours of pushing, hauling and so forth.

"A typical meal consisted of ham, biscuits, tea and without fail, beans—baked and soup. We always had beans and if I do say so, I always relished them and ate them at almost every meal. I did like the bean, I did.

"Back in the camp we'd gather to recall the legendary log jams, then sing of jams and relive the stories of past logging days in the mountains." And just for effect, Earl smiled and broke into a few lyrics:

> We eat, we freeze in the lee of trees
> As the north wind blows its chill,
> And our chuck is froze while we hold our nose
> At the lunch ground on the hill.

"Yes sir, river driving was dangerous. Men could often be heard expressing their feeling that they'd never go up that river again. 'I'm never goin'a come up this river again'—but come next spring the fever was there, of course. It was dirty work and long hours and I knew all that and still I'd go up the river in the springtime. Logging gets in your blood.

"When a river driver is sitting on the bank watching those logs run, the company is making money—logs went into the mill and were turned into boards, shingles, lath. They were once loaded on to ships and sailed downriver—the Hudson—to market. When the river drive came in, the mills started up. Woodsmen and river drivers often signed on for a summer's work. Logs from the mill pond were lifted inside, where they were run through a band saw. Most operations were done by hand and teamwork was highly developed. Boards were edged, tripped and sent out on the loading platform.

"Men who worked in the mill could go on upriver in the fall and work during the winter. "It's almost impossible to describe the esprit de corps you could find in that bunch of men. [Earl surprised me with the use of the colorful foreign phrase. It's funny he'd know French. I assumed he picked it up from a Canadian 'jack. Then again Earl was full of surprises. I was just as surprised when earlier in the day he'd place an unshelled peanut on top of his head, then sat still as a statue until a chipmunk would spot the treat. As soon as the rodent hit the ground on a dead run, Earl lifted the shotgun, killing the little critter. I watched him do this time and again. "Ayuh "satisfied?" he'd tell me. "I could go on doin' this the whole afternoon. I told ya my reason. I won't argue a mite with you if you got any reason against it."] They were all working for their own interest, just the same as if they were an owner in the company. All that remains in the river and some of the mills today are the concrete piers. The downturn in the market happened with the Depression.

"I'm proud I'm a woodsman. I know what to do in the woods and all this and anything there is about it. I like it. I still like it. If I could go in now I would, but I can't do that kind of work no more. I can't go upriver anymore."

Although 93-year-old Earl would never be part of a logging crew again, he greatly enjoyed reliving those days in his memory. As glad as I was to leave his smoke-choked cabin, I will always remember him and appreciate the time he spent telling me about the early days of logging.

Loads on the landing, Adirondack Forest. *Photo by Beach. Courtesy of the Lewis County Historical Society*

CHAPTER 47

Warren Mathis's
Hard-Working Hands

William J. O'Hern

Wood has made Warren Mathis crazy since before the day he and his two brothers, Jon and Rod, took over Mathis Logging, the family business. They successfully manage over 1,000 acres of woodland in Lewis County.

Step into his living room and you immediately understand his passion—why he logs, what it is about walking through a well-managed woodlot that gives him such pleasure, the reason he favors Stihl chainsaws and American wood splitters, and why he's recognized as a Tug Hill Sage for his knowledge and wisdom related to the logging operation and the Tug Hill area.

On meeting Warren and shaking his hand, the first thing you notice is the firm, friendly grip, his calluses, the strength and the size of his hands. "Strong as iron," I thought. The 82-year-old has recently bounced back from a stroke, after his doctor predicted he would probably never walk again or talk well again. My first impression of Warren is that he is a kindhearted person, sharp as a tack and not one bit forgetful despite the stroke of five years ago. Not only does Warren have the BIGGEST logger hands you have ever seen; he is as tough as his favorite native spruce tree that was scored and documented by the New York State Department of Environmental Conservation as one of the top ten spruce trees in the state. He promises, on my next visit, to guide me to this titanic tree.

Along the way I'm betting my bottom dollar I'll hear more tales about German barmaids with hands as large as catcher's mitts that carry five oversized mugs of beer in each hand, and the party times he and Eleanor, his wife, have enjoyed in the enormous beer tents at Munich's Oktoberfest, where Warren and Eleanor have often been guests of the Stihl chainsaw company. Eleanor remains quiet about her experiences in the various beer tents, but Warren doesn't hold back about the veritable blaze of music, the partying and the noticeable aura of alcohol.

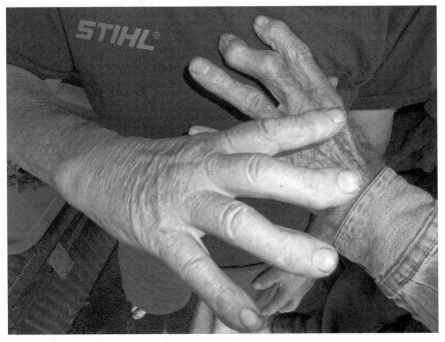

There are 166 years of woodsmen's experience in the gnarled hands of loggers Warren Mathis and Leigh Portner. *Photograph by author*

Types of beer, such as Augustiner, Bräurosl, Hofbräu, Löwenbräu, Ochsen-braterei–Spatenbräu, and Winzerer Fähndl roll off his lips as easily as the names of the many kinds of hardwood grown on the Tug Hill.

Warren is proud of his house. "How good are you with your American hard-wood identification?" he quizzed as we stood in his bright, comfortable sunroom that faces the east branch of the Mohawk River, the walls paneled and floors decked in all different kinds of hardwoods. I recognized a fair number: hard and soft maple, cherry, white and red oak, white ash. "Here's beech, black walnut, cottonwood, red ash, poplar, sycamore, butternut,

Warren Mathis standing next to one of his prized native spruce trees in 2010.
Courtesy of Phyllis W. White, Executive Coordinator, NYS Woodsmen's Field Days

basswood," he said as he pointed out the various boards. He had custom-matched the grain pattern for aesthetic blends. If I were to conjure a moniker for him, I'd call him "Hardwood Warren."

If you want to get to Warren's place and visit, you need to follow Route 26 north to the post office in West Leyden. At that point, turn around and come back a quarter mile. He lives right where the Stihl chainsaw dealership sign sits in his yard. By the way, the peculiar directions give you a sense of the kinds of jokes you will hear from Tug Hill folks.

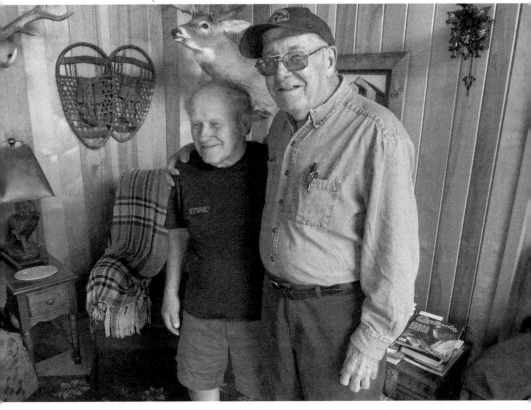

Lt. to Rt. Warren Mathis and Leigh Portner. Former Honorary grand parade marshals of the NYS Woodsmen's Field Days. Among the first wave of loggers who benefitted from mechanized equipment, Warren and Leigh, now "old timers" in their own right although still active in the business, question the future of the forest industry in the face of the heavy, powerful mechanical log harvesters and processors that have replaced manpower and can cause much damage to timberland. "What will the forests of tomorrow look like?" they ask. *Photograph by author*

It would not be an exaggeration to describe Warren Mathis also as "hard-bitten." He's a short to medium-sized man whose occupation has provided a good living for the Mathis family for two generations. I'll tell you about why I believe he is so much like the many other loggers the Tug Hill Country[26] has produced.

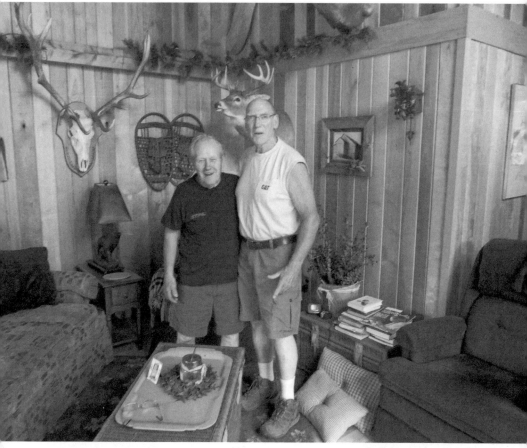

Lt. to Rt. Warren Mathis and the author. Warren's 14-point buck hangs on a golden tone hardwood wall. *Photograph by author*

Warren was born on July 30, 1933. His parents, Otto and Florentine Mathis, raised eleven children in the backwoods of the Tug Hill, living off the land as much as possible.

Warren's backwoods childhood put him in contact with farmers, lumberjacks, saw-mill men, teamsters and road monkeys. He has lived his entire life much like many of the other old-time loggers I have met. Even today, at 82, he continues to actively log with his brother and operate the Stihl chainsaw dealership.

"Warren is the real deal," admirer and family member Emmet D. Abele Jr. reported when Emmet contacted me. "Warren is authentic and humble. A man of great experience in the ways of the woods. He can tell stories about growing up with ten siblings. He's the most interesting with hunting, fishing, logging and just general stories of what it was like growing up essentially living off the land."

It is because of his character, background and experience that Phyllis W. White, the Executive Coordinator of the NYS Woodsmen's Field Days appointed Warren as an honorary grand parade marshal in 2010. White gushed about Mathis in the 2010 Woodsmen's 63rd Anniversary Celebration book:

> *Since his childhood, Warren has had an appreciation for the outdoors. He recalls spending time in the old logging camp #4 in the Tug Hill wilderness. In 1942, his uncles harvested the virgin spruce for Gould Paper Company. The logs were later turned into paper that was used to pack bombs for World War II and used in the B-25s, so when they went down they wouldn't get wet.*

From a boy's perspective, the back end of a work horse looked awfully large. In skidding logs, one end of a log chain would be fashioned to a ring in the middle of the horses' yoke and by means of the chain the horses would drag logs from where they were felled by the lumberjacks to the skidway. *Courtesy of* The Independence

Warren can still remember eating the three-inch fresh pies that the camp cook made! He has seen the evolution and mechanization of the logging industry. Years ago he would use a crosscut saw and work horse to gather the logs on the family farm in order to produce firewood. Today, he uses chainsaws, loaders and skidders to manage the woodlands. He has been an active registered New York State Tree Farmer for over 35 years.

Today, the majority of Warren's time is spent working in the woods or managing his successful Stihl chainsaw dealership. He and Eleanor have sold Stihl chainsaws for over 35 years and have exhibited at the annual NYS Woodsmen's Field Days for almost as many years. However, he still finds time to remain active in the community. He serves as chairman of the Board of Directors of the Region 6 Forest Practice Board; he is a delegate to the Fish and Wildlife board; a member of the board of directors of the Tug Hill for Tomorrow Land Trust; and a past manager for the West Leyden Little League team. When he has a few spare moments, he loves watching Cardinals baseball.

Talking with Warren, you soon realize his love for the woods and waters of upstate New York—the Big Woods, or Tug Hill Country to all who live on the plateau, although it really isn't a traditional hill or plateau.

Many years ago, the Tug Hill saw extensive logging operations. Loggers of all kinds were quartered in camps which were run by men and women who did the cooking and baking and took general care of the cookhouse and bunkroom. Occasionally a few men would cause the cook to complain to their boss that some of the 'jacks were eating more doughnuts than would be expected for breakfast. "Well, just make the holes in them fried cakes a mite bigger and let 'em eat as many as they want," one camp boss was known to quip in reply to the complaint. That is another bit of dry humor that resonates from the kind of sage characters you can still encounter on The Tug.

Warren claims he was working in the woods by the time he was in kindergarten. He clearly remembers those youthful experiences. "Now listen here," he said, "my father and uncles would cut down a tree, then we'd have a mare there, we'd hook her to a log and it was my job to follow her around as she

Adirondack Logging

twitched the logs to the skidway. That horse knew just what she needed to do, but I had to unhook the log, and she'd turn around and go right back around on that skidding trail and she'd be hooked up to another log and out it would come. Why, the horses in Camp 4 had a backend that was as wide as this," and he outstretched his arms to indicate a good seven-foot girth. "Of course, that's how large those behinds looked to a five-year-old kid," Warren qualified before moving on to another memory. "Bess was our mare. Prince was a big white stallion."

In Warren's father's and uncles' day timber was cut with crosscut saws and drawn to skidways the hard way. *Courtesy of Earl M. Kruezer*

Back in those early years, Warren stayed at Camp 4. "That's about six miles up on Swancott Mills," said Mathis. He remembered the first chainsaws and Linn tractors that used to haul out the virgin spruce from the timberlands to the landing. "There were fifty to seventy-five men stayed in camp depending on the year. The camp cook was Lawton. He was from Boonville. Those guys were real lumberjacks. The cracks in the floor boards were so wide dirt could be swept through the openings. Cold wind carried up them cracks. Anyways, we'd walk up there and stay with them in March in the spring of the year. The woods were so dense you couldn't even see the sun. We [his brothers and Warren] would shoot 'porky pines' in the big hemlocks. "They were so big." Warren outstretched his arms again to indicate the spine-needled mammals were as large as spotted fawns. "We'd shoot 'em out of the trees with .22s. As they dropped down, they'd hit the big limbs, bounce up like you would on a trampoline before falling on the next branch below. Everywhere you looked they were in those trees. Golly, there was so many of them critters; they lived in the hemlocks and when they hit the ground with a thud a friend would finish 'em off with a shotgun. Those quill pigs could do some real damage to a lumber camp building, you know."

"The first chainsaw we had was a Craftsman from Sears Roebuck. I never thought those saws would be so popular as they are now. The first chainsaws were terrible heavy. The Diston was a good one hundred fifty pounds. My two brothers and I all had to hang on it. You talk about the hardwood up there, Rodrick Morgan's gang, they were from Port Leyden, they'd cut virgin birch like this." Again, Warren spread out his arms. "Never cut before. I remember across Fish Crick where my homestead was Morgan used D-4 Caterpillar tractors."

Warren continued his rapid-fire recollections, often so quickly one tale interrupted another. "I told the game protector about all the swamps, the rivers, wildlife and fish back then. He said to me, 'Warren I know you don't believe in limits.' We used to go up there fishin' when I was 8–10 years old. We'd walk up the Salmon River, walk down through Swancott Mills and Osceola reservoir and we would catch all the fish we'd ever want to catch and we never threw any of 'em back because there was so many of 'em—why we lived on 'em. We'd come home and fill a dish pan this size around; we' put 'em down cellar and lay wet moss over the top. We lived on trout. Course back then there were no beaver; now it's all beaver ponds. The fishing is all ruined. 'Bout 1940 there was hardly a beaver back then. My father and my uncles and a couple other guys were hunting up in the Brown's Tract, this side of Old Forge. And they were camping back there and there were no deer around the Tug Hill in the 1900s and anyways they were hunting around Middle Branch, it was a popular place for hunting and fishing. They kept hearing the airplanes and they looked up and they see the planes drop the beaver into the ponds. The beaver came from Canada. Now the beaver are all over. Oh, could I tell you about these swamps up 'round here."

When Warren complained about a particular beaver flow that was necessary to negotiate in his truck earlier in the day before I met him, I asked if he ever gave beaver dams a good-sized charge of dynamite to remove the barrier of twigs, poles and earth. He agreed it might be a good idea but cautioned, "It's too dangerous," and could cause too great an expense.

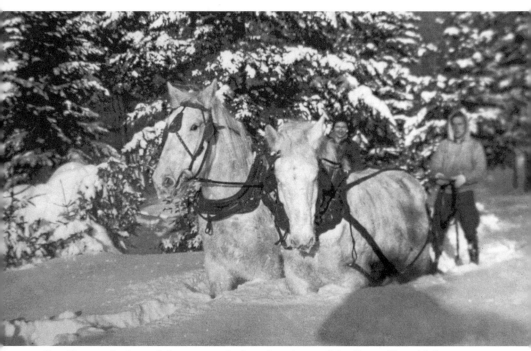

Breaking roads through heavy snow before the advent of the Caterpillar with its diesel engine and wings was a demanding task. *Courtesy of Earl M. Kreuzer*

I'm convinced Warren could go on and on about the wildlife in the Tug Hill region. He has the head of a 14-point buck taken from one of his woodlots hanging on the sunroom wall. But I came to listen about his experiences and to learn about Tug Hill lumbering and the role it has played in the development and economic welfare of the region.

In the beginning, thousands of trees were cut to clear land for farm sites. Soon after, hemlock bark was needed for the tanneries that sprang up. Up to then, hardwood trees were largely ignored as a source of lumber. The period of proper lumbering in the region could be said to have begun in the last half of the nineteenth century. David Swancott was one of the first businessmen who developed a diversified manufacturing enterprise. Later on there was the Gould Paper Company and a thriving lumber business begun by Ebenezer Hooker where Montague is today. There were more, and too many tales to put down.

Warren was an engaging, jolly fellow to talk with. He reminded me of the old-time loggers who came into an Adirondack logging camp looking for work when the wages were small, the going was tough, winter daylight was short and so work would begin long before dawn and go on until after dark. As one old-timer put it, "It was two suppers in one night and hurrah for the brush."

As one tale goes, one adventurous 'jack approached his boss and told him that, come the next Saturday night, he was quitting his job.

"What's the matter?" asked the boss. "Ain't we treated you good?'

"Treated me fine," said the woodsworker.

"Dissatisfied with the grub?"

"Feed is dandy," admitted the man.

"Then what's your reason for quittin'?" asked the foreman.

"Well, I'll tell you," said the lumberjack. "When I come here you promised me steady work. Lately it's been getting' so sometimes I have three-four hours in the middle of the night when I don't have anything to do but sleep."

Warren has some of the same workaholic blood running through his veins and the same kind of moxie as that logger.

Warren tells of a story he told a group of people, about a guy who came to The Tug one day looking for a good breeder. "He wanted horses that could draw wood pulp," Warren related. "Did you ever hear of Joe Issy [sic]?" He asked. "Well this is about his sister. She married a Steinburg and, well, anyways they raised horses and the word was out they owned a good stud. So this guy stopped in and the old lady, she didn't have many teeth I recall, but she always liked me because I drawed four-foot pulp for her. She had a boy my age who passed away and, ahhh, this guy asked for her husband. 'He ain't

Adirondack Logging

here,' she said, 'He's off working in the woods,' so the guy queried, 'I understand you have a good stud here.'

"'Aww, I don't know nothing about it,' she replied.

"'Do you have papers on it?'

"'No I don't know where they are. You got to wait until my husband comes home.'

"Well, anyways as the story goes, he presses, 'You know how far back this horse's pedigree goes?'

"She says, 'I don't know how far back it goes but it comes out this large,'" whereupon Warren once again outspread his arms. "Well you know one lady didn't understand what it meant but she talked it over with some other ladies and said once she understood, she could have crawled right under the table. We partied it up pretty good that day."

Warren guided me though a good portion of his bank of memories that day. I came away from my visit believing he might have acquired his taste for beer back in his "Little Swig" days. It was the job of his older brothers to help cut firewood when they went into the woods with their father. "My father would always bring one bottle of Fort Schuyler beer into the woods when we worked. We boys were allowed to sip from the brew. Each of us would mark on the bottle how much of it each one of us drank. We could never go beyond half the contents. That half was for Dad." Because Warren was the youngest, he explained, "It was my job to chase the mosquitoes away from my father. I had to do that because the insects were so thick. By the time Dad had run the saw ten or fifteen minutes the engine would stop and he'd have to take the coil off and get some spark in it again, so that's why my job was to chase the mosquitoes away. That's the way I was brought up."

There's one particular tree that continues to drive Warren crazy. I promised I would go with him to see it. Warren had to promise he would wangle his son's step-father-in-law, Emmet Abele Jr., to come along. I told Warren I'm committed if Emmet comes on the trip. "It's that giant spruce he often talks about," Emmet told me. "He's been after me for years to see this record spruce. Perhaps this is the impetus to make it happen. It would be fun."

I agreed. It would be fun. It would also be fun to test Emmet's tender skin and mental resolve. I'm sure Warren will have a tale to spin once the Tug Hill pestiferous bull-flies get a taste of Emmet's sweat.

PART FIVE

The Mighty Black River at Rest

William J. O'Hern

On a calm day, the Black River on the flat stretch beyond Gould Paper Company's former mill seems peaceful and benign, but the river has killed an average of one person a year for the last 25 years, admittedly almost always their fault, not the river's. Steamers and canal boats once waddled up her dredged channel, leaving cargo and passengers. Daring white-water men

A Piseco lumber shanty, Circa 1880s–90s. In those early logging operations, millions of feet of virgin logs went tumbling down the headwaters to the hungry mills and log yards in the lower waters. The lumber camps were manned by Adirondack men as tough and rugged as the mountains themselves. *Courtesy if the Piseco Historical Society*

moved pulpwood near its headwaters; sawmills and pulp mills, wood manufacturers, tanneries, and sugar houses lined the banks, and rich farm land was found on the flats along the river.

Gid Perry flushed logs from North Lake through this sluiceway in the late 1880s and early 1890s. By the early twentieth century, the Black and Moose Rivers had an extensive network of dams to impound large volumes of water. Impoundments were necessary. Without dams, loggers were at the mercy of the weather and unpredictable spring runoffs. *Author's collection*

Now and again, in early spring or sporadically in late fall, the Black jumps its banks, inundating many miles of flatland in Lewis County. The flash floods last a few days or hours, causing some negligible damage, but most of the time its central stretch is a quiet old lady lying in the sun and dreaming of her past. And, what a past!

Long before the headwaters dams were built in the 1850s, falls and rapids and rippling white water challenged the skill of the earliest explorers that charted her course, the French *La Compagnie de New York*. In October of 1793, they established small settlements and trading posts, which have since vanished, leaving no trace of their heritage. in the names applied to the Black

River and its tributaries. "From the east, draining the lakes and swamps of the western Adirondacks, the Black River receives the Beaver and Moose Rivers, and creeks bearing such names as Independence, Otter, Crystal, and Fish. Their waters are discolored by organic and mineral matter in solution, thus accounting for the rather unprepossessing name, Black River," reported the VanArnam brothers in their all-embracing history of the era of navigation on the Black River. "Coming into the Black River from the west, draining the swamps of the plateau known as Tug Hill, are the Deer and Sugar rivers, as well as creeks such as the Stoney, Mill, House, Douglass," and others including Whetstone and Roaring Brook, "whose wild gorges are hidden scenic grandeur not surpassed by the more famous glens of the Finger Lakes region in central New York State."

The veneer mill and logs at McKeever, N.Y. *From the postcard collection of Ernest L. Portner*

  *Adirondack Logging*

North Lake, headwaters of the Black River at Atwell, New York. This hospitable environment in the southwest Adirondacks is visited year after year by vacationers to enjoy the natural beauty of the wild-freeing land. *Photograph by author*

"The longest river entirely within the confines of the State of New York is one whose praises are the least sung—the Black. —Edward Hungerford, from Black River... its praises are Least Sung, "North Country Life," Summer, 1947. *Courtesy of Dorothy Payton*

The early decades of the nineteenth century brought waves of immigration from the New England states and from European countries. While the river took its toll of men and supplies, floating boats and breaking bones, settlers, according to the VanArnam history, "in the early decades found the Black River not only the most convenient, but about the only avenue of travel into these northern counties."

Decade after decade the virgin forests yielded to the woodsman's axe; farms were cleared, and thriving towns started.

The Iroquois, the first French settlers, pioneering Welsh farmers, trappers, hunters and fishermen guided by skilled woodsmen, fabulous characters who contributed in small and large ways—all were found throughout in the Black River Valley.

This was the world of Uncle Hatchet, a fictitious character concocted by Edward R. Raymond. "Uncle Hatchet embodies many North Country characters I knew," Raymond clarified. "A composite of truth and fiction."

Outlet of North Lake. "The Black River—sometimes tumultuous, ofttimes calm— is born in North Lake a few miles north of the Mohawk River at Little Falls, passes through Forestport at the rim of the Adirondacks, and makes its way for about a hundred miles, north and west, into Lake Ontario at a point just above historic Sackets Harbor. Until it reaches Carthage much of its way is through a broad gentle valley marked on east by the foothills of the Adirondacks and on the west by the redoubtable Tug Hill, from whose summits splendid views may be obtained of the entire valley." —Edward Hungerford. *Author's photograph*

Born in a backwoods shanty in the little sawmill town of Forestport, New York on July 27, 1905, Raymond lived his whole life in the Adirondack Mountains.

"I lived my first year in a lumber camp," he proudly claimed. "My mother cooked for the camp; Father was a woodsman. He worked as a 'jack cutting mainly spruce, hemlock and pine."

  *Adirondack Logging*

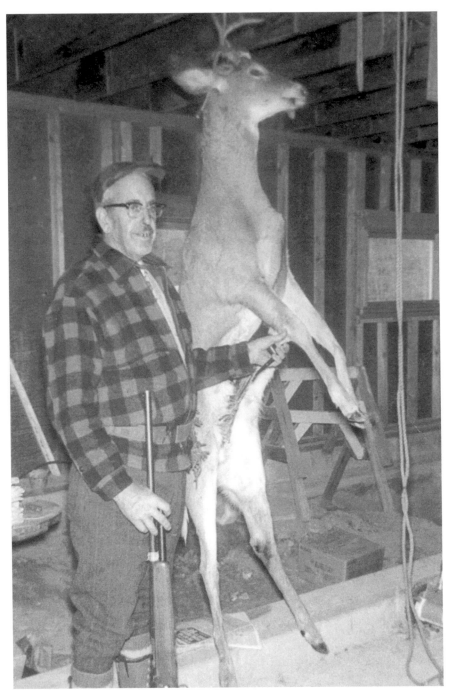

"Big" Ed Raymond, set power poles throughout the central Adirondacks.

Courtesy of Edna Raymond Stalley

Raymond grew up hanging around old "canawlers" and colorful lumberjacks. His childhood heroes were the old-timers who told the tales and kept alive the folklore "told thousands of times with hundreds of variations by many persons" of the far corners of the Black River Valley.

"When Forestport was young," Raymond said, "Blake's Hills was the commons and the cows owned by the town folk were pastured there. It is true that the youngsters did paint whitewashed picket fences with salt brine so the cows on their way to Blake's Hills would stop and lick off the whitewash. Division Street was, for obvious reasons, for many years called Pancake Alley, for through it night and morning passed the cows on their way to pasture, and many a solid oath was uttered by irate citizens who stumbled over a resting cow in the poorly lighted street. It is a fact the younger set once put a line on the steam whistle of a saw mill and kept the good people awake all night."

As an adult "Big" Ed, as he came to be known, could not erase the memory of the days of long ago when his native land was young—the memory of the busy puffing steamers with their tows of canalboats; smoke rising from the myriad manufacturing chimneys and sugar bushes; the snow pack in the mountains and on Tug Hill melting under the spring sun; huge log drives propelled down rushing torrents by intriguing white water men with nerves of steel who lived within his fertile imagination. What cargoes the river carried. What tales old-timers told. They were "like all the folklore heroes of America," recalled Ed.

"Big Ed Raymond was a Niagara Mohawk[27] guy. He was so big that he used to drag telephone poles strapped to his leg," says John Todd Jr., who with his sister, Jeanette, grew up with Raymond's kids.

Edna Stalley, Ed's daughter, confirms that her father was strong: "In Father's tape recording telling the story of his life, he doesn't mention being a wrestler at the local fairs or having rocks broken with a sledge hammer on his chest, but those things happened when he was working for Romy Vaughn, taking horses from one county fair to another during the summer months."

This is only one of the stories told about Ed. Nephew Jim Breen says Big Ed came by his storytelling gift naturally. "I can see him now saying with that wonderful smile that filled his face, 'Now don't this just take the rag off of the bush.'" Breen explained, "When the deer jacker left the woods, he would often tie a rag on a bush so he could easily find his way back in to retrieve his kill. This is according to Uncle Ed, who apparently did plenty of jacking in his time." Ed used the expression whenever he held something was "the cat's pajamas."

Linn tractor with log-loaded sleighs heading out of Camp 7 toward The Haul Road. The Adirondack Timber will eventually reach paper mills along the Black River. Doctor T. Wood Clarke has written charmingly and thoroughly of all the historical lore and tradition of the Black River valley in his excellent *Emigres in the Wilderness*.
Courtesy of Dorothy Payton

In the summer of 1942, Rev. Frank A. Reed, renowned pastor at Niccolls[28] Memorial Church in Old Forge and Big Moose Community Chapel, and founder-publisher-senior editor of the *Lumber Camp News* [later *The Northeastern Logger*], discussed the idea of a clubhouse with a logging crew near Bisby Lake. He was interested in helping lumberjacks. Some 'jacks wisely saved their money. Others, he explained, "spent their hard-earned wages quite unwisely. Alcohol was...[a] major problem." He envisioned a clubhouse where old-time lumberjacks could mingle with their fellow workers. The clubhouse would "provide comfortable beds, good meals, showers and some recreation facilities." Within a short time membership in the venture grew to 600 members.

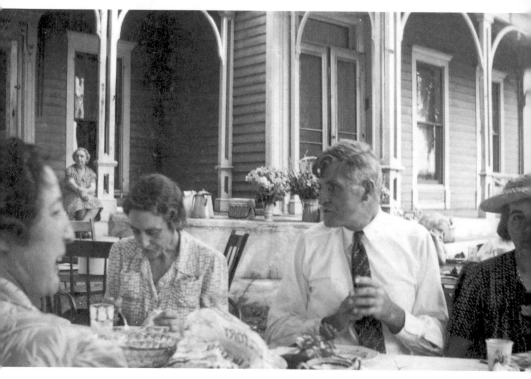

Rev. Reed at a benefit picnic for the Woodsmen's Club. *Photo by Ed Raymond.*
Courtesy of Edna Raymond Stalley

Throughout the winter of 1942 and into the spring of '43, Ed was one of many in the army of volunteers from Boonville, Forestport and Woodgate who displayed a keen interest in the best things of community life—friendliness, unselfish spirit and fine Christian character. Reed recorded in his book, *Lumberjack Sky Pilot,* that they "participated actively in papering, painting... furnishing rooms" and completely repairing the large [Woodsmen's Club] building." Ed Raymond became a charter member of the Woodsmen's Club and served for many years as treasurer. He shared concern for quality-of-life issues regarding retired woodsmen who were living in smaller Adirondack communities. Together with Reed, the men worked on a plan to show woodsmen in the later years of active service how they could provide a more satisfactory program for old age retirement by laying aside some funds in the bank which would supplement Social Security benefits and be available in time of emergency. Besides showing woodsmen how to plan for the day they would

Adirondack Logging

retire from years of strenuous effort in the woods, the men investigated the possibility of the Woodsmen's Club providing for a large vegetable garden where retired woodsmen could supply part of the food for the club table and at the same time earn part of their room and board.

In addition to his work to improve the social life of lumberjacks, Ed was recognized as a person who was interested in regional history and as a well-known tale spinner. Ed was asked by Rev. Reed to write some anecdotes for the enjoyment of the lumbermen who read the *Lumber Camp News*. Edna Stalley recalled, "I think Frank Reed needed something that would interest those men, and my father put down these tales just for the paper. It developed into a lifelong habit." His association with lumbermen, guides and visitors to the Adirondacks and his insight into the ways of the people of the Adirondacks made his tales appealing to all.

Fulton Chain, N. Y. School Building

The Fulton Chain School building Rev. Reed purchased and converted into the Woodsmen's Club. *Courtesy of the Town of Webb Historical Association P0005*

Ed came up with the aptly-named "Uncle Hatchet" stories because the tag had a connection with woodsmen. "The Black River country of the Adirondacks is a tall country," he liked to say. "And the stories have got to grow to match the tall timber and mountains. Why, out about Ice Cave Mountain country—that's the country where the Black River originates—they say there once grew trees so high it took a man a whole week to see the top of them." A tale about Atwell Martin went like this:

> *Speaking of Atwell Martin, that giant of a guide, did you ever hear of the time when he went hunting. Yes, sir—in his youth Old Atwell was the surest shot and fastest runner that ever waded across the Black River. They still talk of him back in Forestport. It seems Atwell sighted a big buck a mile away; it was standing on the edge of Sugarloaf Mountain— and Atwell knew if he shot him, the buck would fall off the edge and down the cliff into North Lake. So Atwell pulled the trigger—and as soon as the bullet left the gun, he ran to where the buck was standing. He ran so fast he got there ahead of the shot; in fact he had to duck his head to let the bullet go by. Yes, sir.*
>
> *And the buck, Big Ed?*
>
> *Oh, the buck was killed, all right. But not by the bullet. When it saw Atwell standing there, that buck was plumb scared to death. It died without waiting for the shot to reach it.*

That's how things happened in Uncle Hatchet country.

Ed valued Reed's invitation to add his wealth of history and love to the minister's newspaper.

Some of the casual-reading Hatchet stories come from the pages of history. Some, from the lips of aged Adirondackers, have the familiar ring of voices of those Big Ed knew who spent their final years tucked away in the quiet woodlands of the Adirondack Mountains.

Before Ed passed, he assembled the finest Uncle Hatchet stories in a privately-printed booklet. He said in its closing: "Let me say that as I look back, there was a lot of hell-raising carried out in [my] …days, but folks did not call them delinquents then, and most of 'em growed up to be good solid people anyhow. That's why I do not despair. History will repeat itself again and again. There's many a tale as yet unspun but I must leave them for another time."

Collection 9
Big Ed's Uncle Hatchet

Edward R. Raymond. *Courtesy of Edna Raymond Stalley*

CHAPTER 48

An American Bedbug

Edward R. Raymond from *The Adventures of Uncle Hatchet*

"One summer I took a job at an Eagle Bay hotel on Fourth Lake," said Uncle Hatchet. "My job was looking after a bunch of 'sports.' I wouldn't call it guiding, but I had some fun anyhow.

"There was an Englishman present—Lord Cecil Cluthbroom was his name. He was a nice fellow and spent a lot of time in the guide house swapping yarns. The only trouble was he was always bragging about England. If we caught a nice string of trout he would say, 'Jove, they are jolly fine but you should see the ones we get in England.' Or, if we saw an extra fine sunrise, he would admit it and then say, 'Beautiful eh, but you should see it rise over the hills of bonnie Scotland, old bean.' No matter what came along, he allowed they had better in England," said Hatchet.

"One day I caught a young snapping turtle," said Hatchet. "He was about the size of a saucer. That evening, I contrived to slip it into his bed unknown to anyone.

"I let on to the rest of the help that there might be some excitement that evening so they all hung around and Cecil did his part by going to bed early. He hadn't been gone more than five minutes when he come down the stairs, his night gown flying out behind him, his bony knees exposed and Mr. Turtle hanging on for dear life.

"'Get the bloody thing off me,' he yelled. 'It will jolly well fang me to death.'

"By this time he was doing a kind of war dance around the lobby. He had always been so much in command of himself. He was so the heart and soul

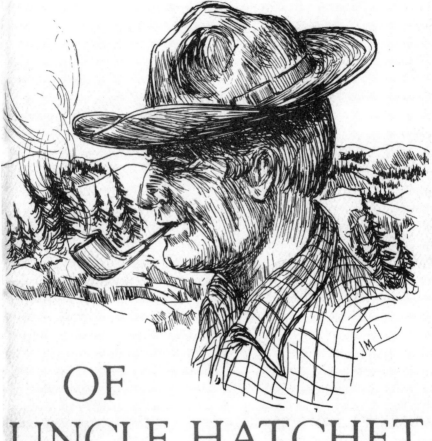

ADVENTURES

OF
UNCLE HATCHET

by Edward R. Raymond

The cover illustration of "Big" Ed's *Adventures of Uncle Hatchet*. *Courtesy of Richard Raymond*

of dignity, that to see him as he really existed, prancing around in night attire, was too much for everyone as they just rocked with laughter. When I finally calmed down, I pried the snapper loose."

"Jove, what was that doing in my bed?" said he.

"That," I replied, "is an American bedbug, and, pray tell me have you anything in England that can beat that?"

The Pulp Mill Dam in McKeever, the way Ed Raymond remembered it.
Courtesy of the Lewis County Historical Society, from Larry J. Myers Collection

Adirondack Logging

CHAPTER 49

A Postscript to Uncle Hatchet

William J. O'Hern

Big Ed's tales are representative of some of the lighthearted reading material loggers enjoyed in the monthly *Lumber Camp News* seventy-five years ago. The humor is representative of his era.

Big Ed never explained how he happened to think up his tales. When I asked his son, Richard in 1998, he didn't know either. Richard only knew the great Northern Forest had Paul Bunyan, West Virginia had John Henry and America's southwest had Pecos Bill. It was only natural that the Adirondacks have its own legendary character.

Ed was a product of his environment. He loved being outdoors. He hunted and fished. Ed would also add that he enjoyed leaning against a wall of a lumber camp bunkhouse and listening to the old timers.

"Sunday!" mused one logger to Ed, "a day fer rest. No logs to roll, ner no bark to peel."

A cook overheard the conversation through a near-by open window and shot back, "I don't see as it is much of a day for rest. You 'jacks are worse than anything the way you eat."

Ed's children attest to his love of the outdoors. Ed wasn't afraid of anything either. They heard stories of their dad grabbing old Dead Eye, the name he gave his rifle, and how he would hear "s'picious crackklin' amongst the dry leaves.

Forestport, a mill town along the Black River. In 1872 there were over one hundred sawmills turning out 150,000,000 feet of lumber. These mills were located not only on the Black River and its two main tributaries, the Beaver and Moose Rivers, but on many smaller creeks such as the Otter, the Fish, and the Independence. *A Beach Photo*

"The next minute," Ed said, "I knew what twas, and in the next minute I saw the black nose o' the all-firedest, dod-burndest biggest bear I had ever encountered."

As the story goes according to Richard, his father blazed away but the bullets never touched the bruin. The assumption is the bear was a scare-dy cat and turned and darted into a hole in some rocks. Ed followed the bear. He fumbled around in the dark, "'spectin' every minute to come to it as I crawled hand over hand when all of a sudden a bit of light comes shining into the end of the cave and away goes that bear up and out the hole."

Richard remembers his dad swore he was telling the truth when he claimed that hole measured eight inches across.

"And how big was that bear?" asked Richard.

"That bear? Why he was the biggest bear black bear I'd ever seen, Son, jest as I told you in the first place."

"How the—" Richard countered, "could a bear that probably measured maybe three feet across the rump get out of an eight inch hole?"

"Why, how'm I to know how he got out? I said he got out didn't I? And that's all there is to it."

Big Ed swore he told his son the truth that Sunday afternoon. And, Richard would be the first to tell anyone his dad always said, "I got respect for the Sabbath or I reckon I could top that there one."

"Now don't this just take the rag off of the bush."

An Informal History of the Revolutionary Linn Tractor

William J. O'Hern

H. H. Linn developed the Linn tractor that so changed the logging industry mostly because he needed to make a living, and saw a way to improve on the way he did that. He could not have dreamed of the impact his innovation would have on a country that was about to bid goodbye to the horse as its main source of power.

Holman Harry Linn's break-through machine. Two Linn tractors lined up outside the Morris Manufacturing Co. ready to be shipped to the Great Northern Paper Company, 1923.

Linns were important to revitalization the nation during the New Deal era. The Bonneville Dam project on the Columbia River in Washington used Linns, and the Tennessee Valley Authority used many of the big machines in numerous public works projects. Closer to home, Linns were used in creating the Stillwater Reservoir.

Courtesy of Ernest L. Portner

Holman Harry Flannery was born on May 7, 1877, to William and Lucretia Flannery. His parents divorced, and H.H. lived with his father in Washburn, Maine, until he left at 16 to live with his mother in Old Town. She had married Robert D. Linn by then, and H.H.'s name was legally changed to Linn.

Imagine a town's excitement when the Linn's Dog Show arrived in town.
Courtesy of Ernest L. Portner

Despite his lack of a high school diploma, Linn was able to make a fairly good living at first as a weaver, as a stitcher in a shoe shop, and then later when he joined a local band that toured the New England states. He soon married, and he and his new wife, Grace, combined their entertainment talents and formed a traveling minstrel road show in early June, 1915. Rene Elliott said, in "Linn Manufacturing Corp: A Brief History," that the show featured "trained dogs and a pony, their own musical and vocal talents, and

Adirondack Logging

the showing of 'moving pictures' each night, for a ten cent admission." The acrobatic animal act was touted as "The LINN DOG SHOW," painted in bold colorful letters on the sides of the coach-type wagon used to haul the show around. As the showbiz couple's reputation and income grew, Linn replaced his horse-drawn wagon with an automobile, which in itself was a crowd draw. Linn fully understood the attraction any mechanical innovation held for the rural citizens of New England.

Work at the Lombard Tractor Co. served as inspiration for H.H. Linn to build a better tractor alternative to the Lombard steam and diesel powered tractor-trucks. His vision was a product that towns, cities, contractors and lumber men would find indispensable.
Courtesy of Ernest L. Portner

In addition to "The Linn Dog Show" advertising blitz, he advertised in smaller but still conspicuous letters on both rear sides of a single track and big-engine vehicle that defined the Linn power unit of the early 1900s: "H.H. LINN Agent for LOMBARD TRACTOR ENGINES."

According to Eric Bracher's "History of the Linn Tractor," Linn's winter employment led him to an even better way to haul his road show around the country.

During the winter layovers, Linn and his wife usually returned to Maine, where he found work with the Lombard Tractor Co., whose plant was situated in Waterville, Maine. Lombard, at that time, was building a

rather curious device, intended to haul heavy logs. It mated a conven-
tional two-wheeled front end with engine to a chassis with a single
continuous-track rear axle drive, which was described as a "lag bad"
or "lag tractor tread." In or around 1911, two such machines were built
for Linn's use. The second version was more successful than the initial
attempt, and Linn used it to pull his show for several years.

During the time he worked at the Lombard Tractor Company, Linn obviously acquired much knowledge and experience, in addition to developing some of his own ideas.

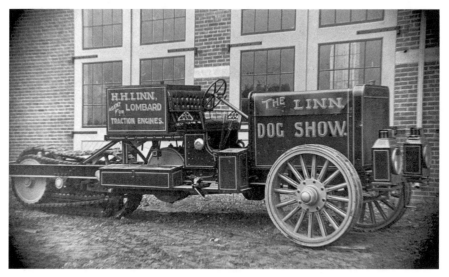

A Linn-designed gasoline-powered outfit using a single crawler track in the rear. The track was a Lombard design. Linn was, at this time, representing the Lombard Company as a traveling agent. His road show coordinated agreeably with his trips to sell Lombard machines. *Courtesy of Ernest L. Portner*

Rene Elliott and Leigh Portner are acquaintances. I consider Elliot a Linn historian. He lives in Morris, N.Y., an earshot away from the former Linn tractor manufacturing plant. Portner, a lifetime logger-mechanic-jack of all trades has been around Linn tractors since childhood. Both men have mechanical knowledge and have acquired much historical information about the manufacture and use of Linn tractors. Portner owns three Linns, all longtime machines acquired during his father's logging days. Any informal history

Adirondack Logging

H.H. Linn's traveling "house-car" or motor home, developed for his traveling road show with trained dogs. This design was inspiration for a 1925 mobile home known as the Linn Highway Haven Pullman. The motor home paved the way for an entirely new industry.

Over time Linn distanced himself from his employer. The split caused legal challenges over patents. *Courtesy of Ernest L. Portner*

of the break-through full, flexible caterpillar tread vehicle would be incomplete without including some of their knowledge about the evolution of early-era hauling-plowing road machinery—a vehicle Elliot describes as an "oddity" of "cobbled together" parts "left over from an age of primitive highways." Elliot writes:

> *A century ago the only widespread improved transportation was in marine or railroad form. So imagine yourself the proprietor of the proverbial dog and pony show in the New England States who realized that towns easily reached by rail or ship were over-saturated, while remote communities were starved for entertainment. Because theatre owners were reluctant to*

Linn's machines proved ideal solutions for road work, snow removal, lumber operations, mining and dam building operations and construction companies. This improved 1921 Linn tractor went to Gould's Camp 7. *Courtesy of Ernest L. Portner*

rent to animal acts and fire codes often prevented the use of electric lights and projection equipment, you have three or four wagons carrying tent, bleachers, props, a dozen dogs, Shetland pony, etc. You build several gas and steam-powered "road engines," only to have their steel tires sink in the mud or slip on the loose bedrock stone of what was claimed to be "improved highways."

After seeing a twenty-ton Lombard "log hauler" with steering sled in front and crawler treads in back under what looked like a small railroad locomotive, you pay Alvin Lombard a visit at his Waterville, Maine, shop to have a smaller, gasoline-powered tractor built for your needs.

While the origins of the crawler tread and thus the claims of inventing the "first practical" crawlers could be a doctoral thesis, Lombard was the first to build such a machine on a commercial basis and have

good success with it. Then, as a result of his working with H.H. Linn,
he would build and sell the first gasoline-powered crawlers, an achieve-
ment that would later be eclipsed by the dispute and rivalry that grew
between them.

Fitting his show itinerary and talents nicely, Linn became Lombard's
sales agent, demonstrator and field mechanic, spending the winter season
in various logging camps throughout Maine and New Hampshire, where
he was dubbed 'The Showman.' But after a while, Lombard's claiming
every improvement Linn made began a rift that climaxed with new
patents received by Lombard. Then Mr. and Mrs. Linn packed up their
show, having traveled through thirteen states and several Canadian
provinces looking for a home to build an even better machine before ending
up in the small upstate village of Morris, New York.[29]

1922 Linn with a 5th wheel trailer. *Courtesy of Ernest L. Portner*

In October of 1916, the Linns wintered over in Morris. Elliot explained, "Severe flooding and the resulting damage held them up long enough that they
decided to spend the winter there. Linn showed movies twice a week in the
Parish Hall, opened a gasoline engine repair shop and did hauling work with
his tractor to earn income. Once, over the winter, he built another tractor with
sled steerage in place of wheels for use on snow."

Portner added to the history. "I think the Morris Fair Grounds he rented to put up his animals and store the wagons and gear suited his tastes as a wintering ground. Linn had considered giving up show business long enough to devote his energies to manufacturing a better tractor. Hargrave Lake could provide needed water power. That's why he formed a company in Morris. His vision was to design a tractor whose caterpillar tread could adapt itself to any kind of terrain."

Linn was a self-taught engineer, Eric Bracher explains, and with a winter's worth of time on his hands he decided to improve on the Lombard house car. The "house car" idea was a forerunner to today's RVs. While his animals and equipment were housed in quarters on the fairgrounds, Linn spent the winter of 1916–1917 in an old wagon and carriage shop assembling his new vehicle.

The first 6 cylinder Linn built in 1926. In the mid-1930s both four- and six-cylinder Cummins diesel engines, as well as Waukesha engines, were offered. In later years big Hercules engines of either 707 or 935 cubic inches were also used. Transmissions used in the Linns were usually either four- or five-speed units, both in forward and reverse. The Linns were expensive pieces of equipment; the average price was approximately $20,000. *Courtesy of Ernest L. Portner*

Linn had the Brennan Motor Co. of Syracuse, N.Y. construct the mechanical components to his specifications. Visually, the most apparent distinction between his truck tractor and the Lombard was his dual-track bed. This Brennan-built machine also featured a fully flexible track unit which

A 1923 Linn with a Champion snow plow. *Courtesy of Ernest L. Portner*

> *Linn designed and later patented. This device, later known as the "Linn*
> *Flexible Traction," used a spring-loaded steel triangle pivoted at its*
> *apex, which allowed its track bed to flex and conform to the contour of*
> *the ground over which the Linn was traveling. This gave the Linn*
> *machine an unparalleled advantage over conventional trucks of the*
> *day when it came to traversing difficult terrain.*

In the spring, Linn and his wife left Morris in their much-improved vehicle
to begin their tour. After only a month, the great polio epidemic of 1917
put them out of business because of quarantines that banned all public gatherings. With no idea how long their road show would be shut down, the Linns
returned to Morris to start a new career in the manufacture of crawler tractors in the repair shop he had used. The building was renovated for use as
a temporary facility while a new factory with water power was being planned
and built. Bracher continues:

A Linn snowplow in action. *Courtesy of Ernest L. Portner*

> *Linn decided to try his hand at manufacturing machines similar to*
> *the one he'd built for his own use. The Linn Manufacturing Co. was*
> *formed in 1917, with its stock held in varying amounts by local residents.*
> *From this point on, the activities of the Linn Manufacturing Co. were*
> *both rapid and impressive.*

Working in an old building on Hargrave Lake that had previously been a
textile factory, Linn built only a dozen machines during the first year. However, as soon as the first tractor was sold to a local lumberman, word quickly
spread about the new machine.

Linn erected a modern concrete-block building, and in 1918 production
began in the new factory. It took a week to build two machines. By 1952, when
production ended, approximately 2,500 had been built.

> *In the first few years the Linn Tractor was introduced to most of the logging,*
> *excavating, heavy-hauling and roadwork industries. Snow removal*
> *was the exception. Not until 1921 did Linn start looking for a suitable*
> *snowplow. Dissatisfied with what was available, he patented his own*
> *and had it built by a Marathon, New York, road machinery company.*

When the Linn Company was at its peak, H.H. Linn sold his interest to the Republic Motor Truck Co. of Alma, Michigan, staying on as a consultant.

The Linn tractor or "half-track," as it became known, was a workhorse of mighty proportions and ability. It was a predecessor of the huge earthmovers built today by such firms as Caterpillar and Euclid. In its ultimate stage of evolution, the Linn was available in a wide variety of forms powered either by a diesel or gasoline engine. Common to all types was the "Linn Flexible Traction," the invention patented by Linn.

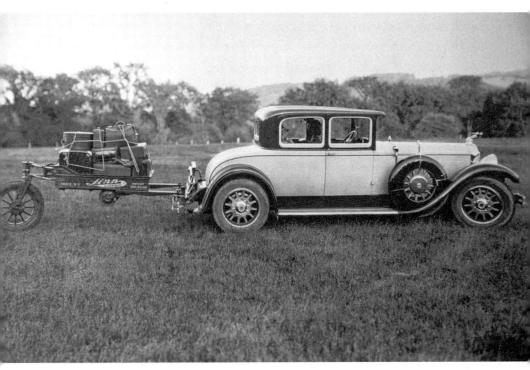

Linn's U-Can-Back line of trailers attached to a car's bumper. Linn's genius covered a wide-range of patented items. *Courtesy of Ernest L. Portner*

Linns were available in a wide variety of body styles. The basic model had a dump body with a rear tailgate and an 8–9 yard dump capacity. Linns could pull long trains of loaded trailers with a total payload of up to 50 tons. In Texas they were used to haul oil pipe castings through the oil fields. In Canada and the Great Lakes states, where snow was present so much of the year, Linn Logging Tractors often had sled steerage units in place of front tires. It was usual for these Linns to pull anywhere from 10 to 16 sleds completely loaded with logs. One Linn that operated at the Hudson Bay Mining and Smelting Co. Ltd. pulled a load of 120 tons of supplies to the company's Flon, Canada, site. Linns were even used to maintain the waterway in the Panama Canal Zone. Perhaps the most surprising purchase of Linn tractors was that made in the early 1920s by the Amotog Trading Co. in Soviet Russia.

Linn sales began to decline as competitors such as La Tourneau and Euclid developed faster earth-moving vehicles. They used immense rubber tires which had recently become available.

Portner pointed out that to move forward in the face of declining sales, "Linn sold his company to the Republic Motor Corporation. Linn stayed on as vice president in charge of engineering." It was during this time he invented a one-wheel automobile trailer called the "U-Can-Back." From this brainchild he created the Linn Trailer Corporation, based in Oneonta. Over time he added other types of trailers to the line.

"In 1931," according to Portner, "Linn returned to the Morris firm. He was responsible for developing new models that included the C-5, a front-wheel-drive with dual front wheels and both a conventional rear axle and a retractable half-track unit that could be raised or lowered as needed. Linn purchasers could select from a wide choice of body sizes and forms and a number of different engines."

In early July of 1937, at the age of 60, the Morris tractor-trailer inventor and manufacturer, his two friends and his pilot were killed when his monoplane crashed and burned shortly after taking off in Morris. The company assets were auctioned off in 1949, but even then it was obvious that the Linn was still useful for logging operations. The Linn Tractors Northwest president came to Morris to oversee the construction of two final Linns from the supply of spare parts that two local businessmen had purchased. A limited number of tractors were built until July of 1952. The last one was sold to the Montgomery County Highway Dept. in Fonda, N.Y.

Thus ended H.H. Linn's American success story.

Leigh Portner's Logging Connection with Linn Tractors

Ernest L. Portner

The Linn tractor played a huge part in ushering logging into a new and much more efficient era. In article, "Adirondack Logging," Rev. Reed meticulously explained the usefulness of the Linn tractors—the new-kid-on-the-block mechanized track machines that replaced old-style horse logging. Reed's dissertation did not say how important the Linn tractor was to the growth of the paper industry in northern New York. Nor did he mention the far-sighted industrial statesman, G.H.P. Gould, who allowed his su-perintendent, John B. Todd, to purchase the experimental machinery that became so important to the Gould Paper Company's success.

As a young boy working in his father's logging business, Leigh Portner recognized the importance of sound performing machinery. As an adult he foresaw the benefit of restoring to working condition two Linn tractors his father once used. Today, at 85, Leigh continues to operate Portner Lumber Company and Sawmill. One of his pleas-ures is to show off his favorite Linn tractor.

Because this book is an informal history, I asked Leigh to write about what he has learned and what he imparts to people who inquire about the line of now-antique Linn machinery.

The first Linn tractors used in the Adirondacks were sold to the Brooklyn Cooperage Co. and John E. Johnson of Port Leyden, N.Y. These early tractors came with a fifth-wheel trailer log sleigh, but the trailer did not work out well. One of the larger companies to use the Linns was the Gould Paper Company of Lyons Falls, N.Y.

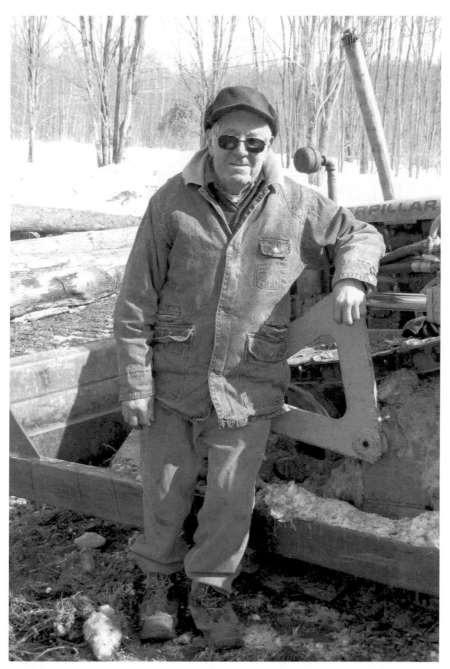

Longtime northern Oneida County logger Ernest L. Portner. Portner Lumber Company once owned six Linn tractors. Portner currently owns three Linns: No. 290, No. 1094, and No. 1290. *Photo by the author*

Adirondack Logging

Gould bought twelve tractors and a number of log sleighs to go with them. Each tractor cost about $5,000 and came with thirty sleighs each. The reason each tractor had three sets of ten sleighs, costing about $160.00 per set, was because of the high degree of breakdowns. Haul-back roads were rough. Between the sleigh's vast weight, the steep grade, and uneven jarring terrain, the equipment took a beating. Broken runners and other parts were a continuous problem. The blacksmith was responsible for constant and necessary inspection and maintenance. They cycled the sleighs: while one set of ten was being loaded, another set was being checked by the blacksmith for breakage, and another set of ten was being unloaded at the landing.

Linn Manufacturing plant before a fire destroyed it. Linn tractors were manufactured in the Otsego County town of Morris, N.Y. and were used extensively for logging in the Adirondacks during the 20th century. *Courtesy of Ernest L. Portner*

Gould bought some larger six-cylinder model Linns in 1926. Each sleigh, once loaded, averaged about ten tons. The haul roads were kept well-iced with sprinkler wagons. On a twelve-mile-long road they used four sprinklers. A sprinkler was built onto a Linn with a trailer sprinkler tank in tow. The trailer sprinkler was sixteen feet long and eight feet tall. The sprinkler box on the Linn was fourteen feet long, eight feet wide and four feet high.

Leigh and Doris Portner by the family's prized Linn tractor No. 1094. After lumber companies and highway departments retired their Linns, the vehicles were bought, repaired, and used by people for a variety of uses. Today collectors of the machinery enjoy displaying their restored motor tractors at antique steam engines and gas shows. *Courtesy of Ernest L. Portner*

Travel on the steep hills was controlled by the sand hill man. His job was to ensure the tractor driver hauling the loaded sleds had a safe descent. He'd shovel little piles of hot sand and scatter straw at regular distances along the sloping snow road to keep the loads from jackknifing on the downgrade. The stuff slowed the tracks on the descent so that the engine would have to pull hard to get the load to the bottom. The sand hill man kept a fire in the sand pit because only hot sand would stick to the sleigh runners to slow

"The snow removal field was opened for Linn in 1921 when Carl H. Fink (founder of Fink Sno-Plows, Inc.) built a crude iron plow for use with a tractor owned by F.W. Carpenter Bus Lines of Black River, N.Y. This helped motivate H.H. Linn to seek a 'working partnership' with Fink, and in 1922 snow plows, designed especially for Linn tractors, became a standard option." —Rene Eliot, "Those Creepy, Crawly Wonderful Linns," *Wheels of Time*, Vol. 6; No. 5. 1985. "Snowplows in Northern New York," *Wheels of Time*, Vol.12, No.6 1991. *Courtesy of Ernest L. Portner*

them down. Gould declared that with a properly iced road, the Linns could pull forty cords up a five-percent grade.

Along with the tractor driver was a whistle punk. He was there to warn the driver if the bull-bows broke and the log load began to buckle. If any of that happened, the driver would have the time of his life exhibiting a bit of fancy steering on a wild ride downhill, trying to get to the bottom with his life intact.

At Camp 7, at Ice Cave Mountain, the tractors were kept in a steam-heated garage. Between this camp and a similar garage at Camp 9, on the river, they kept two mechanics and a greaser busy doing maintenance. All the tractors were greased every night. When the temperatures reached forty degrees below zero, they would have to disconnect the fan belts and cover the radiators to keep them from freezing.

The Linn tractors were started and out by 4:30 in the morning. They tried to make three loaded trips per day to the Moose River landing with each tractor. Each Linn had a driver and a whistle punk who checked the toggle chains and bull pole of each sleigh as well as the binder chains on the log loads. Most of the drivers would put the tractor out of gear on the big hill that went down to the river, and let it rattle full bore. That way they wouldn't pile up the loads on the way down. The tractor drivers of the 1920s and '30s got $4.00 per day, while laborers got only $1.00 per day and board.

The riverbanks were about twenty feet high in this area. The drivers would dump the first loads from the bank into the river, and as more logs came in they would build up a log bridge across the river. They'd freeze the bridge with snow and then build another bridge about 100 feet beyond the first one. As the bridges were completed, the tractors would drive out on them and fill in between the two bridges with more logs. When the ice went out in the spring and the drive started, the logs would roll right along from the landing in the woods to the pulp mill at Lyons Falls.

This 1921 Avery tractor is another early piece of equipment in Portner's expansive collection. *Courtesy of Ernest L. Portner*

The Linn tractors were taken to a maintenance barn in Forestport, New York, each summer for overhauls and other maintenance to get them ready for the next fall. This maintenance cost Gould only about $50.00 per tractor.

Emporium Lumber Company of Cranberry Lake, New York, used Linns to haul from the woods to the mill and also to the railroad. They hauled logs

Adirondack Logging

thirty-five miles to the mill from their timber holdings. I own the No. 3 Linn that Emporium used. I got it out of the woods some years back. It needs a lot of parts, but I am working on it and hope to have it running someday.

Logger and sawmill owner Ernest Leigh Portner, July 2015 standing by his almost century-old office building. *Photo by the author*

My experience with Linns started when I was fourteen years old and my dad let me drive our Linn with a large load of hardwood logs on it. My dad, Ernest Portner, had purchased the timber rights on a large wood lot in 1938. It was the site of a Civilian Conservation Corps camp beyond Hanifin Corners in Empyville. The camp was still active. Most of the men were African-American. He bought it from the State of New York with a successful bid. These woods had never been cut, and the yellow birch and hard maple trees were thirty and forty inches on the stump. All the supplies were hauled in to camp with the Linn, and Dad had a camp built for the men and a horse barn for the teams. We had about twelve men working on this job, and we used the

Linn to haul out to the truck landing, which was about five miles. The snow was four feet deep that first winter, and sometimes the temperature was thirty below. But the Linn would always start with gas in the primer cups and a few good pulls on the crank.

My father worked in those woods three winters and four summers. Through the years Dad had six Linn Tractors: three 4-cylinder and three 6-cylinder. All were either scrapped or sold, except the 1926 4-cylinder. That was used in the winter of 1964 to haul some big pine out to the truck landing. Then it sat outside in back of our sawmill until eight years ago, when I decided to restore it. I also have the 1921 Emporium No. 3 I mentioned earlier, and a 1928 6-cylinder. Both need restoration. This past fall I took my restored 1926

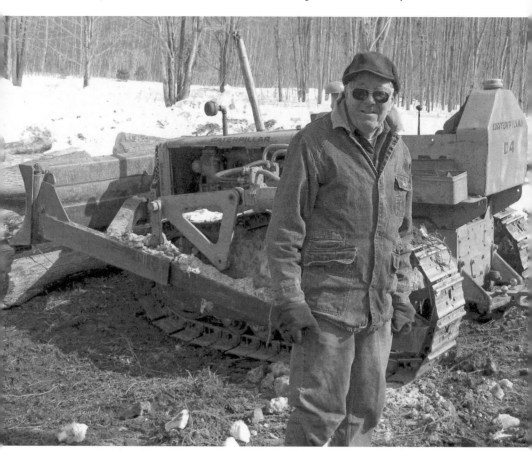

Well into his eightieth decade of life, Leigh Portner continues to log stating he doesn't think he'll quit anytime soon. Spring, 2015. *Photograph by author*

Adirondack Logging

Leigh Portner standing by family business' homemade sign, July 2015. *Photo by the author*

Linn to the New York State Woodsmen's Field Days at Boonville, New York. It made a quite a hit with the crowd.

At one time, my father also had the county snow plowing contract for snow removal on about twenty miles of road. We had three F.W.D. trucks and a 6-cylinder Linn with a V-plow and double sixteen-foot wings. With the dump box full of fifteen tons of ballast, he could plow six and eight feet of hard-packed snow with no problem. Our Linns never needed much repair work, as we kept them in good mechanical condition. They did not go fast, but they'd go through any conditions.

After the 1950s, the Linns went by the wayside as the new skidders and other machines came out. They were last used in the Adirondacks in the late 1950s, and then scrapped.

Other loggers and sawmill men throughout the state and nation also used Linn tractors from the 1930s through the 1950s. Many of the jobbers working for such outfits as Gould Paper Company, Finch Pruyn, and International Paper used Linns, as well as many smaller companies. The Linn Tractors were popular and well-regarded machines amongst the loggers and lumbermen of New York State.

Tribute to the Memory
of Ed Wheeler, Famous Cook

Rev. A.L. Byron-Curtiss, *Utica Daily Press*,
Friday, December 28, 1920

To the editor of the Press:

From far-away California in a Christmas note from "Billy" Graff, one-time bookkeeper of the Gould Paper Company. I have the belated news of the death of Ed Wheeler, for 30 years in the lumber camps. It states that he died on the trail between Camp X and Camp VII in the North Lake country. I cannot refrain from a few words of appreciation of Ed. I would rather write a eulogy of a man like him than pen a panegyric to some famous man of the day. The famous man might deserve it, and again he might not. Ed Wheeler, a humble toiler all his life, deserves at least the tribute of work well done.

Ed began cooking in the camps when salt pork, beans, bread, molasses and boiled tea were the standard of meals. It had expanded before his death into as varied a bill of fare as is served in the average good hotel. Roasted fresh meats, all kinds of vegetables, assorted pastry as well as bread, puddings and coffee are now the regular thing. And it is to the credit of Ed that he kept pace with the expansion of his art, and all within the circumscribed limits of a cookhouse of a lumber camp far removed from town conveniences. The bread had to be baked, the pies made, the doughnuts fried, the vegetables boiled along with hot meats, all on a single range and at a sectional oven, the latter only introduced in the camps within the last 10 years.

But in the seeming excitement of preparing and serving a meal to a hundred hungry, husky men, Ed never batted an eye. He would go serenely from meat block to moulding board, from the oven to the battery of kettles on the stove and have his meals on time, with only the "chore boy" for helper. In the height of "hauling," but one meal, dinner, was served in daylight; breakfast long before dawn, supper long after dark. But Ed was always on the job, once he had started in and had got his stride. Sometimes he halted and hesitated, outside. But once in the woods and he had his wind, he was the benign and efficient cook.

Ed Wheeler (center) at site of the Camp 7 machinery shed where six Linn tractors were lost in a fire. Later spring 1922. *Courtesy of John Todd (The John B. & Scudder Todd Collection)*

Lincoln once said he had noted that men who had none of the vices seldom had any of the virtues either. Well, if Ed had his failings he had his virtues, too. He was a hard worker and the urge of industry was always his. He liked to see garden truck grow and would nurse a few hills of cucumbers and beds of lettuce in the friendly virgin soil of the clearing, and if the time between frosts permitted him to secure enough cucumbers as big as his thumb to go into a salad and enough lettuce to garnish it, he was as happy as J.B. Todd when all the stock was at the river, or Harry Gould when the drive got to Lyons Falls.

Ed has to his credit in heaven the filling of many an empty stomach in quick time, when wanderers in the mountains came to his camp. I have been favored with many a "hand out" by him. If hunting or fishing anywhere within five miles of the camp where he was cook, I always made the haven of his cookhouse, when he would shove the coffee pot forward, stir up the fire and prepare me a meal as ample as my stomach was empty.

While I love the Adirondacks and love to tramp those wild back trails such as Ed passed out on, I would not care to die on one myself. It would be such a bother to get my body out for sepulcher. Yet it cannot be much of a step from such a trail right into heaven. It may be the shortest of all. Who knows? Anyway, we are sure that Ed is on a better trail now, far removed from the distractions and temptations of this lower world.

A.L. Byron-Curtiss
Philadelphia, PA—December 26, 1928

Recipe ED WHEELER'S CALIFORNIA PRUNE CAKE

Ed was a renowned and celebrated 30-year veteran Adirondack lumber camp cook for the Gould Lumber Company. Rev. Frank A. Reed remembered Wheeler once saying, "All I have to do from 9:30 p.m. to 1:30 a.m. is just sleep," when asked what it was like to feed a crew of hungry men at all hours.

Ingredients:

1 cup chopped prunes

1 cup chopped walnuts

2 cups sifted enriched all-purpose flour

414   *Adirondack Logging*

3 teaspoons baking powder

1 teaspoon salt

¼ teaspoon baking soda

½ cup shortening

1 cup granulated sugar

1 teaspoon cinnamon

½ teaspoon nutmeg

¼ teaspoon cloves

2 eggs, beaten

¾ cup prune juice and milk, mixed

Procedure: Make several days ahead, if desired. Heat oven to 350°F. Grease and flour 8 inch x 8 inch x 2 inch cake pan. Combine prunes and walnuts, and set aside. Sift flour with next three ingredients. Cream together shortening, sugar, and spices until fluffy. Add eggs, and continue to beat until very creamy. Add flour mixture, beating smooth after each addition. Stir in prunes and nuts. Pour into prepared cake pan. Bake at 350°F. about 50 minutes or until cake tester inserted in center comes out clean. Let stand 5 to 10 minutes. Turn cake out on rack, and cool. Serve plain, or frost with seven-minute frosting that has been made with prune juice instead of water. [Directions for Seven-minute Frosting were not given. Perhaps it was a recipe any cook would know in 1951, the year this recipe appeared the *The Lumber Camp News.*]

Mr. and Mrs. Lewis Holland's skills were as renowned over a hot griddle as was Ed "Bucky" Wheeler's cooking. *Courtesy of Lyons Falls History Association*

Real Horsepower

William J. O'Hern

In the logging days of real horsepower it was always a question of: How many horses were needed to get the job done?

Substantial care and effort, according to author and long time logger J.C. Ryan, "was given to matching up the horses in color, weight and gait, and no one would allow splitting up a team once they were well matched."

Teamsters who worked year after year for Gould wanted the same team of horses back each year. The men took great pride in keeping their horses in good shape, especially watching out for the animals' well-being when hauling the biggest loads up and down steep grades. Barn bosses were equally vigilant in the care of the many horses under their watch. Good care was the rule of thumb. Each horse was different, right down to how many quarts of oats per day it needed. No one wanted to overfeed, since that was what probably killed more horses than anything else.

To keep a horse in the best of shape, Gould hired a veterinarian to come into camp regularly to float the horses' teeth. Without that dental care, a horse could not properly grind its teeth.

OPPOSITE: Work horses skidded as many as 200 logs a day. It may be readily understood, therefore, that this was not an easy day's work for man or beast. *Courtesy of George Shaughnessy*

Common first aid remedies called for injuries when a horse was "calked" —its ankles stepped on with sharp shoe calks. If this happened, a teamster would apply turpentine or kerosene. It would sting and cause the animal to flounce about, but the cuts would usually heal in a few days' time.

The village blacksmith performed many services beyond being a shoer of horses.
Courtesy of the Lewis County Historical Society, from Larry J. Myers Collection

Old horses were often kept around to haul light loads and firewood. If an animal was disabled, it would have to be disposed of. To Ryan's knowledge, no lumber company he knew of would ever "let one of its horses that had worked for a number of years be sold for mink or fox food."

Adirondack Express writer Mart Allen told a distressing story in his "Men and Horses Teamed Up to Cut Adirondack Timber" column. He expressed the reality of yesteryear when he said, "Both man and horse shared the many dangers of woods work, and accidents were common… Occasionally, a horse was injured to the extent that it would have to be euthanized."

The following incident reported by Allen happened during a logging operation in a remote wooded private park. He said the practice was reaffirmed by Mickey Freeman, who was a forest ranger. At that time the gun was the accepted method to dispatch a horse, but the use of firearms was prohibited on many of the private parks.

Allen learned that the strange solution came as a result of a horse whose back had been broken by a falling tree. The landowner was very adamant about no guns being permitted on his land, so an injured animal would be subjected to prolonged suffering waiting for someone to obtain permission to retrieve a gun when dynamite was a staple on most logging jobs.

Allen's story says "Its suffering was ended by a stick of dynamite being tied to its head and detonated."

Despite the upsetting nature of this story of the "old ways" of dealing with animals, things have changed a great deal when it comes to animal welfare and business profit.

Petro-fueled horsepower meets real horsepower. *Courtesy of the Lewis County Historical Society, from Larry J. Myers Collection*

Barbara Bird's Defense
of Lumberjacks' Drinking Sprees

William J. O'Hern and Barbara K. Bird

arbara Kephart Bird's husband, Royal G. Bird, was a long-time forester for the Gould Paper Company. Barbara often accompanied her husband into Gould's lumber camps. The couple lived in a little log cottage on the shoulder of Ice Cave mountain. Over the years Barbara met or came in contact with most, if not all, of the lumberjacks who worked in Camps 5, 7, 8, 9, and

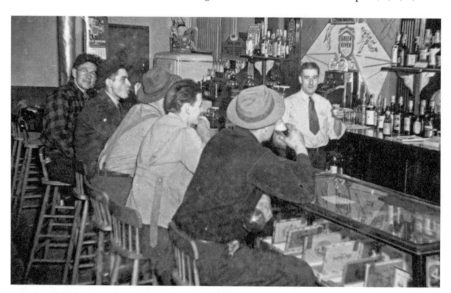

There is a perception that a lumberjack was right at home in a saloon. That was true enough for some men who enjoyed mugs of beer and shots of whiskey. *Courtesy of Harold Link*

  *Adirondack Logging*

10. She knew their lives were not easy or safe. She has said, "Lumberjacks work hard, live hard, die hard." Her opinion of a forester's life wasn't much different. She recognized it too was neither safe nor easy. Royal also "works long and laboriously, faces hazards and endures hardships," she has said.

"Ma" Getman's Hotel, Forestport, N.Y. Spruce fever often drove the 'jacks crazy and out of the Black River headwaters when they got a two- or three-hundred dollar stake. Then, stake-bound, they headed out of the woods. Sometimes they made it as far as Utica, where the saloons and the women along Water Street got their money. Sometimes they only made it as far as Ma's Place, a roadhouse in Forestport. *Courtesy of Leola Schmelzle*

Bird witnessed first-hand the work of Rev. Reed as "The Lumberjacks' Sky Pilot." She attended his church-building services in camp, listened to his sermons addressing protection against their weakness for alcohol, and was outspoken against tavern owners who filled their saloon tills with lumberjacks' money and often turned a blind eye when a 'jack was rolled and robbed of his stake while in a stupefied condition.

Barbara Bird said this about the loggers.

> *The men in the remote camps were professionally superior, and they took great pride in their work. They did not drink while in camp. This abstinence coupled with the lack of diversions during long months in the woods, may account for the drinking sprees in which many of them indulged*

when they reached town. The additional fact that they were then in pos-
session of several months' accumulated pay did not help the situation.

I suspect that the average lumberjack is best known to civilization when
he is in town on a spree. He is an all-too-evident object of contempt at
that time, and unfortunately the impression persists in the minds of
most people who run across him. Hence he has acquired a bad name for
himself. It is undeniable that many lumberjacks drink. It is also unde-
niable that, when he is under the influence of liquor, the lumberjack is
promptly fleeced of his hard-earned cash by creatures who prey on him.
If any contempt is warranted, it might better rest on the human vul-
tures who make their living by enticing men to drunkenness and then
robbing them. The lumberjack earns his pay with sweat, skill and hard
work. He is in no sense malicious. At his worst, he is not as bad as the
parasites who exploit him and consider themselves smart in doing it!

Although they earn their money so arduously, lumberjacks spend it
freely. That is their idea of real fun. I know of one lumberjack who
labored for months to earn eight hundred dollars. At the end of ten days
in town it was all gone. I have seen another lumberjack who had several
twenty-dollar bills wadded around some greasy pliers in his hip pocket.
He bought a watch for eighty dollars when he went to town, and two
days later, while drunk, he gave it away.

There was one lumberjack who made it a practice to buy a second-
hand car whenever he went to town. Then he would go out and wreck
it. One time he hired a man to drive him around. They went from one
saloon to another till someone asked our lumberjack friend why he did
not buy a drink for his chauffeur. Hs reply was emphatic. "Hell! One
of us has to stay sober to drive the car!" Eventually he grew less careful.
He went out alone with the car one day and broke his neck.

New York State
Woodsmen's Field Days

Edited and with Commentary by William J. O'Hern

I n the editorial column, page two of the *Lumber Camp News*, July 1948 issue, Rev. Frank A. Reed succinctly defined a first-of-its-kind event that the Woodsmen's Club[30] promoted—"its first Field Day at Old Forge on July 17." Reed suggested, "This may be the first in a series of such events promoted annually in the area. It might easily become one of four or five promoted in the Northeast."

Fourth from Lt. Rev. Frank Reed in a late 1940s NYS Woodsmen's Parade in Tupper Lake. Tupper Lake was considered the capital of New York's lumbering industry. Lumber companies, paper companies, lumber operators, the State Conservation Department, the U.U. Forest Service, Adirondack woodsmen, the forestry colleges, and the local community all cooperated to make the event a success. *Courtesy of the Goff-Nelson Memorial (Tupper Lake) Library*

The lumberjack field day did meet with enthusiastic success. And true to Rev. Reed's prediction it continues to this day as a nationally-attended NYS Woodsmen's Field Days event.

The first field day was held in Old Forge, N.Y., in 1948, conducted to raise funds for the benefit of the Woodsmen's Club, founded by Rev. Reed. The fledgling event was a great success, with over 1,300 attendees and a profit of $600.

In 1949, because of lack of adequate facilities in Old Forge, a decision was made to move the Field Days to Tupper Lake, N.Y. It was held there for the next thirteen years.

A parade is the first event on the program. Shown is Grand Marshall Leigh Portner and his Linn in the 2000 N.Y.S. Woodsmen's Field Day Parade in Boonville, N.Y.
Courtesy of Ernest L. Portner

Page 45 in 67th Anniversary Celebration NYS Woodsmen's Field Days Souvenir Program provides a concise historical review of the event.

Tupper Lake was fortunate in having dedicated men who promoted, produced and improved the Woodsmen's Field Days for participants, exhibitors and spectators. In 1962, the Woodsmen's Field Days were moved from Tupper Lake to Boonville, N.Y., with the understanding that the event would be sponsored every other year by each North Country community. Boonville was chosen because of the excellent facilities available at its Oneida County Fairgrounds.

Until 1971, the event was hosted by Tupper Lake and Boonville. However, in 1972, the Tupper Lake Chamber of Commerce found it impossible to sponsor the 25th annual Field Days. On being notified of Tupper Lake's decision, the Boonville Area Chamber of Commerce elected to sponsor the Field Days on an annual basis rather than let them lapse.

Due to the event's size and the planning work involved, it was segregated from the Boonville Area Chamber of Commerce and became incorporated as a non-profit organization, the NYS Woodsmen's Field Days, Inc. Today, the corporation employs two full-timers and one part-timer throughout

67th N.Y.S. Woodsmen's Field Days, August 15, 2015. The three days are consumed by the various activities—a parade which includes floats depicting logging processes and other phases of Adirondack life both past and present; the crowning of a queen; demonstrations of logging equipment; and numerous contests in which experienced lumbermen and lumberwomen from New York and other states match their skill and strength. The contests include chopping, cross-cut sawing, buck saw, horse-pulling, chain saw, log rolling and tree felling to name a few. *Photographers George Capron and Betty Haig. Photos courtesy of the Boonville Herald*

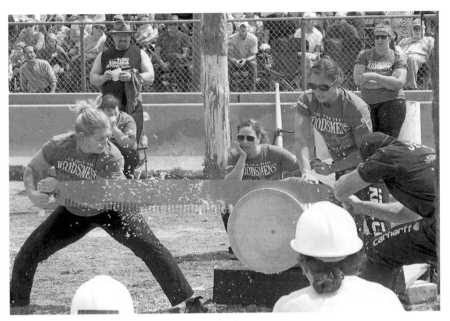

Lumber Jill and Lumber Jack competitors come from all over the United States.
Photographers George Capron and Betty Haig. Photos courtesy of the Boonville Herald

the year. In 1982, the corporation purchased a building on Main Street in Boonville and through efforts of volunteers and donations from forestry-related businesses and organizations, it was restored and named the Rev. Frank A. Reed Memorial Building. It is home to the offices of the Boonville Area Chamber of Commerce, the NYS Timber Producers' Association and the NYS Woodsmen's Field Days, Inc.

Held annually the third weekend in August, the three-day action-packed event now attracts over 40,000 spectators to the Village of Boonville. It is billed as one of the top three lumberjack shows in the United States by professional lumberjacks who compete in fierce competition throughout the weekend.

During the Field Days, you can mix business with pleasure. Exhibitors throughout the United States and Canada display and demonstrate the latest forest industry tools, technology and equipment. Visitors can watch wood carvers and visit wood-related businesses in the area. Other activities include forestry-related seminars, a wood crafts show, a foot and classic canoe and kayak race, a beard contest, hydraulic loader and skidder contests, judging of log trucks, a parade, a horse-skidding competition, a tug-of-war, a greased pole climb, the World's Open Lumber Jill championship log rolling, chain sawing, axe throwing, crosscut log rolling, dinners and dancing, music, fireworks and more.

There is no way this event could take place without the help of volunteers, and today there are over 300 members in the "Field Days family" of volunteers. The corporation business is conducted by a twelve-member Board of Directors, all of whom are volunteers. Meetings are held each month throughout the year. The Woodsmen's Planning Committee consists of over 26 volunteers, each responsible for some part of the weekend. The Planning Committee meets in February and then again starting in June, through September.

The three-day event highlights the old and the new. *Photographers George Capron and Betty Haig. Photos courtesy of the Boonville Herald*

Through the generous support of sponsors, donations from forest industry businesses and the untiring efforts of the volunteers producing the weekend, the NYS Woodsmen's Field Days, Inc. is able to further its goals and objectives. The proceeds from the Field Days are used to further promote the forest industry. The corporation hosts a number of scholarships in area

The men who were proud to call themselves lumberjacks were a hardy bunch, able to endure most everything that came their way—whether it was long periods away from their families or Mother Nature thrashing them with snowstorms and deep bone-chilling temperatures.

Rev. Frank Reed talks with a Watertown television reporter about his nostalgic and historic logging films, and it's safe to assume they discussed the "Spruce Fever" that some loggers sought to cure after months in the lumber camps and the end of the spring log drive.

Reed's 1930s and '40s films, shot by the sky pilot who visited lumber camps through-out the Adirondack-North Country, was a project between WPBS television and Rev. Reed.

Photo by C. Wesley Brewster, Syracuse, N.Y. Courtesy of Phyllis W. White, Executive Coordinator and Debi Ryder, Executive Assistant of the NYS Woodsmen's Field Days, Inc.

schools for students majoring in forestry and/or conservation. Seminars, a "safety days" brochure and safety video, and hosting workshops for the purpose of training future lumberjacks are just a few of the projects that have been completed and carried out by members of the corporation.

The Woodsmen's Club, still in existence today, is a non-profit organization dedicated to helping woods workers and maintaining cemetery lots in several Adirondack communities for woodsmen without families. The club also funds substantial scholarships to students attending Paul Smith's College.

The Impact of
Logging's Mechanization

William J. O'Hern

The lumberjacks who felled the Adirondack timber worked for logging enterprises like the Gould Paper Company. Commercial logging followed the expansion of America as companies strove to keep up with the rapid pace of progress. For well over a century, timber harvesting became one of the top industries in the Adirondack Mountains.

The loggers used double-bitted axes, two-man cross cut saws, pike poles, peaveys and calked shoes, horses and other early methods to bring the trees down and drive the logs down waterways to the mills. Rapidly improving technology throughout the 20th century allowed more trees to be harvested in less time. Transportation also caught up to the task of moving the massive tonnage of softwood and later hardwood logs. Railways and mechanical tracked vehicles replaced oxen, horses and sleighs.

The gradual mechanization of America's logging industry from the introduction of the Linn tractors in the second decade of the twentieth century greatly changed the way lumberjacks worked and interacted with forest ecosystems. Business owners like H.P. Gould understood the benefits of introducing machinery. Gould was aware that it would affect employment, as more reliance on machinery would mean less need for manpower. Forest silviculture was teaching lower impact selective methods on timber jobs. In addition to the use of machinery to harvest timber, Gould brought on board formally trained foresters like Royal G. Bird—whose wife, Barbara K. Bird, is the author of *Calked Shoes, Life in Adirondack Lumber Camps,* 1952.

Foresters, like today's forestry consultants, had a healthy respect for the Big Woods. Properly executed management plans would provide sustainable yields of high-quality timber for years to come. None of these changes came about, however, without conflict. There was and still is often heated discussion between two worldviews: first, a belief in the "old" methods that often focused on short-term profit, and second, the emerging "new" ethic of restraint regarding impact on the environment .

As petroleum-fueled machines harvested and removed trees with rising regularity, one might have drawn the conclusion that the business of harvesting timber was going to negatively affect the forest environment. Crews regularly built roads, skidways and landings, and those logging sites did have an impact on the land, often making regeneration a longer process in the high-impact areas. But H.P. Gould and his foresters made serious efforts toward forest conservation. They did not want wildlife habitat to be adversely affected; they made efforts not to have ecosystems negatively altered by wind and rain; and they knew how to handle the forest floor properly so the soil was not made less fertile by nutrients depletion. Sustaining forest resources was a Gould Company priority. However, as it is today, even with all the early cautionary techniques used at the time, there were complaints and divergent philosophies—such as that the land was left unattractive, that logging activity might adversely affect tourism, and that there was an inherent richness in sustaining woodland. Similar heated debate continues today. People still struggle with these divergent philosophies and continue to search for common ground between them.

Forest owners and loggers Ernest Portner and Warren Mathis worked in logging during the time when the forestry industry became increasingly mechanized. Now into the eighth decade of their lives, they continue to see the number of logging jobs decrease as the number of 21st-century machines used for logging purposes increases. They have raised their voices questioning what the future for logging will be like in the face of ever-larger kinds of machinery being used and forestry practices being followed today.

Portner and Mathis are outdoors-oriented people. Their collective hearts have developed strong personal connections with the logging woods. They

In the modernized logging industry, diesel powered trucks have replaced old-fashioned real horse power and water-powered river drives to transport logs from forest to mill.
Photograph by Jim Pakin/Dollar Photo Club

also see the Big Woods as a place for their physical and spiritual nourishment, and yet one hears a favorite declaration on the subject: "What is going to become of the woodland for tomorrow?"

They saw the first chainsaw rapidly replace the bucksaw and axe as the 'jacks favored means of felling trees after the mid-1950s, and they witnessed

Adirondack Logging

increasingly complex machinery to fell, delimb, process, and transport wood to the mill sites. These methods not only eliminated even more jobs, but also reorganized the way loggers worked. The introduction of the wheeled skidder in the 1960s is just one example of how a single piece of machinery eliminated the need for teams of loggers. In fact, one owner-operator could act as a 'feller' who cut the trees, then become a skidder operator who hauled the logs out of the forest, and then the 'buck,' one who chopped the logs into smaller segments at the landing where logs would be loaded onto trucks for transport to the mill site. Logging has become more mechanized with the introduction of slashers, feller forwarders, and single-grip harvesters.

As previously mentioned, older and younger generations of loggers differ in their opinions, knowledge and skills. But listen to Wayne Kwasniewski, a timber harvester and forestry consultant who provides management plans and appraisals. He has heard his share of philosophizing, cogitating, procrastinating and complaining. His slant gives me faith in the correctness of the future path of the timber industry in the Adirondacks and on Tug Hill.

"Yes, I've heard all the same complaints from old-timers like Warren and others. I guess it's just human nature why people feel the way they do.

"I remember when my uncles (J&C Lumber Co.) finished cutting off the Gould/Georgia Pacific property, which is now the Corrigan Tract, the old-timers then thought the same thing. That property has been cut two or three times since and we are harvesting there now. Other than the skid trails being wider, with all of the BMP's [best management practices] and regulations in place today, I'm not sure there is any more or less impacts on the forest today with the advent of mechanization. It has made the industry much safer.

One thing I find ironic is as far back as the 1930s and continuing into the '60s, streams and brooks on Tug Hill were bulldozed and used for truck roads and river drives. During that time frame most were teeming with brook trout and anyone could drink from them without the fear of giardia. Today, after 50 years of the government protecting the water quality, the trout are all but gone and you don't dare drink from the streams.

"Look, there are way more environmental controls on the forest industry now than there ever were in the old days. Most foresters and loggers today adhere to the best management practices outlined by the DEC. Plus today many loggers are trained as certified New York State loggers.

"On the 30,000 acre Corrigan Tract that I work on, the property is SFI [sustainable forestry initiative] certified and we get audited on a regular basis by a third party. We flag a 100-foot buffer along all classified streams, wetlands and vernal pools. We can have limited harvest inside these buffers, but only high-grade trees are cut if they can be extracted with limited impact. The shade integrity and water quality is a priority. Along both branches of the Salmon River there is a 200-foot no-cut buffer. We mark wildlife and heritage trees to be left in the residual stand. We are professionals and we know what we are doing.

"It makes me laugh when I hear non-industry people complain about current harvest and management techniques. I've heard it all my life. When Gould's, Lyons Falls Pulp and Paper, etc. sold these properties, lay people said, 'There's no timber left.' Funny we are still harvesting on these properties, and the trees are growing while I write this e-mail.

"As usual, people criticize what they don't understand.

"In a nutshell, eight years ago when I started working for Molpus Woodlands Group on the Corrigan Tract, I thought where the hell am I going to find any timber to cut after Wagner woodlands got done managing it for the former investor? Well, 30,000 acres is a big chunk of land, and I've even surprised myself with just how much timber volume there is left on this tract. We harvested a 300-plus acre sale last summer (2014) that had not been cut since the 1970s and have another 300 to 400-acre sale set to harvest next summer that also hasn't been cut since the 1970s. Currently we are harvesting a 700-acre sale that too has not been cut since the 70's. We are harvesting less than 1000 acres annually on this property, so it's easy to see we can work on a 30-year harvest rotation, plus our management plan is approved by the state Department of Environmental Conservation."

Modern practices will continue to be talked about—even denounced and demonized by some. Environmental impact regulations and technological advancements in the logging industry have had both negative and positive effects on forest ecosystems. Logging can cause irreparable harm to both the environment and the wildlife population, but with education and state and federal forestry acts that enforce conservation measures, I believe loggers I know will continue to take a stand for conservation. After all, it is the only way their industry can continue.

Ernest Leigh Portner's Old Iron Disease

William J. O'Hern

I ron, steam and diesel engines, oil, grease, and gasoline seem to be in the blood of folks who enjoy restoration of century-old machinery. History ties together generations of men and women creating a network of "family-types" of collectors, restorers and general-interest men and women throughout America—i.e., some collect tractors, some collect hit-and-miss engines, some only certain manufactured brands.

I razz my long-time friend, professional logger and Linn collector-enthusiast Leigh Portner, telling him he likes anything with tracks, wheels and a motor. It started when he was a young boy working in his father's logging business.

I am kidding, in a nice way, when I say Portner is a character with "old iron disease" who loves vintage machinery. Leigh and I have bushwhacked into some rough backcountry to find remnants of early motorized logging machinery. It's easy to see why the logger admires the antique machinery.

Besides tramping the unmarked depths of the far reaches of forest, with Leigh in search of former logging sites for discarded Linn parts and logging equipment, we hope to stumble across an intact Linn vehicle some day. Leigh calls them "ghosts in the woods."

I tell Leigh he needs to write a book about his passion. He says, "No one book can tell all the hardship and the practical knowledge acquired, and"— he adds as he hands me a snapshot of a big gas-powered Lombard-tracked motor home with a string of wagons from his extensive collection of heavy steam and gasoline track-related photos—"it'd be awful difficult to write a comprehensive nuts-and-bolts type history because it would need to be extensively detailed to be completely thorough.

"The history of steam-powered crawlers goes at least as far back as 1854 in California. We're talking about so far back in the movement, when Holman Harry Linn and Alvin Lombard crossed paths, when Linn needed a road engine."

My knowledge doesn't come to the kneecaps of Leigh's, but like other people I enjoy hearing and learning about the change in methods in forestry practice that gave rise to the Linn gasoline-powered vehicles, and the evolution that then made the use of the Linn obsolete.

Without Leigh's help about the line of now-antique Linn machinery and his generous offer to share his collection of logging pictures and memorabilia, this work would never have been as complete.

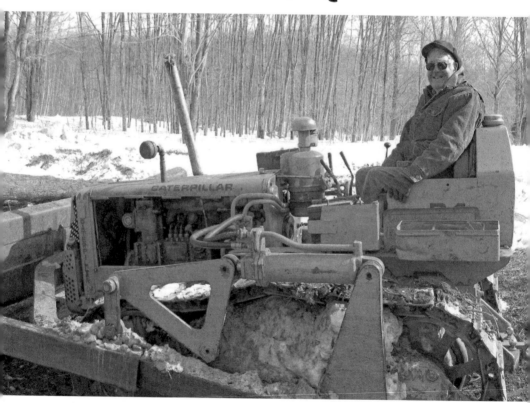

Leigh Portner, spring 2015. *Photograph by author*

ACKNOWLEDGEMENTS

The majority of the people who helped me in this historical story are mentioned in the text, but it is important to acknowledge everyone for their assistance—whether large or small—for without their help *Adirondack Logging* would not have been possible to develop.

I extend my gratitude to Katherine K. Lewis, Director of the Goodsell Museum, Town of Webb Historical Association, and Kristy Rubyor, Town of Webb Historical Association Administrative Assistant, who were extremely helpful in both looking for photographs from their association's archives and allowing me to poke through the association's files. Thanks also to Ernest Leigh Portner, Phyllis W. White, and Eric Johnson.

A very special thanks goes to my friend, Mary L. Thomas, and to Neal Burdick. Mary has been my invaluable resource from the outset of the manuscript's development. Mary's sound advice is valuable for anyone who has a story to tell. She reviewed and edited the initial draft and made composition and creative suggestions as well as last-minute additions that crept in right up to the time of printing.

Neal Burdick edited the final draft. His constructive comments and observations tightened and focused each chapter.

I would also like to express a sincere thank you to Emmel D. Abele Jr.; Mart Allen; Edward Blankman; Gerald Bourdage; Eric Bracher; Jim and Terry Breen; Janet Burt; George Capron; George R. Cataldo; Dick Cox; John Donahue; Rene Elliott; Clifford H. Gill; Betty Haig; Sandy Hrim; Rob Igoe, President of North Country Books, Inc.; Dr. Martha Tyler John; Gilbert H. Jordan II;

Joe Kelly, owner-publisher of the *Boonville Herald*; Debra Kimok, Special Collections Liberian, Feinberg Library, Plattsburgh State University of New York; Wayne Kwasniewski; Warren Mathis; Peg Mauer, Librarian, Goff-Nelson Memorial Library, Tupper Lake, N.Y.; M. Lisa Monroe, Editor of the *Adirondack Express*; Bambi K. Norman; Jane N. Lormore; Daniel P. McGough, Resource Manager, Lyons Falls Pulp and Paper; Catherine Mooney; Mallory Norris, Lewis County Historical Society volunteer and Director of the Mennonite Heritage Farm; Carol Nortz; Jerry Perrin, Office Manager/Curator and Board Member of the Lewis County Historical Society; Mary Pesez-Kames; Cindy Pritchard; Erich Ruger; Gail M. Simmons; Ken Sprague; Edna Stalley; John Todd Jr.; Scott Todd; Shirley T. VanNest, Lyons Falls History Association; Stormy Wylie, *Wheels of Time* magazine editor; Roy E. Wires; and Lee Young, American Truck Historical Society Archivist.

Last, I would also like to acknowledge, posthumously, Frederick J. Allsup; Mrs. Aunsworth [sic]; John Carney; George Glyndon Cole; Matthew J. and Madge Conway; Rev. A.L. Byron-Curtiss; Maitland C. DeSormo; O. Lovell Day; Arthur S. Draper; Mary Rita Gadway; Bertha Gill; Helen Ireland Hays; Dr. Harry F. Jackson; Dr. Silas C. Kimm; Ernestine Koenig; Nellie Lance; George Lanktree; William H. McCarthy; Orison Street Marden; Dorothy Mooney; Irene Munger; Patrick O'Brien; Bill Okusko; Marjorie Z. O'Hern; Carlton B. Olds; Roselle Putney; Edward R. Raymond; Henry Ruber; Erich Ruger; George Shaughnessy; Leola Schmelzle; Ruby Donahue Stevens; Harriet Sweeney; Casber C. Thompson; Dante O. Tranquille; Ethel Tripp; Robert A. Wells; Florence E. Western; Mary Ruth White; Howard Wieman; Emily Mitchell Wires; Lawton Williams; Fred Worden; and Ethel S. Zysset.

I have made every effort to acknowledge the assistance of everyone who helped with this project; any omission is an unintentional oversight.

FOOTNOTES

1. For more on Rev. Reed, see Collection IV. (pg. 3)

2. A rosser was a man who, when a tree had fallen, came up with an ax to remove the bark, halfway around, from one end of each of the logs into which the tree would be sawn. Whether the log was drawn to a nearby skidway or snaked out, the peeled end of the log would considerably ease the labor of the horses. (pg. 18)

3. A Jack Works is a pond where four-foot or twelve-foot logs are taken out of the water on a trough. A man stands on a platform out over the water and directs logs using a long pike pole into a chain-driven chute or elevator. Logs are lifted out of the water and deposited at a railroad siding. (pg. 24)

4. The term refers to loggers brought into the United States to take positions vacated by Americans who joined the armed forces. The Gould Paper Company, Finch Pruyn and other logging employers paid the bond to the federal government as an assurance that foreign workers stayed in the country for only a certain period of time. When the 'jacks, returned home, the bond was returned. It acted as an insurance policy that a foreign worker would not stay illegally. (pg. 31)

5. Charles W. Pratt was a long-time active in Northern New York industries. Pratt was recognized as a keen businessman whose interests were closely allied with the paper making and lumber industry. He was in part responsible for the formation o the Black River Telephone Company in 1900. (pg. 38)

6. The McCarthy brothers, Bill, Jim and Pat contracted with the Gould Paper Company for the removal of Gould's last stands of spruce and hemlock from their Tug Hil tract. (pg. 47)

7. "M" stands for a thousand board feet. A board foot is 1 inch thick by 12 inches square. Logs taper. For instance a ten foot log 12 inches on the small end is 49 board feet. On a Doyle-Scribner scale, 60 logs make up 2,800 to 3,000 board feet. (pg. 48)

8. A very important job in getting logs out of the woods. A swamper kept logs moving—he cut off limbs from the sawed off-logs and made skidding trails into the fallen logs for the horses. Quite often swamping was done by older men who had slowed down some but knew how to handle and plan a good swamping job. (pg. 57)

9. A "work horse." An organized, efficient person who sees that the work is done properly. (pg. 57)

10. Colvin was a big-time lumber business operator in the Tug Hill area and throughout the Adirondacks. See "George Colvin'sLogging Operations," *The Northeastern Logger*, August–September, 1952. (pg. 58)

11. See "C.J. Strife Adirondack Operations," *The Northeastern Logger*, November, 1952. (pg. 58)

12. The Lombard Steam Log Hauler Co. and Holt-Best caterpillar tractors were competitors of Linns. (pg. 62)

13. Sizing or size is any one of numerous specific substances that is applied to or incorporated in other material, especially papers and textiles, to act as a protecting *filler* or *glaze*. Sizing is used in papermaking and textile manufacturing to change the absorption and wear characteristics of those materials; it is the term used for oil-based surface preparation for gilding (and is also known as mordant in this context); and it is used by painters and artists to prepare paper and textile surfaces for some art techniques. —from Wikipedia, the free encyclopedia. (pg. 105)

14. Rev. Byron-Curtiss' experience is recorded in Ch. 26 "Life in a Lumber Camp," *Under an Adirondack Influence: The Life of A.L. Byron-Curtiss 1871–1959*, The Forager Press, 2008. (pg. 114)

15. The proposed Higley-Panther Mountain dam battles began in 1945. The proposal was made by the Black River Regulating District Board and approved state agencies. In 1955 the people of New York State decisively defeated the proposed amendment to Article XIV of the State Constitution, which would have permitted the construction of the dams on the South Branch of the Moose River. It was one of the longest and most costly battle in

Adirondack political history. *The Forest Preserve 1945–1955*, authored by Paul Schaefer, provides an in-depth review of those ten critical years in the history of the Adirondacks. (pg. 138)

16. Joe McDermott of Port Leyden became a logging operator later in life. (pg. 143)

17. William H. "Bill" McCarthy. (pg. 145)

18. "'Uncle' Jack's bear story" in *Adirondack Stories of the Black River Country*, 2003. (pg. 241)

19. The book became a best-seller. It has been reprinted multiple times. See *Under an Adirondack Influence: The Life of A.L. Byron-Curtiss 1871–1959*, The Forager Press, 2008. (pg. 241)

20. See *Adirondack Stories of the Black River Country*, North Country Books, Inc., 2003. (pg. 242)

21. Details of this Iowa-owned company is found in "The Rice Veneer Company Adirondack Operations," *The Northeastern Logger*, June, 1952. (pg. 246)

22. Further history about Swancott Mills and an indepth story of the lumbering industry on Tug Hill Plateau can be found in "On Tug Hill Lumbering," *Tug Hill Country: Tales from the Big Woods* by Harold E. Samson, North Country Books. (pg. 250)

23. Cookees were assistants to the cooks. They washed dishes, built fires, assisted in the food preparation, and delivered meals when lumbermen were too far from camp to return to the dining hall. (pg. 252)

24. Griffin wasn't alone in his praise for this Forestport Station community leader who was always ready to help the sick, call for a doctor, mail letters or deliver a message to a neighbor. Jesse LaPatra described James's generosity in an undated article that appeared in the *Boonville Herald*.

Saw Sharpening. *Courtesy of Lyons Falls History Association*

"Most of the men in the community were lumberjacks and there would be little or no money while they were in the woods until the man who drove the tote-team or tote-tractor came out for supplies and brought with him 'chits' for the families to pay bills with." (pg. 288)

25. Barbara Kephart Bird's father, the late Horace Kephart, authored *The Book of Camping and Woodcraft; Our Southern Highlanders; Camp Cookery; Sporting Firearms*, and other books. He was a recognized authority on the subject of camping and life in the wilderness. *Our Southern Highlanders*, first published in 1913, was reprinted for a third time in 2001. (pg. 300)

26. A long explanation of just what constitutes Tug Hill Country is best read in the 1971 book *Tug Hill Country: Tales from the Big Woods* by Harold E. Samson. Samson does not list Warren in the acknowledgements, but he did note Rev. Frank A. Reed and other men and women who had a connection with Warren. Regional historian Samson

would have heard such a gamut of true stories and tall tales from Warren that it might have provided him with a third book on the region's history, the place where Warren has been slammin' through the trees for a lifetime. I wouldn't doubt ole Warren might have even discovered a few subspecies of supernatural hardwoods in his travels—woods like wormy beaver bark in Boyston, pecker-hole jackpot maple in Redfield, and the Martinsburg sideways-leaning maple that grows along one of the many streams that begin in the tremendous watershed of The Tug—of course foresters might consider his claims more folklore than reality.

Their arguments wouldn't deter Warren. As I said, Warren has been around. (pg. 365)

27. National Grid today. (pg. 380)

28. Niccolls Memorial Church was named in honor of Dr. Samuel L. Niccolls of St. Louis, Missouri, who had a camp on First Lake. (pg. 381)

29. As an interesting tangent to enthusiasts who find these early era motor vehicles fascinating subjects, Don Chew points out in his article "Tracks and Screws?—A.O. Lombard and H.H. Linn" article: "At the same time that Lombard and Linn were working on their tracked vehicles, up the road in Bangor, Maine, Mr. Peavey was busy developing a different idea. From 1900–1905, he worked on designing a vehicle which moved across both frozen and unfrozen ground on a pair of large screws. Peavey's log haulers excelled at pulling logs on snow and ice, especially when going uphill." (pg. 397)

30. Rev. Reed worked tirelessly to establish a club house for the old-time lumberjacks. He believed "Such a club-house should provide comfortable beds, good meals, showers and some recreation." The chapter "The Woodsmen's Club" in *Lumberjack Sky Pilot* explains the need for such a facility. (pg. 424)

SOURCES

Sources and Suggested Reading About Logging

CORRESPONDENCE

William J. O'Hern and Rene Elliot,
August 07, 2010.

William J. O'Hern and Rene Elliot,
February–March 2011.

William J. O'Hern and Jim Breen,
December 2010.

William J. O'Hern and Scott Todd,
December 2010.

William J. O'Hern and Edna Stalley,
November 2010–January 2011.

William J. O'Hern and Richard Raymond,
December, 1998.

MAGAZINES, BOOKS AND NEWSPAPERS

_____. "Adirondack Rivers and Lumbermen."
[Regarding the Court of Appeals Moose
River Case.] *Albany Journal*, June 7, 1899.

_____. "Logging with Linns: Methods and
Practices Employed by the Cascade Limber
Co.'s Contract Loggers." Magazine and
Date Unknown.

_____. "To Protect Pulp Lands." *The Paper
Mill and Wood Pulp News*, October 11, 1909.

_____. "Back River Telephone Co."
The Journal and Republican, 1909.

_____. "New Telephone Rates." *The Journal
and Republican*, March 24, 1910.

_____. "Dix As Governor To Drop Business."
The New York Times. November 11, 1910.

_____. "No Debt To Pay To Any One—Dix."
The New York Times. November 13, 1910.

_____. "Three Die in Flames as
Plane Crashes Near Morris Airfield."
Oneonta Daily Star, July 6, 1937.

_____. "Lumberjacks' Clergyman
Accepts Forestport Call."
Source unknown. April 22, 1942.

_____. "John B. Todd, 78 Dies at His
Home." *Daily Sentenial*, Rome, N.Y. March
18, 1943.

_____. "Scudder Todd, Prominent
Citizen of Lyons Falls, Died Suddenly
in Watertown." Unknown source and
year. November 7, _____.

_____. "McKeever Dam Washes Out."
Lumber Camp News. June, 1947.

_____. "Logging on the Moose."
North Country Life, Spring 1948.

_____. "Rice Veneer Company Buys
McKeever." *Lumber Camp News*. August, 1949.

_____. "Gould Paper Company Sold."
Source and date unknown.

_____. "Paper Making at Lyons Falls."
North Country Life, Fall 1949.

_____. "Gould's Old-Time Logging
Operations." *The Northeastern Logger*.
Vol. 1; No. 7, February 1953.

_____. "Holman Harry Linn (1877–1937),
Showman: His Lombard Connection."
(unknown source).

_____. "A 1900 View of New York's
Lumber Industry Part II." *York State
Tradition*, Summer 1953.

_____. "Rev. Frank Reed's Dream 'Come
True.' Woodsman's Club Opens Tonight at
Forestport." Source and date unknown.

_____. "Robert A. Wells, 56, Expires Suddenly." The Utica *Daily Press*, February 24, 1962, 1974.

_____. "Bygone Years." The *Booneville Herald*, April 3, 1974.

_____. "Reed Would Have Been Proud of His Memorials." *The Northern Logger*, March 1981.

_____. "The Linn, a New England Truck: Workhorse Around the World." *Double Clutch*, A publication of Antique Truck Club of America, Inc. Volume 16, No. 6, January/February 1986.

_____. "The Rev. Frank A. Reed Dead at Age 85." Source and date unknown.

_____. "The Last Log Drive," *Moose River Quarterly*, Page 16–17 [no date given].

Ackerson, Robert C. Linn tractor history found in manuscript form in the archives at Rough and Tumble Engineers Historical Association at Kinzers, Maine.

Allen, Mart. "Food Was One Of Few Amenities Offered At Early Lumber Camps." *Adirondack Express*, October 24, 1995.

Allen, Mart. "'Gee' And 'Haw' Guided Logging Horses At Work." *Adirondack Express*, October 31, 1995.

_____. "Men And Horses Teamed Up To Cut Adirondack Timber." *Adirondack Express*, November 7, 1995.

_____. "WWII Machinery Development Influenced Lumber Industry." *Adirondack Express*, November 14, 1995.

_____. "Rev. Frank A. Reed, Lumberjack Sky Pilot." *Adirondack Express*, June 14, 2005.

Allsup, Fredrick J. "A Christmas Fire." *Lumber Camp News*, December 1948.

Bird, Barbara Kephart. *Calked Shoes: Life in Adirondack Lumber Camps*. Prospect Books, 1952.

Bracher, Eric. "The History of the Linn Tractor." *TimberTimes* magazine, Issue 20. [No date listed.]

Byron-Curtiss, A.L. Nat Foster Lodge Log Book. May 9, 1927–July 31, 1932.

Carmer, Carl. *Listen for a Lonesome Drum*, Part IV, "Road-Monkey and Whistle-Punk," Farrar & Rinehardt, Inc., 1936.

Chew, Don. "Tracks and Screws?—A.O. Lombard and H.H. Linn." American Truck Historical Society's *Wheels of Time*, March/April 1997.

Chisholm, J.F. "Alvin Lombard's Tractors." *Antique Power*, Date Unknown.

Conway, Matthew J. "Highmarket, As You Were: Two Hundred Years of Tug Hill." [self-published], 1977.

Conway, Matthew J. "Port Leyden: The Iron City, a Passing Glance." Tug Hill Books, 1989.

Cook, David. "Pulpwood." *The New York State Conservationist*, February–March 1948.

Day, O. Lovell. "Lumbering at Days Mills." *North Country Life*, Summer 1958.

Delutis, Conse R. "Cat Skinners—Whistle Punks." Rome *Daily Sentinel*, February 8, 1939.

Delutis, Conse R. "Cat Skinners—Whistle Punks." Rome *Daily Sentinel*, February 9, 1939.

Delutis, Conse R. "Cat Skinners—Whistle Punks." Rome *Daily Sentinel*, February 10, 1939.

Delutis, Conse R. "Cat Skinners—Whistle Punks." Rome *Daily Sentinel*, February 11, 1939.

Draper, Arthur S. "In the Adirondack Country." *Lumber Camp News*, December 1946.

Drew, Hazel. "Tales from Little Lewis," date unknown.

Elliott, Rene. "Those Creepy, Crawly Wonderful Linns." American Truck Historical Society's *Wheels of Time*, Vol. 6, No. 5, September/October 1985.

_____. "Some Postscripts on the Linns." American Truck Historical Society's *Wheels of Time*, Vol. 7, No. 2, March/April 1986.

_____. "Linn Manufacturing Corp. A Brief History." *New Berlin Gazette*, September 18, 1986.

_____. "Snowplows in Northern New York." American Truck Historical Society's *Wheels of Time*, Vol.12, No. 6, November/December 1991.

_____. "The C-Series Linns." American Truck Historical Society's *Wheels of Time*, Vol. 13, No. 6, November/December 1992.

_____. "The Linn Trailer & Van. Co." American Truck Historical Society's *Wheels of Time*, Vol. 15, No. 3, May/June 1994.

_____. "The Linn Tractor." Hays Antique Truck Museum's *Old Truck Town News*, January 2000.

Goodwin, James, A. "Lumbering High on the High Peaks." *Adirondac*, Volume XLVI Number 7, September 1982.

Gove, Bill. *Logging Railroads of the Adirondacks*. Syracuse University Press, 2006.

Ham, John M. and Timothy R. Mayers. "The New York Central in the Adirondacks." *Stony Clove and Catskill Mountain Press*, 2015.

Hays, Helen Ireland. "Sleigh Bells on the Camel's Hump." *York State Tradition*, Winter 1972.

Jackson, Dr. Harry F. "Branding and Driving in the Adirondacks." *North Country Life*, Spring 1960.

Kling, Edwin M. "McKeever in the 'Teens.'" *Lumber Camp News*, September 1949.

Landon, Harry L. "The North Country: A History Embracing Jefferson, St. Lawrence, Oswego, Lewis and Franklin Counties, New York." Historical Publishing Company, Indianapolis, Indiana, 1932.

Lawrence, Philomena. "Old Tractors Live on In Unique Collection: New York Collector Specializes in Lombard & Linn Logging Tractors," *The Northern Logger & Timber Processor*, May 2006.

Lewis, Audrey. "Hard Work, Low Pay, Good Food," Utica *Observer-Dispatch*, August 26, 1991.

O'Hern, William J. *Under an Adirondack Influence: The Life of A.L. Byron-Curtiss 1871–1959*. Cleveland, N.Y.: The Forager Press, 2008.

_____. *Adirondack Stories of the Black River Country*. Utica, N.Y.: North Country Books, 2003.

O'Donnell, Thomas C. *Birth of a River, An Informal History of the Black River Headwaters*. Black River Books, 1952.

Olds, Carlton B. "Timber Rafting on the St. Lawrence." *North Country Life*, Fall 1952.

McDermott, Marion H. *Abundant Harvest: St. Patrick Catholic Church in Forestport, New York*. A Syracuse Catholic Press Association Book, 1991.

Mason, Clarence W. "The Coming of the Tractor." Old Forge, N.Y.: *Lumber Camp News*, May 1949.

_____. "The Sky Pilot's Corner." Old Forge, N.Y.: *Lumber Camp News*, May 1949.

Marden, Orison Street. "This One Thing I Do." *Lumber Camp News*, December 1951.

Masters, Peg. "McKeever Early History." Town of Webb Historical Association. www.webbhistory.org/McKeever_Early_History.htm

Mihalyi, Louis. "Lumber Camp Cooks." *Adirondack Life* magazine, May–June, 1988.

Moose, Ed. "Linn of Morris." *Oneonta Past & Present*, (unknown newspaper), 1962.

Nortz, Carol. "Editorial." *Adirondack Life* magazine, June, 2014.

Portner, Ernest Leigh. "Logging with Linn Tractors in Upstate New York." *TimberTimes*, Issue 20. [No date listed.]

Reed, Rev. Frank A. "Planning One's Life." *Lumber Camp News*, August 1947.

_____. "Editorial." *Lumber Camp News*, August 1947.

_____. "I am the Door." *Lumber Camp News*, September 1948.

_____. "Thanksgiving." *Lumber Camp News*, November 1948.

_____. "God's Work." *Lumber Camp News*, February 1949.

_____. "Jesus, the Healer." *Lumber Camp News*, September 1949.

_____. "Editorial." *Lumber Camp News*, September 1949.

_____. "Editorial." *The Northeastern Logger*, February 1953.

_____. "Adirondack Lumbering." New York State Ranger School, *Alumni News*, 1948.

Reid, Alan D. "Ranger School Has Alumni Reunion." *Lumber Camp News*, Vol. 10 No. 5, September 1948.

Gadway, Mary Rita. "Life in the South Woods Lumber Camp." Reprinted from *The Chateaugay Record*. *North Country Life*, 1958.

Ryan, J.C. *Early Loggers in Minnesota, Vol. I*. Minnesota Timber Producers Association, 1975.

_____. *Early Loggers in Minnesota, Vol. II*. Minnesota Timber Producers Association, 1976.

_____. *Early Loggers in Minnesota,*
Vol. III. Minnesota Timber Producers
Association, 1980.

Sisson, Stanley H. "Use of Tractors in
Winter Log—Hauling." *Empire State
Forests Products Association* Bulletin No. 12.
December 1921.

Sprague, Ken, "History & Heritage,"
Adirondack Express, December 18, 2001.

_____. "History & Heritage,"
Adirondack Express, January 8, 2002.

_____. "History & Heritage,"
Adirondack Express, January 15, 2002.

_____. "History & Heritage,"
Adirondack Express, January 29, 2002.

_____. "History & Heritage: The Rev. Frank
Reed." *Adirondack Express,* June 18, 2013.

_____. "History & Heritage: The Rev.,
Religion and the Logger's Life."
Adirondack Express, August 13, 2013.

_____. "History & Heritage: Logging Camp
Life." *Adirondack Express,* August 27, 2013.

Stevens, Ruby Donahue. "Mike's Mill."
York State Tradition, Winter 1954.

(The Triple C.) "The Gould Paper Company."
Old Forge, N.Y.: *Lumber Camp News,* Vol. 10
No. 5, September 1948.

The Ranger School, A Century in the Forest, Jim
Coufal, Arnie Lanckton and Brian Woodward,
eds. SUNY-ESF Ranger School, 2012.

Thompson, Casber C. "An Adirondack
Logger. From The Editor's Mail." *North
Country Life,* Spring 1950.

Trimm, Lee S. "The Bark Peelers."
The New York State Conservationist.
August–September 1953.

VanArnam, Ralph N. and Lewis S.
"The Era of Navigation on Black River,"
Part I, *North Country Life,* Winter, 1945;
Part II, Spring, 1949; Part III, Summer,
1949: Part IV, Fall, 1949.

VanValkenburgh, Norman J. "Forest
Management? Or, Not?" *Adirondac,*
Volume XLVII Number 1, February 1983.

Wallace, Oliver P. "Is Your Horse
Pulling His Load on the Logging Job?"
The Northeastern Logger, September 1954.

Wells, Robert A. "Big Tracts in 3 Counties."
Watertown Daily Times, Feb. 13, 1928.

_____. "Snow Taxi Follows Forest Trail to
Lumbering Camp." *Watertown Daily Times,*
Feb. 14, 1928.

_____. "Many Difficulties Face Men Driving
Tractor Log Trains." *Watertown Daily Times,*
Feb. 15, 1928.

_____. "Thousands of Logs Piled
on Ice Awaiting Spring Drive."
Watertown Daily Times, Feb. 16, 1928.

_____. "Veteran Woodsmen Describe
Entire Lumbering Operation."
Watertown Daily Times, Feb. 17, 1928.

_____. "Colorful French-Canadian
Lumbermen Disappearing."
Watertown Daily Times, Feb. 18, 1928.

White, Mary Ruth. "Tug Hill Lumbering
Then and Now." Reprinted from the
Lumber Camp News. North Country Life,
Winter 1953.

Williams, Emily. "Good as Gold."
Adirondack Life, March/April 1998.

Wolfgram, Steve. "The Forest Products
Industry in the Adirondacks." *Adirondac,*
Volume XLVII Number 5, June 1983.

INTERNET

"Adirondack Journal—Lumber Camp
Cook," http://www.adkmuseum.org/about_
us/adirondack_journal/?id=289

"Life in Logging Camps," www.reynoldstonn
ewyork.org

"Lost Generations in the Adirondack Forest,"
from 1998 Spring News of the Association
for the Protection of the Adirondacks,
www.colgate.edu

"The Adirondacks Logging," https://www.
pbs.org/theadirondacks

"Work in the Woods: Logging the Adirondacks," http://adkmuseum.org/exhibits_ and
_events/permanent_exhibits/detail/?id=8

www.reynoldstonnewyork.org

RECORDINGS

Cassette tape recording of interview by
Janice Oatman and Cathy Farrell with logger
Rupert Lamphear of Indian Lake, N.Y.,
Adirondack Museum Library

A

Adams, Sherman: 18, 170

Adirondack(s): i, ii, iii, v, vi, vii, viii, 3, 4, 6, 17, 18, 19, 22, 26, 27, 29, 30, 31, 32, 39, 40, 47, 52, 53, 54, 55, 56, 58, 61, 70, 73, 74, 75, 77, 78, 86, 91, 101, 113, 115, 117, 118, 119, 121, 132, 143, 150, 152, 153, 158, 161, 162, 163, 164, 165, 166, 167, 169, 170, 172, 175, 178, 183, 186, 187, 188, 193, 194, 196, 198, 199, 200, 202, 207, 209, 213, 217, 218, 221, 223, 227, 229, 232, 238, 241, 242, 243, 250, 253, 262, 268, 282, 284, 287, 288, 289, 294, 300, 301, 302, 304, 312, 314, 316, 321, 322, 324, 327, 330, 334, 336, 338, 339, 340, 353, 354, 361, 372, 374, 376, 377, 378, 379, 381, 382, 383, 384, 389, 403, 405, 411, 414, 418, 424, 426, 429, 430, 431, 433, 438, 440, 442, 443, 444, 445, 446, 447, 454

area: 58, 172

camp(s): 29, 187, 198, 209, 221, 454

communities: 382, 429

community: 199

country: viii, 334, 443, 454

crew: 218

days: 17

division of the New York Central: 119

early natives: 340

foothills: 304

foothills village: 304

forest: 158, 354, 361, 445

hermit Noah John Rondeau: 29

history: 338

lake country: 241

logger: viii, 314, 445

logging: 22, 55, 77, 193, 199, 300, 302, 312, 372, 403, 445

logging camp: 193, 199, 312, 372

logging camp cookery: 199

logging camps: 47

logging lore: 302

logging operations: 77

logging town of McKeever: 300

lumber camp: 339, 340

lumber camp cook: 414

Lumber Camp Parish: 75, 167

lumber camps: i, ii, 17, 170, 178, 227, 300, 431, 443, 446

lumber woods: vi, 53, 178

lumbering: iii, v, 17, 31, 444

lumbering enterprises: 249

lumbering operation: 217

Lumberjack Parish: 165

men: 374

Operations: 440

past: 194

political history: 440

pulpwood: 18

region: 284, 321, 327, 340

reminiscences: 302

river-driving: 6

rivers: 27, 322, 442

section: 32

sky pilot: 162, 166

strawberries: 143, 289

streams: 27

timber: 381, 418, 430, 443

Tomato Soup Cake: vii, 207

villages: 31

wilderness: 75, 454

woods: 175, 200

woodsman: 238

woodsmen: 30, 424

Adirondack Apples: 243

Adirondack Capers: 242

Adirondack Logging

Adirondack Logging

Adirondack Logging

Available at www.adkwilds.com or www.adirondackmountaintraders.com
or by phone: North Country Books 1-800-342-7409